INTERNATIONAL SOCIETY, GLOBAL POLITY

SAGE was founded in 1965 by Sara Miller McCune to support the dissemination of usable knowledge by publishing innovative and high-quality research and teaching content. Today, we publish more than 750 journals, including those of more than 300 learned societies, more than 800 new books per year, and a growing range of library products including archives, data, case studies, reports, conference highlights, and video. SAGE remains majority-owned by our founder, and on her passing will become owned by a charitable trust that secures our continued independence.

Los Angeles | London | Washington DC | New Delhi | Singapore

INTERNATIONAL SOCIETY, GLOBAL POLITY

An Introduction to
International
Political Theory

CHRIS BROWN

Los Angeles | London | New Delhi
Singapore | Washington DC

Los Angeles | London | New Delhi
Singapore | Washington DC

SAGE Publications Ltd
1 Oliver's Yard
55 City Road
London EC1Y 1SP

SAGE Publications Inc.
2455 Teller Road
Thousand Oaks, California 91320

SAGE Publications India Pvt Ltd
B 1/I 1 Mohan Cooperative Industrial Area
Mathura Road
New Delhi 110 044

SAGE Publications Asia-Pacific Pte Ltd
3 Church Street
#10-04 Samsung Hub
Singapore 049483

Editor: Natalie Aguilera
Assistant Editor: James Piper
Production editor: Katie Forsythe
Copyeditor: Clare Weaver
Proofreader: Imogen Roome
Marketing manager: Sally Ransom
Cover design: Francis Kenney
Typeset by: C&M Digitals (P) Ltd, Chennai, India
Printed in Great Britain by Henry Ling Limited at
The Dorset Press, Dorchester, DT1 1HD

Library of Congress Control Number: 2014941631

British Library Cataloguing in Publication data

A catalogue record for this book is available from
the British Library

ISBN 978-1-4462-7282-4
ISBN 978-1-4462-7283-1 (pbk)

TABLE OF CONTENTS

TABLE OF CONTENTS

ABOUT THE AUTHOR

Chris Brown is Emeritus Professor of International Relations at the London School of Economics and Political Science. An LSE graduate (BSc (Econ) International Relations, 1968), he returned to the Department of International Relations at the School as Professor in 1998 and 'retired' in 2014. He held the Chair of Politics at Southampton University from 1994–98, and before that was a Lecturer and then Senior Lecturer at the University of Kent at Canterbury. He is the author of numerous articles and book chapters on international political theory and of *Practical Judgement in International Political Theory* (2010), *Sovereignty, Rights and Justice* (2002), *International Relations Theory: New Normative Approaches* (1992), editor of *Political Restructuring in Europe: Ethical Perspectives* (1994) and co-editor (with Terry Nardin and N.J. Rengger) of *International Relations in Political Thought* (2002). His textbook *Understanding International Relations* (2009) is now in its 4th and final edition and has been translated into Arabic, Chinese. Portuguese and Turkish. He was Chair of the British International Studies Association from 1998–2000.

PREFACE

This book can be, and I hope will be, read in different ways. On the one hand it presents a particular reading of the shifts that have taken place, and are taking place, in the normative framework of international relations, summarised here as a putative movement from seeing the world as an international society, to seeing the world as a global polity. On the other hand, it can be, and I hope will be, used by students of international political theory to develop their own reading of this shift, or perhaps to reject the very idea that such a shift is taking place. These two objectives are not incompatible. In my experience teaching this subject over two and a half decades students want their teachers, and the books they recommend, to have views and to be willing to share them – always provided that they are open to hearing other opinions and provide the means by which different takes on the subject can be developed. Since this is a book that expresses a particular view of the world, it is written with minimal referencing in order not to disturb the flow of the text, but since I want to give plenty of opportunities for the reader to develop his or her own views, each chapter is followed by a guide to further reading.

ACKNOWLEDGEMENTS

I have been writing on these topics for longer than I care to think, and a certain amount of auto-plagiarism is, I think, inevitable – there are only so many ways one can outline Rawls's *Law of Peoples* in a paragraph or two, and I have employed all of them over the last 15 years. Specific borrowings that are worth noting appear in Chapter 8, which draws some material from Chris Brown (2013b) *Global Responsibility to Protect*, 5 (4): 423–42, and Chapters 3 and 9 which draw on Chris Brown (2013a) 'Just War and political judgment' in Anthony Lang, Cian O'Driscoll and John Williams, and an unpublished paper written in honour of Jean Bethke Elshtain.

I am grateful to a number of friends and colleagues at LSE, Aberystwyth University and St Andrews University for many conversations over the years on the topics discussed here – I must identify by name Toni Erskine, Tony Lang and Nick Rengger but there are many, many others without whose input this would be a different and much weaker book. My students at LSE on IR306, IR462 and IR463 will recognise much that is on offer here – I have tried out everything that this book has to offer on them, and it is a better book as a result; I'm very grateful, and to Elke Schwarz for help with the bibliography. Last, but not least, Natalie Aguilera has been an exemplary editor, always supportive, likewise James Piper, Katie Forsythe, Sally Ransom, Clare Weaver and all the Sage team.

1
INTRODUCTION TO THE STUDY OF INTERNATIONAL POLITICAL THEORY

Realist International Relations theorists tell us that international politics is about states, power and interest and there is no reason to believe that this is not the case, but one of the founding principles of all the different variants of International Political Theory that will be examined in this book is that this is not the whole story. International politics is also about values and norms, and states are not always the most significant international actors. Another belief of International Relations theorists – this time liberal as well as realist – is that the discipline of International Relations is a twentieth-century construct, generated by the two World Wars. Again practitioners of International Political Theory do not deny that as a university discipline, International Relations emerged after 1918, and re-emerged, revitalised after 1945, but they also hold that thinking about topics that we now call 'international' has a long and deep history. Conventional International Relations theorists acknowledge the existence of a few forerunners to their discourse – Thucydides, Machiavelli, perhaps Hobbes and Kant – but International Political Theory draws on a much wider intellectual constellation, including many thinkers who are not obviously 'international' as that term has come to be understood in modern times (Brown et al., 2002). To summarise these differences, for International Relations scholars, their discipline is either a sub-field of contemporary Political Science (the dominant American view) or a cross-disciplinary focus informed by history, philosophy and law (the characteristic British view) but for International Political Theory, the study of the international is an exercise in Applied Political Philosophy. Just what kind of an exercise is the subject matter of this book, and this introductory chapter is designed to set the scene for what is to come, expanding these programmatic statements, clearing away some misunderstandings and confusions, and identifying key issues.

The normative framework of international relations

International Political Theory focuses on the normative framework within which international relations takes places. This involves some quite complex ideas but, and this cannot be stressed too often, it also involves getting down and dirty with the messy reality of international politics. There is obviously the potential for disjuncture here between the more high-flown realms of discourse and the very down to earth detail of day-to-day international relations, but part of the task of the international political theorist is not to allow a gap to emerge here, or at least not to allow it to become so wide that it distorts our understanding of either theory or the world. This will sound very abstract to the newcomer to the subject, so in the next few paragraphs one or two illustrations of the ways in which the normative framework of international relations both raises deep questions and impinges on the real world will be offered. In each case the short discussion offered here is a kind of taster for what will come later because all of the topics raised will be considered at much greater depth in later chapters.

Consider first the role of force in international relations – the modern discipline of IR arose from the ashes of the First and Second World Wars so this is an obvious starting point. The use of force is often approached instrumentally – we ask whether a particular tactic will bring about the result we want it to – but it is almost never approached solely from this perspective. There are figures in modern world history who have had a purely instrumental approach to force – in the twentieth century Hitler, Stalin, Mao – but they are rarely seen as appropriate role models. Rather, most people – statesmen and women, soldiers, citizens – want to think that when force is applied it is done so for good reason, and in an appropriate way, and there is a body of philosophical literature that addresses precisely the question of what constitutes a 'good' reason and what is an 'appropriate' way. Buddhists, Hindus, Muslims and Jews have their own traditions to fall back on, but in the European West that body of literature revolves around the notion of 'Just War' and is deeply rooted in both Medieval Christian and modern secular thought. The categories of Just War thinking were established centuries ago by figures such as Saints Augustine and Thomas Aquinas and have been adopted and sometimes transformed by modern international lawyers and political philosophers and part of the task of International Political Theory is to grasp these categories in all their philosophical depth. However, this would be an arid exercise if these categories, and the wisdom that has gone into developing them over the centuries, are not put to work in examining contemporary uses of force. We need to be able to relate such notions as 'just cause', 'right intention' and 'proportionality' to decisions which have been made, and have to be made, on the conflicts of our age. We need to find a way to work from the thought of Thomas Aquinas on the one hand to the decision by President Obama to employ pilotless drones to carry out targeted killings in the Yemen on the other. If we don't have anything to say about drone warfare then we will have failed in one way, but if what we have to say could have been said in an op-ed piece without being informed by the philosophical discourse then we will have failed in a different way. International Political Theory is an exercise in applied political philosophy and all three words are important.

For a second example, consider the issue of global social justice. For political philosophers, social justice is a topic that has never disappeared from view, and in the modern era one work, *A Theory of Justice* (1970) by John Rawls has dominated thinking on the subject. Rawls actually developed his theory in the context of bounded societies which were assumed for the purposes of the theory to be self-contained, but most theorists who have approached the subject since Rawls have regarded this as a strange, indeed perverse, way of approaching the subject, and many 'Post-Rawlsian' theorists have produced quite complex notions of global social justice, as will be explored later in this book. Some advocate quite dramatic changes in the global international economic order, others look to a change in the behaviour of individuals, arguing that large-scale transfers of wealth from the global rich to the global poor are required. The arguments presented by these political philosophers are sometimes simple, sometimes complex and often are counter-intuitive and require a genuine change in the way we think about the world – and this is good, because part of the purpose of any exercise in political philosophy ought to be precisely to unsettle established patters of thought. However, again, this would be an arid exercise if the work of these thinkers were not to be related very closely to the kind of campaigns for social justice that are conducted in the real world. Proposals to 'Make Poverty History' need to be related to the academic debates on global social justice, and criticised (and perhaps supported) from the perspective of these debates. Celebrities such as Bono and Bob Geldof and various other UN Special Ambassadors can make particular causes fashionable and, others, by means of omission, unfashionable, and one of the important tasks for International Political Theorists is to subject their thinking to the same kind of critique that is called for by, to take the above example, the US decisions on drone warfare. Looked at another way, when we write of the normative framework of international politics we are concerned not just with state behaviour but with the ways in which civil society groups promote particular normative positions, and we are not simply concerned with the 'high politics' of war and peace but also with the 'low' politics of e.g. AIDS prevention in Africa. These are themes that will be addressed in the main body of the book, but also explored in detail in the Further Reading sections.

International Political Theory, International Ethics and Normative IR Theory

Having attempted to make these connections between International Political Theory and the world of political action, it is now necessary to step back somewhat and examine a rather more abstract issue, that of nomenclature. The phrase International Political Theory employed in the preceding paragraphs is only one way of describing the subject matter of this book. Alternatives that are widely employed in the literature include 'International Ethics' and 'Normative International Relations Theory' and before getting down to more important matters it may be worth explaining why these terms are not employed widely here. This may seem pedantic, but terminology is important; the words we use have connotations in ordinary language which may be misleading and so it is important to get things straight from the outset.

'International Ethics', or variants thereof such as 'Ethics and International Relations', is a formulation that is quite widely used in book titles and – perhaps especially in the United States – in the context of university courses on such subjects as 'The Ethics of Foreign Policy'. It also has the cachet of contributing to the title of a very important think-tank and policy institute *The Carnegie Council for Ethics & International Affairs*. The Council, which among its many activities publishes the key journal *Ethics & International Affairs,* is a very important resource for international political theorists, with the same kind of significance for the subject that the US *Council on Foreign Relations* or the British *Royal Institute of International Affairs* ('Chatham House') has for the study of foreign policy. So why is International Ethics unsatisfactory as a way of summarising the field?

The danger here is that an emphasis on ethics – at least as the term is understood nowadays – is rather limiting. Ethics is about shaping moral conduct, distinguishing right from wrong and, while it is good that we should think of such matters in an international context, this is too restrictive an account of what International Political Theory has to offer. More important, there is a danger that defining the subject matter in ethical terms will lead to the error of confusing analysis with advocacy. Scholars may sometimes choose to act as 'norm entrepreneurs' promoting a particular vision of how the world should be, but such an activity is, or ought to be, secondary to the task of analysing norms, discerning how they work and what effect normative change will have. To confuse the two distinct roles is potentially dangerous in so far as the tendency will be to take the wish for the deed. Such was the error of those Inter-War scholars who later came to be identified, somewhat unfairly, as 'idealists' or 'utopians' (Long and Wilson, 1995). They wanted to bring about a world governed by the rule of law and principles of justice, which is, of course, commendable, but they sometimes fell into the trap of behaving as though such a world already existed, which it does not. Because international political theorists are actually and nec-essarily concerned with norms, it is particularly important that they do not fall into this trap, even if, at times, the result is that they will seem not to be responding adequately to the bad things that go on in the world. The key point is that there is a difference between being a scholar and being an advocate. This may seem rather abstract and an illustration of the point may be helpful.

As will be considered at some length in Chapters 7 and 8, humanitarian intervention, that is an intervention by one or more states into the domestic affairs of another for ostensibly humanitarian reasons, is a deeply contested notion. In 2001 an *International Commission on Intervention and State Sovereignty* produced a report entitled 'The Responsibility to Protect' (sometimes summa-rised as R2P) which was designed to find a non-contentious pathway through the thicket of issues that surround the idea of humanitarian intervention, a pathway that was partially adopted in the World Outcome Summit Document adopted by the UN General Assembly in the Autumn of 2005. A Co-Chair of the Commission was the Australian statesman Gareth Evans who became a major advocate for the ideas it contained and in 2008 produced a comprehensive book on the subject, *The Responsibility to Protect: Ending Mass Atrocity Crimes Once and For All*. The Queensland-based journal *Global Responsibility to Protect* invited three academics – Michael Barnett, Robert Jackson and the current writer – to contribute short essays on the book, to which Evans would reply (see Vol. 2, No. 3, 307–27). Of the three academics, Michael Barnett is a regular co-author with Thomas Weiss, one of the academic authors of the *ICISS* Report, and gave a sympathetic review of the book, Robert Jackson is a leading English School 'plu-ralist' (on which see Chapter 3) and was predictably hostile while the present author produced an essay that was sympathetic to the aims of R2P but critical of the delivery mechanism. As one might expect, Gareth Evans was favourably disposed towards Barnett, hostile to Jackson and, to a lesser extent to Brown, but what is of interest in the present context is the tone of exasperation in his response. Clearly, the way he saw it was that his book was dedicated to 'ending mass atrocity crimes once and for all', a noble aim that his interlocutors, even the sympathetic Barnett, were responding to inappropriately by raising con-cerns that he regarded as 'academic' in the pejorative sense of the term. In this we can see the difference between advocacy and analysis – and the case is made more interesting by the fact that, before he became Attorney General and later Foreign Minister in governments formed by the Australian Labour Party, Evans was himself an academic lawyer; the point is he had himself changed his role from analyst to advocate whereas the three academics in question had stayed on their side of the fence that exists between these two vocations.

To return to the wider point of this story, the term 'international ethics' with its inevitable emphasis on morality, 'doing the right thing' and distinguishing between right and wrong encourages the scholar to become a moralist. Since we all have tendencies in that direction, anything that pushes us that way needs to be resisted. Turning to the next alternative to International Political Theory, 'Normative International Relations Theory' does not have quite so moralising a connotation as International Ethics (although it does tend in that direction) and it also features in book titles including, rather embarrassingly given the current argument, as a sub-title to the first book on the subject by the present author, *International Relations Theory: New Normative Approaches* (1992). International Political Theory is certainly concerned with norms, so on the face of it 'normative theory' sounds as though it is helpfully descriptive. What's the problem?

In order to explain why the term 'normative' is actually unhelpful it is necessary to shift focus somewhat and look at the term 'theory', which, in the social sciences is understood in a number of different ways. The original Greek meaning of the term theory (*theoria*) involved contemplation and reflection and was contrasted with practice (*praxis*) which involved doing something; in the modern (natural) sciences a theory is a set of well-substantiated propositions about the world which have been tested and, for the time being, are considered to be true. These propositions take the form of law-like statements linking one set of observations (variables) with another, thus they involve propositions such as 'if "x" (the independent variable or, loosely, cause) and "a", "b", "n" (intervening variables) then "y" (the dependent variable or, loosely, effect)'. A great deal of ink has been spilled on the subject of whether this formulation can also be applied to the social sciences.

One very influential answer to this question was offered by the economist Milton Friedman in a 1953 essay 'The methodology of positive economics', which draws on the distinction between 'is' and 'ought' statements probably best set out by the Enlightenment philosopher David Hume in the eighteenth century (Friedman, 1966 [1953]; Hume 1739/1985). Friedman distinguishes *positive* economics, which he believes tells us how things actually are, from *normative* economics, which purports to tell us how things should be. Thus, to take a famous albeit simplistic example, the Phillips Curve was an exercise in positive economics which attempted to explain the relationship between the rate of inflation and the level of unemployment in a society – essentially lower unemployment was associated with higher inflation. If the curve is accurately described (which nowadays is doubtful, but that's irrelevant in this context) it should be possible to predict the level of employment associated with any particular inflation rate – this is positive economics, but what it cannot tell us is which particular combination of the two variables is desirable; that, according to Friedman's distinction, is a matter for normative economics. It is not something that can be decided by a fact-based calculation because whatever combination is chosen there will be winners and losers and deciding whether to punish savers with high levels of inflation, or disadvantage job seekers with low levels, is a policy decision that reflects values not analysis.

On the face of it, this positive/normative distinction seems very useful, and has in fact been adopted by many non-economists, including scholars of

International Relations, and including those scholars who engage in what they call normative International Relations theory. So, again, what's the problem? In fact there are two problems, one concerned with the philosophy of the social sciences, the other with the sociology of academic disciplines. To take the latter point first because it is less important, for many social scientists, including Friedman, and for most mainstream International Relations scholars, although both positive and normative theory are, in principle, seen as legitimate activities the former is regarded as more serious, in a sense more real, than the latter. For these scholars 'real' theory is explanatory theory – this is where the rigorous work is done, and normative theory is seen as a decidedly second-rate activity. In effect, scholars who describe their work as normative theory are marginalising themselves, pushing themselves into an academic backwater while the real deal is going down elsewhere.

This would not matter, were it not for the fact that, in any event, the distinction between normative and positive theory is by no means as clear cut as the position outlined above would have it. The Friedman account of a positive social science is clearly based on the model of the natural sciences, yet there are important ways in which the natural and social sciences differ. In the natural sciences non-reflexivity is the rule – to put it crudely, the subject matter of a natural science theory is not conscious of the fact that its behaviour or nature is being theorised, and is not capable of reflecting on the implications of this fact. Human beings are so capable; they can adapt consciously in ways that the objects of natural science cannot. Neo-positivist theorists of international relations are, of course, conscious of this difficulty and do their best to adapt their theories to take it into account, and with some success – but it remains the case that the distinction between normative and positive theory is blurred. Norms and values permeate human behaviour and they permeate the behaviour of states and while it is not necessary to go as far as those who argue that as a result all theory is normative it would certainly be unwise to encourage the idea that there is a clear dividing line between the normative and the positive (Frost, 1996).

These are reasons why alternative names such as International Ethics and Normative IR Theory do not work, but there are also good positive reasons for thinking about our subject matter as International Political Theory. Aside from avoiding prescription and standing apart from the normative/positive distinction, International Political Theory invites links to past and present bodies of work that are very much relevant to what we are investigating, and it discourages the idea that the study of International Relations is *sui generis*, that is, significantly distinct from other areas of the social sciences. This *sui generis* assumption has deep roots in one of the most important ways of addressing norms in International Relations, the 'English School', and is very harmful. A key text here is a famous early, provocative, paper by Martin Wight 'Why is there no International Theory?' published in the collection *Diplomatic Investigations* in 1966, but first presented in 1960 as a foundation document for the British Committee for the Study of International Theory, a group of scholars who later became known as the founders of the 'English School' (Butterfield and Wight, 1966; Dunne, 1998). Wight argues that very few of the great political philosophers and political theorists have written about international politics, because political theory is essentially a theory of the state, and a discourse that is premised on the idea of progress, both of which characteristics are inimical to the international, which is the realm of 'recurrence and repetition'. The second of these alleged characteristics will be challenged in later chapters of this book, but the first needs to be scotched here and now. Political Philosophy is not now nor has it ever been simply focused on the state; relations between 'insiders' and 'outsiders', obligations to 'others' as opposed to our fellow citizens, or co-religionists, or co-nationals – these are topics that have exercised some of the greatest minds for millennia (Brown et al., 2002).

To bring this point home in more specific terms, consider the incorporation of Classical Greek thought into contemporary thinking about international relations. Wight in his essay makes the point that it is Thucydides, the historian of the Peloponnesian War rather than the great philosophers such as Plato and Aristotle, who speaks to modern international concerns – and it is indeed the case that Thucydides, that 'most politic of historians' as Thomas Hobbes described him, does provide us with an account of the causes of war and the operation of the balance of power and, in the so-called 'Melian Dialogue', with a proto-realist account of the relationship between norms and power (Thucydides, 2009). Still, Wight's point only works on a very restrictive account of the subject matter of international politics. One of the core issues in political life then and now is the relationship between the 'universal' and the 'particular' and the Greeks had a great deal to say on this matter. Both Plato and Aristotle did in fact lecture on the nature of inter-city war and the like, but more importantly they also presented an account of political life which was tied to the bounded community, in their case the city and which drew a very sharp distinction between fellow-citizens and others (including slaves, women, resident aliens and citizens of other cities). A key topic for both thinkers was how this 'communitarianism' (to use a modern term rather anachronistically) could be reconciled with such Pan-Hellenic activities as the worship of the Gods and the pursuit of the virtues. They resolved such dilemmas in favour of their cities, but their successors – the Stoics in particular – no longer lived in the kind of city which could give meaning to people's lives and they thought in universal terms. Their aim was to be a citizen of the world, or 'cosmopolitan', a term that was revived two millennia later at the time of the European Enlightenment.

The relationship between cosmopolitanism and particularism will be a focus of much of the rest of this book – the point here is that Greeks have much more to offer us than simply Thucydides' thoughts on war, interesting though the latter are, and to describe what we are about as International Political Theory is more conducive to exploring this wider agenda than the alternatives, and less likely to cause us to think that the classics of political thought have nothing much to say to us. The same point also applies when it comes to modern political thought. As will become apparent later in this book, global social justice has become a major focus of contemporary political philosophy posing all sorts of interesting questions in ways which mainstream International Relations scholars find rather uncomfortable – sometimes for good, sometimes for bad, reasons. The core point is that the *sui generis* assumption simply does not hold and has to be abandoned unless we are to lose contact with the wider world of thought, and defining the field as International Political Theory is one way to keep the discourse plugged into that wider field.

States, communities, nations and individuals

The next section of this introduction offers some preliminary thoughts on the building blocks of International Political Theory, the various units that, individually, or in combination, go to make up the referent object of the discourse. For the last three centuries or so 'the state' has been the central unit through which international relations has been conceptualised, but terms like 'community' and 'nation' have also been used to describe the collectivities whose relationships are at the heart of the matter – the difference between these terms needs to be clarified. More recently, especially since 1945, these collective terms have been joined by 'the individual' as possible foci for the study of International Political Theory – the international human rights regime and international criminal law have been central to this development. These four primary units of International Political Theory – state, community, nation, individual – are joined by secondary units, international institutions, governmental and non-governmental and together, in various combinations, they coalesced to produce alternative conceptions of how the world works. More on these conceptions in the next section – here the focus with be on the primary units.

The modern *state* is a territorially based political unit which claims sovereign status, that is to say which recognises no external superior, and no internal equal. It used to be said the sovereign state became the norm in Europe after the Treaty of Westphalia, whence came the term 'Westphalia System' as a convenient description of the European order after 1648. Nowadays it is widely recognised that this characterisation rests on a misunderstanding of what that treaty entailed, but it remains the case that a change did take place in the sixteenth and seventeenth centuries out of which emerged the modern state. There is, of course, much, much more to be said about the state but this basic definition is all we need for the moment.

A *community* is a social group bound together by a degree of mutual trust, even affection. Communities may be based on actual interactions, in which case they are generally less extensive than the state, or virtual interactions in which case they can be more extensive – consider, for example the Muslim *Ummah* or community of all believers – or functionally based (the academic community would be a good example here).

A *nation* is a community that is linked to a territory, whose members believe that they possess inherited qualities that distinguish them from all others. Nowadays, this quite often, but not always, leads to the belief that the nation should possess sovereignty, that is form a state. With very few exceptions – North Korea and Iceland perhaps – all states are actually multi-national, but nationalist sentiment remains strong.

These three terms – state, community, nation – are the source of a great deal of confusion in International Political Theory, which is why it is necessary to stipulate definitions at the outset. *State* and *nation* are very frequently taken as synonymous, perhaps actually run-together as in *nation-state*. The very term 'international' makes this mistake – it was coined (by Jeremy Bentham) at a time when nation and state actually were treated as synonymous, before, that is, nationalism as a political ideology differentiated them. Again, the main global family of institutions is incorrectly described as the United *Nations* – for obvious reasons the more accurate description United *States* was not available (and the *United* part is not very accurate either, but that's a different point). Confusing *state* and *community* is a less common mistake in ordinary speech, but one that quite frequently occurs in contemporary political philosophy. Thus, it is not uncommon for arguments that explore the rights and duties of political communities to be applied wholesale to states, even though most actual states do not coincide with a political community.

The fourth primary unit of International Political Theory is the *individual*. Historically, individuals have only featured as objects of international relations rather than as actors in their own right. In terms of conventional international law, diplomats as individuals have a particular, protected status and, at the other end of the social scale, pirates also have a status, very much unprotected, as the enemies of humanity who can be detained and punished by any country that lays hands upon them – and in the days when sovereignty was personal, sovereigns also had a role as actors in International Relations. Since 1945 this has changed. The Universal Declaration of Human Rights made by the General Assembly of the UN in 1948 was simply the initial stage in the development of a very elaborate international regime for the protection of human rights, giving the individual a standing in international relations not present before that date. The development of International Criminal Law has also worked to the same effect, although this time not necessarily to the advantage of particular individuals – heads of government and other officials can no longer claim immunity from the consequences of their action on the basis that they were simply acting as office-holders; in certain circumstances they can now be held personally responsible before international tribunals such as the International Criminal Court for their conduct in office.

The relationship of individuals to the three collective bodies, states, communities and nations, forms a large part of the subject matter of contemporary International Political Theory. Which of these primary units should be normatively privileged? Liberal, cosmopolitan International Political Theory assumes that the individual comes first and that ultimately the justification for states, communities and nations is that they serve the interests of individuals; however, there are liberal nationalists such as David Miller, Yael Tamir and Michael Walzer who see the nation as the means whereby the interests of individuals are served. Republican (Neo-Roman) political theorists understand individual liberty rather differently from the way it is understood in liberal theory, and communitarians and Hegelians refuse to see the individual and the community as independent of each other – for them the notion of a pre-social individual makes no sense.

As this 100-word summary of 200 years of political theory should make clear the relationship between states, communities and individuals defies easy summary. In the 1990s it was quite common for international political theorists to write of a debate between liberal cosmopolitans and communitarians, shadowing a similar debate in contemporary political theory – but as a number of writers have demonstrated, the assumptions necessary to make this idea of a debate work are too many and too implausible for this to be a good way to approach the subject. Instead, this book will be organised around a different distinction, still an over-simplification, but a productive one I hope – the distinction between an international society (or society of states, the terms are used here synonymously) and a global polity.

International society and the global polity

For some scholars of International Relations states are the central actors in world politics, and the way they interact is solely determined by material forces, that is by the interplay of power and interest. These scholars – most obviously self-identified nowadays as 'structural realists' – acknowledge that the interactions of states leads to regular patterns of behaviour such that one can talk about an *international system*, but these patterns of behaviour are simply created by the iteration of ends-means calculations over time (Waltz, 1979). There is no normative component to the international system; from this perspective states may enter into agreements with one another, but such agreements are adhered to only for so long as they remain in the interests of the states who entered in to them – international law has no binding force outside of the will of states. Such a conception more or less denies the possibility that International Political Theory could have anything useful to say about international relations. Fortunately there are other ways of understanding the relations of states; it is possible to conceive of states forming an *international society* rather than an international system.

The notion of an international society is nowadays associated with the so-called 'English School' (on which more in Chapter 2) but the term actually has a long history and in using it English School scholars have simply plugged themselves into a notion that has been central to thinking about international relations for at least 300 years. The notion of a society of states shares much with the notion of an international system, in particular the belief that states are the central actors in world politics; the difference is that the pattern of relationships they create by their interactions is understood to be, at least in part, normatively governed. International law has governing force, it creates genuine obligations, even if these obligations are not always met in full. Norms such as that of diplomatic immunity are binding on all states. Even the practice of inter-state war is governed by norms. Whereas in an international system a balance of power may emerge fortuitously because of the distribution of forces, in an international society the balance of power is recognised as a normatively desirable end which states will adjust their policies to achieve (Bull, 1977). It should be said that the nature of norms and how they are formed is an interesting topic and the Further Reading associated with this chapter will provide pointers to the literature here.

Of course, this picture of a functioning international society could be seen as rather fanciful, obviously painted as seen through rose-tinted glasses. As we know, not all states regard international law as binding, certainly not all the time, and the norms of international society are quite frequently violated – although it is unusual for them to be rejected outright; for that a Hitler is required, someone who genuinely sees no potential limits to his power. The notion of a society of states is a Weberian 'ideal-type'; in *On the Methodology of the Social Sciences* (1949: 90) Weber explains:

> An ideal type is formed by the one-sided accentuation of one or more points of view and by the synthesis of a great many diffuse, discrete, more or less present and occasionally absent concrete individual phenomena, which are arranged according to those one-sidedly emphasized viewpoints into a unified analytical construct...

In this case it is the normative nature of inter-state relations that is one-sidedly accentuated for the purpose of creating the analytical construct of a society of states.

In any event, the notion of a society of states has a history that can be traced back to the political practice and the political and legal philosophy of the seventeenth and eighteenth centuries – it stands as the most readily available alternative to a power-political approach to International Relations and was recognised as such by the 'classical realists', although its most self-conscious modern commentators self-identify as the 'English School'. International society is a flexible concept, which can incorporate war as an institution of the society of states via the Just War tradition and its modern proponents such as Michael Walzer, as well as humanitarian concerns and the notion of human rights; the most influential modern theory of justice and rights, that of John Rawls, rests on the idea of a Society of States, although he calls it a 'society of peoples' (Walzer, 2006; Rawls, 1999).

The society of states has a long history, but the modern version was established in 1945 with the signing of the United Nations Charter, most of which sets out in institutional and legal form the principles by which international society has been governed over the years. But the UN also set in motion challenges to the notion of an international society, challenges which have become more and more salient in the 70 years since 1945. The two most important of these challenges are, first, the attempts which have been made to extend the scope of international law into international criminal law; new institutions such as the International Criminal Court have attempted the 'juridification' of international politics, changing the legal relations between states in a quite dramatic way. At the same time, second, a new kind of humanitarianism has emerged, focused on the causes of suffering rather than simply the relief of suffering, and extending the idea of human rights and, unlike the Universal Declaration of Human Rights in 1948, increasingly defining them against the state, rather than as something to be achieved through the state.

The new human rights regime focuses on economic, social and collective rights, and the new humanitarianism has led to 'humanitarian wars' and the emergence of a new understanding of sovereignty, sovereignty as responsibility. As part of this shift the notion of a 'Just War' has changed, with older notions of e.g. non-combatant immunity and the moral equality of combatants being challenged. And, perhaps most fundamentally in the realm of ideas, theories of global justice have been developed which reject the Rawlsian willingness to think of an international society composed of states, and look instead to a global society composed of individuals. Putting all these changes together, we can see emerging an alternative ideal-type to the society of states – the notion of a *global polity* incorporating states, but with the individual as the most important referent object, and with sets of institutions which are creating networks of global governance such that increasingly the sovereignty of states is limited and curtailed.

These two notions, of a society of states and a global polity, are the poles around which this book is organised. The rest of this chapter will set out the way in which this is to be carried out, but before moving to this task it is crucially important to get across one central proposition. Although in what follows we will follow chronology and look at the society of states before the global polity, it is NOT to be thought that the latter has replaced, or is replacing, the former. The most important single fact about the normative foundations of contemporary world politics is that an international society and a global polity exist together in the modern world – both analytical constructs represent a reality about contemporary international politics. We live in a world of states *and* we live in a global polity. This is not a comfortable state of affairs. On the contrary it is a source of a great deal of conflict and disharmony. Cosmopolitan thinkers sometimes ignore the existence of the society of states, and their ignorance goes a long way towards robbing their work of serious value; statist thinkers sometimes write about the modern world in terms appropriate to the world of 1815 rather than 2015, and their work is equally misleading as a result. The coexistence of an international society and a global polity is a central fact about our age, but we cannot study both at once and so the organisational principle adopted here is chronological. The book will be organised in two parts.

Part I: International Society

The aim of Part I is to elaborate the points made above concerning the normative account of IR as an international society as theorised by thinkers from the seventeenth century through to Hedley Bull and the English School, and to show how this notion is also supported, albeit for different reasons, by some modern political theorists such as Michael Walzer and John Rawls. It will be demonstrated that the society of states can also support an ethics of war, and a politics of human rights and humanitarianism. Finally, some new developments in international criminal law and the politics of humanitarianism that pose a serious challenge to the notion of a society of states.

Chapter 2, *International Society and International Law* will examine the origins of international society and international law in the sixteenth to eighteenth centuries, the normative foundations of sovereignty and non-intervention and the modern English School and the different varieties of international society offered by 'pluralists' and 'solidarists'.

Chapter 3, *War as an Institution of International Society* will focus on the 'Just War' tradition from Aquinas to Michael Walzer and the notions of *ius ad bellam* and *ius in bello*. Walzer's understanding of the rights of political communities will be seen as offering a contemporary basis for the society of states.

Chapter 4, *Human Rights, Humanitarianism and the Society of States* will examine the notion of 'Classical' humanitarianism and the work of the International Committee of the Red Cross as a development within international society in the nineteenth century. The emergence of the notion of human rights in the early twentieth century, leading up to the *Universal Declaration* and the *Genocide Convention* of 1948, will be plotted. In the second part of the chapter the work of John Rawls will be presented – Rawls is, in some respects, the last 'Westphalia' political theorist, someone whose work on the Law of Peoples and basic human rights represents a modern version of the society of states.

Chapter 5, *Challenges to the Society of States* will explore the attempted juridification of world politics, the development of international criminal law, universal jurisdiction, the ICC and other international courts. As part of the same process, the New Humanitarianism, the rejection of the norm of non-intervention and the emergence of political NGO activism will be examined.

Part II: The Emerging Global Polity

Part II develops these challenges in detail looking at the notion of economic rights and the rights of peoples, identifying some contradictions within these new ideas, and examining attempts to resolve them. Then the politics of 'humanitarian intervention', the successes and failures of the 1990s and the later doctrine of R2P will be examined along with developments in the ethics of war and violence in a contemporary context. Proposals for global justice and international institutional reform will be examined.

Chapter 6, *The New Human Rights Regime* will examine new understandings of human rights as something defined against the states rather than claimed from it. Culturist and Feminist critiques will be examined along with attempts to defend and redefine rights, in particular the pragmatist Richard Rorty's notion of a 'human rights culture', and Martha Nussbaum's presentation of human capabilities as a (universal) alternative to rights.

Chapter 7, *Intervention: The 1990s Learning Curve* will look at the first generation of post-Cold War humanitarian operations, in particular the response to the wars of former Yugoslavia and to state failure in Somalia and the failure to respond to the genocide in Rwanda in 1994.

Chapter 8, *The Responsibility to Protect* explores the way in which the notion of a 'responsibility to protect' emerged out of the 1990s experience, especially that of Kosovo in 1999, partly on the initiative of the International Commission on Intervention and State Sovereignty which reported in 2001. R2P was established as an official UN doctrine in 2005 – its record since then in Libya, Cote d'Ivoire and Syria has been mixed.

Chapter 9, *The Ethics of War and Violence in a Post-Westphalian Age* examines the conduct of war in the twenty-first century along with the War on Terror. Non-combatant immunity and 'new wars', targeted killing and drones and the struggle to control information are themes here. Finally, modern analytical Just War theory will be explored and critiqued.

Chapter 10, *Global Justice* will explore Kantian and Utilitarian notions via the work of Peter Singer, Charles Beitz, Brian Barry and Thomas Pogge. Cosmopolitan proposals for institutional reform and global governance represent the most developed account of a global polity currently available.

Conclusion

Chapter 11, *The Return of Realism in Theory and Practice* examines critiques of liberal cosmopolitanism and global justice, also the so-called 'new political realism'. Finally the impact of the normative framework preferred by the emergent powers, and especially China, will be examined along with the possibility that moves towards a global polity will actually be reversed in the years to come.

Further Reading

There are a number of readable introductions to international political theory: unsurprisingly, Chris Brown (1992) and (2002) have some similarities to the present volume, although my thinking has moved on in the intervening years – see e.g. Brown (2006a) and (2006b); Mervyn Frost (1996) presents his neo-Hegelian take on the discourse – Frost (2009) is a slimmed down more popular introduction; Edward Keene (2005) approaches the subject as a historian of ideas; Kimberly Hutchings (2010) offers the approach of a feminist political theorist and Richard Shapcott (2010) that of a critical theorist. Kwame Anthony Appiah (2007) isn't a textbook, but is a very thoughtful introduction to many of the issues international political theorists study.

Charles Beitz (1985) collects a number of classic articles in international political theory, many of which are also to be found in two invaluable collections of papers brought together by Thomas Pogge and Keith Horton (2007) and Pogge and Darrell Moellendorf (2008). See also Bell (2009) and (2010).

For IR theory in general and its relationship to international political theory, David Boucher (1998) provides an excellent history. Chris Brown (2009) is a text on IR by the present author. The collection of essays edited by Ken Booth and Steve Smith (1995) is still useful and a new edition edited by Booth and Toni Erskine is on the way. Erskine's account of 'Normative IR Theory' (2009) is very valuable and presents a good contrast to the approach outlined in this book.

This book is concerned with norms in action, as it were, but there is now a very strong literature, largely constructivist, on the formation and spread of norms from a more theoretical viewpoint. Key texts here would include Friedrich Kratochwil (1989), Jeffrey Checkel (1998), Martha Finnemore (1996) and Finnemore and Katherine Sikkink (1998).

The most important specialist journal in international political theory is *Ethics & International Affairs*, the Journal of the Carnegie Council for Ethics & International Affairs; the *Journal of International Political Theory* is relatively new to the field but is establishing a strong reputation; *Millennium: Journal of International Studies* publishes a great deal of IPT from a critical viewpoint, while the *European Journal of International Relations* leans towards constructivism; the *Review of International Studies* publishes good material across the board; for theoretically informed commentary on issues of current importance *Foreign Affairs*, the journal of the Council of Foreign Relations in New York, and *International Affairs*, the journal of the Royal Institute of International Affairs ('Chatham House') are both very valuable.

The blogsphere changes at a rate that makes it likely that recommendations here will be out of date before read, but there are one or two sites which must be mentioned: www.carnegiecouncil.org/index.html is the site of the aforementioned Carnegie Council and is an excellent resource; www.foreignpolicy.com is the site of the magazine *Foreign Policy* and has much information on current affairs and links to many useful blogs; www.whiteoliphaunt.com/duckofminerva is the site of the 'Duck of Minerva', which is uneven but at its best is outstanding; the political science profession is represented at www.washingtonpost.com/blogs/monkey-cage/. The Stanford Encyclopaedia of Philosophy http://plato.stanford.edu is a first point of call for many of the issues discussed in this book. More specialist sites will be identified in the following chapters.

PART I

INTERNATIONAL SOCIETY

2

INTERNATIONAL SOCIETY AND INTERNATIONAL LAW

In this chapter the emergence of the 'Society of States' will be examined along with the simultaneous emergence of what later became known as 'International Law'. The emergence of the society of states was a process that took a century and a half – the so-called 'long sixteenth century', 1492–1648, and was largely theorised in the century after 1648; International Law took on a recognisable shape in the same period, but has roots in the high Medieval period, and perhaps earlier. In the second half of the chapter, the work of the English School will be examined; the English School is nowadays the branch of IR theory most closely associated with International Society – in fact, as will be made apparent, there is very little that is specifically 'English' about the concept, and the association is largely based on the fact that other branches of IR theory which once were content to use the same terminology no longer do so.

The emergence of international society

A long view of human history would suggest that for the last 10,000 years human beings have mostly lived in small relatively isolated communities or in empires; state systems are the exception rather than the rule, and state systems that last for several centuries are a subset with only one member, and that member is the system that has been in existence for more or less the last 400 years. Quite possibly, this unique status is attributable to the fact that this system is actually a *society* of states rather than the kind of state-system that briefly existed in, say, the Hellenic period between the fall of Alexander's Empire and the rise of Rome, or the period of the 'Warring States' in China. In those systems, each of their members desired to be the basis for a world-empire, and relations were conducted solely on the basis of power and interest. Power and interest have been important components of the international order that emerged in Western Europe in the long sixteenth century, but the survival and growth of that system to its current world-encompassing dimensions is attributable to the fact that these have not been the only important components of that order. The nature of the additional factors that have created longevity is of real interest here, as are the conditions that created them.

The key to this issue is the fact that the conditions under which the European state system emerged in the long sixteenth century were very unusual. Generally when systems of states emerge it is a result of the collapse of an imperial system and, in a way, that is true in this case – but the collapse of the Roman Empire actually took place 1,000 years earlier and it is the complex system of social relations that replaced Rome that is the seedbed for the new order. The Roman Empire collapsed in the West in a long drawn out process that was more or less complete around 500 CE, but left behind one universal institution, the Catholic Church, and after 800 CE and the coronation of Charlemagne as the Holy Roman Emperor, a kind of imperial structure was reborn with the Church's approval. However, this new combination of a universal religious authority and a putatively universal political authority never possessed the kind of effective power that a more conventional empire would exercise, partly because the two wings, secular and religious, rarely operated together and, indeed, were often in conflict. As well as these two universal institutions, some territorial political entities, kingdoms, managed to establish effective control, especially in the West of Europe, a patchwork quilt of local magnates were often effectively independent even of these kings and, as the years went by, the Medieval scene was completed by the emergence of independent cities, guilds and universities (Holmes, 1992). The most important universal institution, the Church, had branches everywhere, and was the largest land-owner in Europe, with monasteries and bishoprics exercising a high degree of independent power – it was, in effect, in today's terms, a very powerful international business enterprise (Lynch, 1992).

The result was a unique political order, with multiple centres of power linked together in chains of obligation. Even the strongest secular rulers answered to someone, and ordinary individuals understood their identities in both local and universal terms, for example as a member of a guild, or liegeman of a local lord, and as a Christian. This changed in the long sixteenth century. Gradually local and universal identities faded along with local and universal sources of power; instead, identities and power gravitated to medium-sized territorial units, recognisably states in the modern sense of the term. This change took place because of a combination of factors. The Protestant Reformation challenged the authority of the Church and removed an important unifying factor in European life, but the beneficiaries of this shift away from the universal were medium-sized political units rather than small-scale local polities. Partly this reflected a shift in military technologies; the Medieval system rested on the dominance of cavalry, armoured knights who were maintained by small-scale estates and only came together under the command of a king on occasion, but in this period the battlefield came to be dominated by trained infantry and by the new artillery made possible by the use of gunpowder, and these technologies were too expensive for local magnates to afford. The new medium-sized rulers were able to afford this weaponry partly because of the influx of silver from the new world; Spain carried out the conquest of the Americas but the silver imported into Europe rarely stayed in Spanish hands, but rather gravitated to the newer centres of industry in Northern France, the Low Countries and England.

The exact mix of these factors, ideological, military and economic, that produced the modern state is still debated by historians, and probably always will be, but from our point of view what is crucial is that a new European order was created in which the major players came to understand themselves as the rulers of territorially based 'sovereign' states. They came to believe that they should acknowledge no external superior – even Catholic rulers were no longer prepared to allow the Pope anything more than spiritual authority (except in the lands where the Pope himself was sovereign) – and no internal equal. This latter claim was resisted by the old aristocracy in most countries, and led to more than one civil war, but only in a few countries, most obviously England and the United Provinces, were the old magnates able to preserve a degree of independent power, elsewhere being restricted to the role of 'courtiers', residing in the presence of the sovereign and dependent on his goodwill. The new rulers were usually literally 'sovereigns', that is actual individuals who held power, but 'sovereignty' as a notion gradually in this period came to be understood as a property of states rather than something possessed by individuals. Even though it was still possible for Louis XIV of France to claim 'L'État, c'est moi' – or at least for people to believe that he had said this, there being no reliable evidence that he actually did – in fact, even Louis, the very model of an absolute monarch, could be, and was, distinguished from France. The sovereign state was not simply the expression of a particular personality, it was, instead a key invention of the modern era.

Sovereignty, international society and the law of nations

Some 'realist' writers, Stephen Krasner in particular, have challenged the idea that something critical happened in the long sixteenth century; their argument is that rulers have always attempted to rule without acknowledging external superiors or internal equals – to put the matter crudely, they just became better at it in this period, gathering more resources to themselves and asserting their independence more effectively (Krasner, 1999). There is some truth to this – clearly many medieval rulers wanted to think of themselves as separated from the chains of obligation that composed medieval society, and some actually came close to achieving the status of a sovereign in the modern sense of the term. Krasner goes on to argue that sovereignty is a very confusing term, with several different meanings and, again, he has a point. But what all this misses, or at least downplays the importance of, is that sovereignty is not just a matter of the absence of *external superiors* and *internal equals* – crucially, the concept of sovereignty as it emerged in the modern period involved also recognition by *external equals* and this was, and is, a key feature of the society of states, indeed it is what makes the society of states possible. Part of the story here is about the emergence of international law, or the law of nations as it was originally called – and this will be considered later is this section – but it was also about the emergence of, and limits to, a norm of non-intervention.

The idea behind the norm of non-intervention is clear, even if in practice things are considerably more complex. Non-intervention involves a sovereign recognising the right of other sovereigns to be sovereign in their lands as a necessary corollary to his (or her, but usually his) right to be sovereign in his lands. An important point here is that non-*intervention* is not the same as non-*aggression*, which did not become a fully-fledged norm of international society until the twentieth century. The taking of territory by conquest was part of the operation of international society from its very beginning – the point is that sovereigns could, and did, fight wars against each other without challenging their respective rights to rule, their legitimacy. Of course, aggression can become intervention when the point of the action is to overthrow a sovereign and change the nature of the polity against which war is being made but the majority of wars do not take this form. Thus, the Spanish Armada of 1588 and the descent of William of Orange on England 100 years later were interventions designed to bring about regime-change – unsuccessful in the first case, successful, albeit with a lot of local support, in the second – but they stand out in English and European history precisely because they combine aggression and intervention, notions that were normally kept apart.

The long sixteenth century changed the nature of monarchy in Europe; the rulers of the new territorial states enhanced their ceremonial status quite deliberately in this period. Language is interesting here; the Plantagenet Kings of England were referred to as 'Your Grace', a title they shared with Dukes and Bishops – the Tudors demanded to be called 'Your Majesty', a title they shared with no other Englishman, but, crucially, was shared with other kings. Monarchs came to refer to each other using fraternal titles ('My brother', 'Mon frère') – and in many cases, of course, they were related to each other, if not as brothers then as cousins, although after the Reformation inter-marriage among European royalty became more restrictive, with Protestants marrying Protestants and Orthodox Christians, and Catholics, Catholics. Such was not always the case, but marrying out of one's religion often did not end well – Charles I of England and Scotland was happily married to a French Catholic princess, but, partly as a result, his sons Charles II and James II became Catholic and the latter lost the throne to his, Charles I's, Protestant grandson and granddaughter William and Mary.

So, sovereigns thought of themselves as part of a wider family of sovereigns – but as most of us know, being part of a family does not preclude considerable hostility, and family members quite frequently intervene in each other's affairs, so how did the norm of non-intervention arise? There are two answers to this question, operating at different levels; sovereignty and non-intervention can be seen as pragmatic solutions to the problem of religious diversity, or they can be seen as a principled response to new – or rather revived – ideas about property and political power.

The pragmatic dimension is not difficult to grasp. The very forces that were creating territorial states in the long sixteenth century were also sources of great tension in virtually all European societies. The level of hostility that existed between Protestants and Catholics – and, for that matter, between Lutheran Protestants and Calvinist Protestants – is difficult for modern Europeans to grasp, although those who live in Northern Ireland have a better chance of doing so than most. In the early sixteenth century, North German Protestant princes fought the Catholic Emperor in a series of bitter religious wars, but the divide between Protestant and Catholic did not fit neatly with existing borders, which meant the possibility of adding civil strife to inter-state warfare was very high; a Peasants' revolt in the same period added to the distress of ordinary people throughout the Empire. When, finally, a kind of temporary truce was established by the Peace of Augsburg of 1555, the principle was established that each ruler would decide on the religious identity of his own realm; the religion of the king would be the religion of the people, *cuius regio, ejus religio*.

This was a very crude principle, an extreme form of non-intervention, and one that could produce a great deal of misery for divided societies – in England in the mid-sixteenth century the religion of the monarch swung from full-blooded Protestantism under Edward VI, to rigid Catholicism under Mary and then a rather less extreme, but equally intolerant Protestantism under Elizabeth, with ordinary people being obliged to pretend to change their beliefs with each incoming ruler. England was not part of the Empire but its rulers applied *cuius regio, ejus religio* whenever they could – in France, also not part of the Empire, the division was too great for religious uniformity to be applied easily but the desire to do so led to great violence and atrocities such as the St Bartholomew's Day Massacre of 1572. Moreover, the principle was not actually followed by the princes of Europe who continued to intervene in each other's religious affairs when they considered it opportune to do so.

Cuius regio, ejus religio was thus not an very successful principle, but the general idea that the way to end the seemingly endless and horrific conflicts of the sixteenth century was to strengthen the authority of secular rulers took hold, and became the basis for the work of some of the first theorists of the concept of 'sovereignty', such as the French political philosophers known as the *politiques* and, ultimately in the next century, the greatest of all theorists of sovereignty, Thomas Hobbes. Hobbes's work defies any quick summary, but the core principle of 'no external superior, no internal equal' is central to his conception of the sovereign, and a very large part of his *Leviathan* is devoted to an attack on the Catholic Church which focuses not on its theology as such, which would have been the focus a century before, but on its claim to universal jurisdiction. Hobbes's sovereign is created by the people who contract one with another to create a ruler who is not himself bound by a contract with his people and it is intolerable to Hobbes to think of this ruler being undermined by outside forces (Hobbes, 1651/1994; Springborg, 2007).

Pragmatically then, sovereignty is a solution to a problem – the problem of maintaining order in a world where religion is no longer a unifying but potentially a dividing force. However, the brutality of the principle of *cuius regio, ejus religio* does not actually survive into the modern world, at least not in that extreme form. The Peace of Westphalia in 1648, the Treaties of Osnabrück and Münster, which ended the religious wars of the seventeenth century – the 'Thirty Years War' – actually regulate and refine the principle rather than simply restate it. Rather than simply declaring that the sovereign can decide the religion of his or her people, Westphalia actually provides quite extensive protection for minorities, authorising intervention on their behalf by external powers if necessary for their protection. This is an interesting shift, which makes it clear that, contrary to the views of the older generation of IR scholars who saw 1648 as establishing the principle of an untrammelled sovereignty (which could hardly be the basis for an international *society*), what was done at Westphalia was to regularise and formalise a much more sophisticated notion of sovereignty, one based on the idea of non-intervention, but a non-intervention norm that recognised the possibility of certain exceptions to the rule. Non-intervention was not to be seen as simply a necessary concomitant to the idea of sovereignty, but rather as a norm the terms of which were to be established by collective agreement and custom in the evolving European society. Brendan Simms and David Trim in their pioneering work on humanitarian intervention have shown how that norm evolved through the examination of numerous cases where it was, apparently, breached, including cases where the protection of local populations from oppression was the reason for overriding the norm (Simms and Trim, 2011).

The principle of sovereignty was a response to the pragmatic needs of a divided European society, but it was also a reflection of wider changes in the way in which contemporaries thought about the world. Here the important shift is not so much the Reformation but the Renaissance and the revival of interest in and knowledge of the classical world, especially of Rome. A key element in this revival is a changing account of the meaning of 'property'. In the medieval world property ownership is almost always conditional in some way; land, the most important form of property, was held conditional on service to a liege lord who in turn owed obligations to a grander magnate, and so on up to the highest levels in society. At the very top of the social anthill the Emperor and independent kings were under the sovereignty of God – and his earthly representative, the Pope, if the latter was powerful enough to make this a reality. The obligation of service went both ways – the king's liegemen were expected to turn out in his support but he had obligations to them and so on down the chain.

Of course, things were never quite that clear cut, and as Krasner and other realists have pointed out, rulers often did their best to break the chain and assert their independence, but the power of ideas is very great and limited their ability so to do. The revival of Roman thinking, and in particular the Roman law of property, *dominium*, changed all this. Roman property owners were not caught up in such a chain of obligation – they owned property outright and could do what they willed with it, answering to no one for their behaviour. Friedrich Kratochwil has argued in a very influential paper that the territorial princes thrown up by processes outlined above understood their rule in terms of *dominium* (Kratochwil, 1995). Sovereignty is understood as meaning that the state is the property of the ruler who can do with it what he or she wills. Outsiders have no right to intervene in the conduct of rulers.

On the face of it this would seem to set in place a very strong doctrine of sovereignty and non-intervention, but, in fact, it underscores the idea that sovereigns should accept each other as equals. Property owners can do as they wish with their property – except in so far as their behaviour impinges on the property rights of other property owners. The claim to own property outright carries with it the logical implication that other property owners also own property outright. It also carries with it the logical implication that if a property owner behaves in a way that affects the property rights of other property owners the latter have the right to prevent him from so doing. In short, sovereignty as *dominium* is a normative principle and non-intervention is a norm to which exceptions may sometimes be found. The circumstances under which they could be found are very nicely summarised in an unexpected place, the UN Charter of 1945, Chapter VII which sets out action to be taken in the case of threats to international peace and security. Article 2(7) of the same document establishes the general principle of non-intervention in the jurisdiction of states, but when what is happening within that jurisdiction constitutes a threat to international peace and security the norm may be breached.

Thus it is that a combination of pragmatism and principle produces a doctrine of sovereignty and non-intervention, which simultaneously establishes independent political units and determines that relations among them should be normatively governed – a unique combination and the feature that distinguishes European international society from other state-systems. Alongside this change was another of equal significance – the development of international law, or, as it was known in the early modern period, the Law of Nations. The 'Law of Nations' is a straightforward translation of the Roman *ius gentium*, but by the seventeenth century the meaning of these two terms had drifted a long way apart. The Roman Empire was a hotchpotch of territories governed at the level of politics and the individual by Roman law, but at the social and economic level many territories retained this original legal system; *ius gentium* regulated relations between territories at the level and thus was close to what we now call Private International Law rather than to Public International Law which governs the relations of states. If anything, the notion of the Law of Nations was closer to the Roman idea of *ius naturale*, 'natural law' that is principles of law recognised by all human beings, or at least all civilised people. To add to the confusion, medieval thinkers took over the notion of Natural Law but understood it rather differently – for the Scholastics 'natural law' was law generated by human reason, based on human nature, and contrasted with God's law, based on revelation.

Gradually, over the course of the long sixteenth century these various sources of law coalesced into what we now think of as the Law of Nations. Initially the 'Salamanca School' of Spanish jurists, in particular Suarez and Vitoria, developed the Scholastic idea of natural law to respond to the unique problems posed by the conquest of the Americas by Spain, turning the medieval notion into something that looks much more like the modern idea of a law that governs relations between independent polities. However, the Salamancans rejected, or rather did not even contemplate, the idea of sovereignty – for them as for the Scholastics, sovereignty rested with God alone; this was a shift achieved by Protestant scholars such as Gentili (an Italian Protestant who moved to England for health reasons) and the Dutchman Grotius. As Richard Tuck has documented, Grotius produced an account of sovereignty very close to that of his near contemporary, Thomas Hobbes – he also revolutionised the notion of a Just War, as we will see in the next chapter of this book (Tuck, 2000 and 2002). In the late seventeenth and early eighteenth centuries a succession of legal philosophers, Pufendorf, Wolff and especially Emerich de Vattel developed the idea of an independent law of nations, still linked to the idea of natural law, but with its own identity (Brown et al., 2002).

Vattel is the writer who comes closest to setting out the legal basis of a Society of States in language that is recognisably modern. It is Vattel above all who establishes that the key subjects of the law of nations are states rather than individuals and, crucially, that sovereignty implies sovereign equality. Vattel recognises, of course, that states are not actually equal in terms of their powers, that is their capacity to affect events, but he sees very clearly that they can still claim legal equality – in an interesting figure of speech he notes that just as giants and dwarves are both men, so big states and small are both sovereign. Like all of his predecessors, Vattel still links the Law of Nations to Natural Law, but the link is now easily broken, and in a later period, the nineteenth century, it breaks and the Law of Nations becomes simply something created by states for their own convenience. By then the Law of Nations has been renamed by Jeremy Bentham International Law. Most of Bentham's many neologisms did not stick, but this one gradually came to supplant the earlier coinage, and the link to Natural Law was pushed even further into the past, although, as we will see, arguably it has returned in the modern period.

The Society of States: Europe and the world

The Society of States is a fully operating mode of interaction between states in the eighteenth century. This is a period when Europe does resemble the 'one great republic' that both Edward Gibbon and Edmund Burke described, the latter at the point at the end of the century when this description was rapidly becoming outmoded by the attempt of the French Revolutionaries and later Napoleon to change the rules of the game. This was the period described in Carl Schmitt's *Nomos of the Earth* when wars between states came closest to resembling duels between sovereigns, when ordinary individuals were relatively uninvolved unless they were unlucky enough to live in the territories where battles were fought (Schmitt, 2003). The English writer Laurence Sterne in *A Sentimental Journey* tells of arriving in Dover en route to Paris having quite forgotten that George II of England was at war with Louis XV of France – fortunately he finds a French aristocrat returning from a trip to London under a safe-conduct pass who provides him with the same for his trip to Paris. Sterne exaggerates for comic effect but still one gets a sense of a coherent rather cosmopolitan world, which would soon be disrupted by the French Revolution and the rise of nationalism (Sterne, 2008). After 1815, nationalism disrupts somewhat International Society; even where sovereigns survive they mostly find themselves embedded into national political systems where the people are seen as the ultimate source of constitutional power – but this is a less radical change than might have been expected; Thomas Hobbes in the seventeenth century saw no necessity that sovereignty be invested in a single individual, although he did believe that things worked better if it was.

A more interesting shift in the society of states in the nineteenth century actually concerns not nationalism as such, but relations between Europe and the rest of the world. As will have been apparent from the previous discussion, one of the features that held the society of states together was a shared past, European and Christian. With the Reformation the Christian element of this past was fractured but the basics held fast – Catholics and Protestants differed on much, but held the same core beliefs. In the eighteenth century the old description of Europe as 'Christendom' was no longer much used, but it was taken for granted that members of international society were Christian. The great 'other' of Medieval Christendom was Ottoman Turkey and in the long sixteenth century the status of the Sultan actually illustrated very clearly the changes that were taking place in Europe. Unlike the kings of the West, the Sultan was not prepared to accept the status of an equal – as holder of the Caliphate and, as he saw it, inheritor of the empire of Rome, the Sultan regarded his status as far more exalted than even the grandest of European kings. Moreover, the European monarchs were equally clear that they did not want to include him in their club, even though occasionally they were prepared to ally with him as part of the game of politics. In the eighteenth century when Ottoman power was on a sharp decline the Sultan made advances towards the club of European sovereigns, but was rebuffed – Europe may not have been Christendom any more but it was still composed of Christian powers.

Relations with the Ottomans were only a small part of Europe's relations with the rest of the world in the early modern period. This was the age of the conquest of the Americas, and of European expansion into the rest of the non-European world. In the case of the Americas, the Europeans were technologically more advanced than the locals and dominated from the beginning – the picture was much more complex in the East. Powerful rulers on the Indian sub-continent and in China and South East Asia were more than able to hold their own against the incomers until towards the end of the eighteenth century, and Europeans were able to operate only on the edges of these worlds, technologically superior only at sea where their gun-bearing ocean-going galleons could deal with most opponents. Powerful or not, what is clear is that from the beginning Europeans treated their relations with non-Europeans as different in kind from their relations with each other. The notion of sovereign equality that came to be the defining feature of relations within Europe was never applied outside of the continent. Moreover, relations between Europeans were conducted differently in the non-European world – for example, the struggle for supremacy in the East Indies between Dutch and English merchant-adventurers was conducted on a no holds barred basis regardless of the state of relations between the two naval powers in Europe, where they were often allied against Spain or France. 'Beyond the line' things were different. The radical conservative German philosopher Carl Schmitt in his *The Nomos of the Earth* tells one version of the story, the English School writer Edward Keene in his *Beyond the Anarchical Society* tells another, but they both agree that different rules apply within and beyond the limits of Europe (Keene, 2002; Schmitt, 2003).

In the nineteenth century there are a number of changes that take place in the relationship between Europe and the rest of the world. In the first place, European technological superiority changes the nature of the game; the European outsiders are now able to lay down the terms of any interactions with the locals and, in some cases, most obviously with the British in India, formal imperialism takes place and foreign rule supplants local control. Even where formal imperialism does not take place, norms of non-intervention which are still considered valid in Europe do not apply in the rest of the world. Gary Bass and Martha Finnemore have set out the ways in which explicitly 'humanitarian' interventions are conducted in the nineteenth century, usually on behalf of Christians persecuted (or allegedly persecuted in some cases) by non-European rulers (Finnemore, 2003; Bass, 2008). But while these acts of imperialism were taking place, it was also the case that the terms of membership of international society were being rethought. Gradually the key qualification ceases to be being European and Christian, and becomes instead being 'civilised' – of course, civilisation itself was defined in Christian and European terms so one could argue that only the packaging is being changed here, but the shift is nonetheless crucial. In this period where racism permeated all thinking, non-European could not change their skin colour and become European, and becoming Christian would require changing core beliefs, but becoming civilised was something that lay within the realms of possibility.

The idea of the 'standards of civilisation' is a product of this thinking (Gong, 1984). When Europeans encountered non-European states which they had no wish to actually conquer – or where intra-European politics precluded this option – they would impose these standards instead. The basic idea was that these states would not be treated as equals until they were in possession of the right sort of institutions and attitudes; the key requirements were that they instituted the rule of law, and provided protection for individuals and property – the needs of European traders being evident in these requirements. Until such time as they complied, these states were subjected to various restrictions, such as external control of customs offices, and extraterritorial jurisdiction over locally based Europeans. These restrictions were, of course, deeply resented and shaken off as soon as was practicable – in the Ottoman Empire in 1856, in Japan by treaty in 1899, although in China not until 1944 – but an important point is that it was possible for them to be ended; 'civilised' status was actually achievable, however demeaning the process.

The idea of imposing extra-territorial jurisdiction in this way faded in the twentieth century but it left behind two important residues. First, it established that sovereignty was not simply a matter of being able to assert the right of non-intervention. In terms which later were proposed by the English School theorist Robert Jackson, sovereignty was not just a matter of the *negative* right to be left alone, it also involved the *positive* notion of being capable of self-government (Jackson, 1990). In the nineteenth century European countries declared themselves all to be in possession of such a positive capability, but in the twentieth century this division of the world into the capable and the incapable on the basis of racial or geographical origins became unacceptable – but the issue of capacity did not go away, and Jackson's point that many of the 'quasi-states' left behind by decolonisation did not possess positive sovereignty is certainly valid. The second point that should be noted is that, although it goes without saying that the idea of Europeans telling Japan and China that they were not civilised is patently absurd and offensive, still the requirements of the standards of civilisation are not so obviously obnoxious. Establishing the rule of law in countries where this did not exist, where, for example, the lives of ordinary people were in the hands of an aristocracy that could dispose of them at will, is, taken out of context, on the face of it a good idea, even if it goes against local cultural mores. The clash between universal values and local standards of behaviour carries through into the twentieth and twenty-first centuries in the idea of human rights, which even a strong supporter of the current regime, Jack Donnelly, has termed the new 'standards of civilisation' (Donnelly, 1998).

The rise of the international human rights regime and its implications for the idea of an international society will be the subject matter of Chapter 4 of this book; what needs to be noted now is that the process by which the conditions for membership of international society move from being European to being civilised paved the way for the expansion of the society of states in the twentieth century, and especially after the Second World War with the establishment of the United Nations. Membership of the society of states was no longer to carry a cultural price tag – instead all states were to be understood as members of the new enlarged international society; the geographical, spatial and cultural restrictions plotted by Schmitt and Keene were no longer to apply. The key issue here is whether international society could survive without these restrictions. This has been one of the preoccupations of the major source of thinking on the society of states in the twentieth century, to which we now turn, the 'English School'.

The English School and the Society of States

In the 1950s the Rockefeller Foundation financed Committees on the theory of international relations on both sides of the Atlantic – the American Committee appears to have focused their efforts on a major conference, the proceedings of which have recently been published in a collection edited by Nicholas Guilhot, but this side of the Atlantic the British Committee met regularly over the next few years, produced edited collections, and developed what became a distinctive approach to International Relations (Dunne, 1998; Guilhot, 2011). The leading lights of the British Committee included the historian Herbert Butterfield, the theologian Donald McKinnon, Martin Wight, Reader of International Relations at the London School of Economics, the military historian Michael Howard and a younger scholar, Hedley Bull, who later made the most important and influential contribution to the committee's work.

The key text produced under the explicit auspices of the British Committee was a collection of essays published in 1966, *Diplomatic Investigations* (Butterfield and Wight, 1966). These essays on topics such as Western values and international relations and the balance of power drew on the European tradition of statecraft, focused on norms and values and defended traditional modes of scholarship in International Relations – Law, History and Philosophy. The central questions they posed revolved around the idea of an international society understood more or less as outlined in this chapter. Such a conception of the subject matter of international relations theory became increasingly controversial in the face of the rise of the behavioural sciences in the United States, and the British Committee writers, especially Bull, became standard bearers for what they called the classical approach, which Bull set out at some length in what is still the single most important text of this school of thought, *The Anarchical Society* (Bull, 1977). The title perfectly catches the core idea of a society of states – that international anarchy need not be devoid of social rules. This approach was controversial, with critics arguing that it represented a characteristically English take on the 'two cultures' with a rejection of the scientific mode of thought. In 1981 the (Welsh) political scientist Roy Jones as part of such a critique named the scholars who followed this tradition the 'English School', and the name stuck as a label its adherents were happy to accept (Jones, 1981). In fact the English School is English only in the sense that it was based in England (in other words, in the same way in which the Frankfurt School got its name) – its adherents have been Australian, American, South African, Canadian, Scottish and Welsh as well as, occasionally, English.

It might be thought that the emphasis of the School on norms and values is particularly appropriate for a country whose power in more conventional terms has been on a steady decline for some time, but, in fact, the English School approach to international society in essence continues a long European tradition of thinking about international order. It stands out as distinctive because this long tradition fell out of favour in the twentieth century in continental Europe and in the United States. Continental European thought oscillated between a hard-line power politics (for example, in Nazi Germany and Soviet Russia) and a radical rejection of international society in Western Europe post-1945. The US case is rather different. Wilsonian liberalism post-1918 was actually consistent with a strand of thought on international society but understood itself as a radical critique of the old order; more interesting is the fate of American realism. Post-1945 figures like Hans J. Morgenthau, Arnold Wolfers and John Herz were actually theorists of international society, a term they all used quite freely, but the turn to structural realism heralded by Waltz's *Theory of International Politics* in 1979 downplayed normative theory, understood international relations in terms of the interplay of objective material forces, and valorised science in a way that the classical American realists specifically rejected (Morgenthau, 1947; Waltz, 1979). In effect, the English School represents the continuation of a tradition of thought that has been abandoned elsewhere – although interestingly the New English School refounded by Barry Buzan in the 2000s has made much more of an effort to connect with some strands of the American academy, especially constructivism (Buzan, 2004, 2014).

As the inheritors of the European tradition, the English School has been the place where thinking about the society of states has been most conscious of the need to respond to the twentieth-century shift from a European to a global international order. The original British Committee were very much Eurocentric and Christian in orientation; McKinnon was a leading British theologian and both Butterfield and Wight were explicitly Christian thinkers – this is a dimension of their thought which is often understated in twenty-first century, post-Christian Britain, where it is difficult to recall how important Christian theology was to all currents of British intellectual life in the mid-twentieth century (Cochran, 2009). Hedley Bull was not a Christian thinker, but in *The Anarchical Society* he treats the institutions of international society (diplomacy, international law, the balance of power) as European cultural artefacts. The English School were very interested in *The Evolution of International Society*, as expounded by Adam Watson in 1992, and in *The Expansion of International Society* an influential collection edited by Bull and Watson in 1984, but they approached the topic from an essentially Eurocentric perspective. From an International Political Theory perspective on cultural diversity the most interesting English School writer is Edward Keene whose work *Beyond the Anarchical Society* is referenced above. He links the formation of a Society of States in Europe explicitly to colonialism outside of Europe, and traces the way in which the notion of toleration of different political orders has interacted with the promotion of civilisation – with both positions coming together in the modern post-1945 political settlement in which self-determination and human rights are uneasy bedfellows.

The nature of international society:
Solidarism and pluralism

English School writers agree that there is an international 'society' which is, at some level, rule-governed, but disagree as to the normative basis of this international order; what makes a society of sovereign states desirable? On what basis is the norm of non-intervention defensible? These have become key questions partly because of the expansion of international society – it is no longer adequate to describe the practices of international society as simply based on the ways in which European political life evolved in the early modern period. The pragmatic case for the normative value of sovereign states in an age of religious intolerance and the heritage of Roman law are specific to a time and a place (although religious intolerance, unfortunately, is still with us) and if the institutions they created are to remain relevant they need to be justified in terms that resonate with a non-European world. Whether this can be done is still an open question, but two attempts have been made by English School writers to do exactly that; 'solidarists' and 'pluralists' both draw inspiration from classic English School texts, but in very different ways.

The *solidarist* position is nicely summarised by a statement from Hedley Bull's *Hagey Lectures* of 1984, where he describes sovereign governments as 'local agents of the common good' (Bull, 1984b). The idea here is that government is a necessity for human flourishing, but problems of scale rule out the possibility of a single, universal government and therefore 'local' governments are legitimate, and a society of sovereign governments constitutes a rational political order for humanity. But, the *telos* of the international society thus justified is to promote human flourishing, therefore its ultimate referent objects ought to be individual human beings rather than states. This means, for example, that the rights of sovereigns cannot be employed to justify large-scale human rights violations; sovereignty norms and human rights norms are not, and cannot be, in conflict. Mervyn Frost's neo-Hegelian constitutive theory of individuality is a version of this argument – the state and the individual are co-constituted (Frost, 1996). Solidarists have no principled objection to humanitarian intervention and support initiatives such as that represented by the *International Commission on Interventional and State Sovereignty* Report, 2001 which advocated a Responsibility to Protect (R2P). A number of writers fall into the solidarist camp – R.J. Vincent's work on human rights is usually taken to be a foundational solidarist text, and Tim Dunne and Nicholas Wheeler in the 1990s were the writers who drew out the distinction between solidarism and pluralism (Vincent, 1986; Wheeler and Dunne, 1996); Wheeler's work on *Saving Strangers* is a key solidarist text, perhaps the single most important (Wheeler, 2000).

Solidarism stresses the notion that international society instantiates a universal notion of the good; *pluralist* English School theory sees the point of international society is that it allows *different* conceptions of the good to flourish. One of the most interesting versions of this position is set out by Terry Nardin in *Law, Morality and the Relations of States* (Nardin, 1983). He sees international society as a 'practical association' as opposed to a 'purposive association', this is a re-working of Michael Oakeshott's distinction between 'civic' and 'enterprise' associations, set out in the latter's *On Human Conduct* (Oakeshott, 1975). The root idea here is that the purpose of international society, its *telos*, is to allow states to live together under conditions of peace and justice while following their own conception of the good. Practices and norms such as non-intervention, the legal principle that treaties must be considered binding (*pacta sunt servanda*) and diplomatic immunity must be acknowledged by any state that wants to be recognised as such. This is a well thought through position, which has important implications for contemporary debates – for example, do human rights norms imply a common project beyond co-existence and thus violate the idea of international society as a practical association? 'Gross violations of human dignity' as the old expression has it may violate the terms of practical association, but this is minimalist in the context of the modern human rights regime – this is a topic which will be returned to in Chapter 4 below. Other leading pluralist scholars include Robert Jackson and James Mayall, both of whom are actually more closely associated with the English School than Nardin, although the latter's work, and his reliance on Oakeshott, puts him squarely within the tradition, even though the institutional links are fewer in his case than with the other writers named here (Mayall, 1990; Jackson, 2003).

Solidarism assumes and valorises the existence of universal values and common notions of the good; pluralism assumes and valorises the existence of different conceptions of the good. Both positions have points in their favour, but both positions also gloss over the fact that many (pessimistically, most) states are not dedicated to *any* conception of the good whether local or universal. Both positions simply assume states are 'well-ordered' and their rulers are oriented towards some conception of justice, be it universal or local, but a sceptic might say that the rulers of many states in today's world are simply power-seeking kleptomaniacs, with no discernable interest in the welfare of 'their' people. Still, the division between solidarists and pluralists is a useful way of looking at English School writers, especially when issues of intervention are at stake, although it should be noted that not all English School writers fit into one or other category. Apart from the new English School most associated with Buzan, Richard Little and Ole Waever, major writers such as Andrew Hurrell and Ian Clark are not easily assimilated to the pluralist/solidarist divide (Hurrell, 2007; Clark, 2011). Like most binary divisions, this one obscures as much as it clarifies.

Conclusion: International society, the English School and modern political theory

The English School represents the best that the European tradition of thinking about statecraft, a tradition that goes back four centuries at least, can offer in the modern age. The central question though is whether that best is good enough given contemporary conditions. Solidarist and pluralist versions of English School thought draw on that tradition to address the issue of the shift to a global international society, and recognise that the society of states needs to be justified in terms that could appeal to states, rulers and peoples for whom European history and values have no resonance or authority. And, to reiterate, this matters because so much of the work of the English school rests on the proposition that culture matters, that the institutions of international society are cultural artefacts created by a particular history, and in so far as this is true, it matters if this history and culture is being experienced at best at second hand.

Is it possible to produce a defence of the notion of the society of states that is not culturally based? This is an open question, and one that will be explored in the next two chapters where the work of two modern political theorists, neither of whom is associated with the English School, or indeed with International

Relations theory more generally, will be examined. The context for this examination will be an exploration of two areas where the society of states comes under particular scrutiny. In the next chapter, the issue of war and violence will be the focus. Rather counter-intuitively, war is actually an institution of international society – that is to say it is a regular pattern of behaviour which plays an important role in the ways in which international society operates; how is this compatible with the idea that international society is norm-based? The answer lies in the notion that war, although always representing a breakdown of social norms, could nonetheless be regulated normatively. The notion of the Just War is central to this regulation and is itself one of the oldest traditions of thought about international society – indeed the oldest in terms of those traditions that are still current – but it has also stimulated modern political theorists to explore not just war, but also the nature of the international society of which war is a part. Michael Walzer is foremost among such thinkers, and will be the focus of the second part of the next chapter. In his account of the rights of political communities he offers an alternative version of international society to that of the English School. In the following chapter the focus will be on human rights and international society. For some modern thinkers human rights and the liberal framework within which they make sense are a reason for abandoning the idea of an international society and moving to a different normative framework – but for the most important liberal thinker of the last 50 years, John Rawls, this is not so; instead in his *Law of Peoples* he sets out another version of international society to set alongside that of Bull and Walzer. It may be that all three versions fail to meet the requirements of the twenty-first century, but before we reach such a conclusion we need to give the idea of the society of states the best defence we can.

Further Reading

There are innumerable histories of international society, very few of which are as politically savvy as A.J.P. Taylor's classic *The Struggle for Mastery on Europe* (1971), but Brendan Simm's outstanding *Europe: The Struggle for Supremacy* (2013) covers a wider time-frame and is equally enjoyable to read, even if his belief in the supremacy of international factors sometimes goes too far. Paul Kennedy (1989) presents a controversial thesis on the rise and fall of nations which certainly deserves consideration. On the early history of international society Andreas Osiander (1994) and (2001), Daniel Philpott (2001) and Samuel Barkin and Bruce Cronin (1994) have good stories to tell. John Hobson (2012) is a root and branch critique of

(Continued)

(Continued)

the kind of story told in this chapter – readers will have to decide for themselves whether the Eurocentrism to which he refers is actually as serious a problem as he would have us believe. On sovereignty, in addition to the references in text, Hent Kalmo and Quentin Skinner's collection (2011) is very valuable, as is the work of Jens Bartelson (1995) and (2014). Again, apart from the references in the text, further discussion of the norm of non-intervention will be found throughout the rest of this book.

The general literature on international law is equally vast. Jan Klabbers (2013) is an introduction to the subject that is IPT friendly. Political scientists David Armstrong (2007) and Christian Reus-Smit (2003) and (2004) present valuable theses about the relationship between international relations and international law. The essays in Friedrich Kratochwil (2014) should be required reading for all students of international political theory. Martti Koskenniemi is an international lawyer who crosses the boundary between law and international relations with ease; see particularly (2002) and (2011) but also (1990). James Crawford and Koskenniemi's *Cambridge Companion to International Law* (2012) is very useful. Gerry Simpson (2004) and (2007) are also cross-over works of great wisdom. Peter Wilson (2009) presents a short account of the English School's approach to international law.

Most of the key references to the English School are given in the text. Alex Bellamy (2005) is a useful collection as are Cornelia Navari (2009) and (2013). Barry Buzan's revival of the English School (2004) and (2014) focuses in particular on World Society and so is less to the point than many of the sources quoted in this chapter, but the website and bibliography of English School works he has created is simply outstanding, an invaluable scholarly tool: www.polis.leeds.ac.uk/research/international-relations-security/english-school. Richard Little (2000) and (2003) is part of the 'new' English School, but perhaps a little less focused on world society than Buzan. Andrew Linklater and Hidemi Suganami (2007) present a judicious assessment of the English School and Linklater (2011) combines English School history with process sociology and the work of Norbert Elias.

3

WAR AS AN INSTITUTION OF INTERNATIONAL SOCIETY

The central premise of the society of states is that relations between states are norm-governed, not simply the product of power politics or the interplay of material factors, force and interests. At the same time, relations between states in this international society often involve violence. Interstate war has been a consistent feature of European international relations since the origins of international society in the long sixteenth century, and remains so in the global international society that has developed post-1945. Jack Levy, John Mueller and others have documented the fact that interstate violence has actually fallen over the years – a position recently popularised by Steven Pinker is his bestseller *The Better Angels of Our Nature* – and in Western Europe, the original home of international society, states no longer calculate the possibility that they will go to war with each other, but still war is an important feature of the modern world (Mueller, 2004; Levy, 2010; Pinker, 2012). Moreover, it could be argued that war is not a contingent feature of international society, something that could be abolished without affecting the system as a whole, but essential to its functioning. One of the defining features of international society is the absence of an authoritative mechanism for conflict resolution; international law and arbitration offer such mechanisms but only in circumstances where the state parties to a conflict agree to their use, and even then there is no enforcement mechanism at their disposal. As a result, war has been used as the *ultima ratio regnum*, the last argument of kings, the final method of pursuing the equivalent of a civil suit in domestic society, and for this reason until recently was recognised in international law as a legitimate act of state.

Things have changed somewhat in the post-1945 international society. The very high cost of interstate war in the industrial age led to a number of international measures which were designed to undermine the legality of war. The Covenant of the League of Nations restricted severely the circumstances under which states could legally resort to force, in the Kellogg-Briand Pact of 1928 states agreed not to engage in aggressive war, and in the Treaty of London of 1945 which established the Tribunal at Nuremburg to try Nazi leaders, the waging of aggressive war was declared to be a criminal offence. The UN Charter completed and codified the outlawing of aggression. Unfortunately the reason why war existed as a legitimate institution of international society, the absence of an authoritative conflict-resolving mechanism, was not addressed with the same comprehensiveness with the result that states have continued to make war – although nowadays the term 'war' is rarely used for legal reasons, and all acts of force are described by their perpetrators as defensive. In fact, most wars nowadays do not actually resolve conflicts, but force is still resorted to with some frequency.

All this points to the importance of establishing a normative framework for consideration of the role of violence in international society, and a framework consistent with the idea of an international society as a norm-governed entity. Two quite common approaches to the use of force fail to meet the latter requirement; realism and pacifism. For the realist – at least of the Clausewitzian variety – war is simply an act of policy, a political instrument, to be judged solely on consequentialist terms, but this is surely inconsistent with the idea of a *society* of states. Violence is destructive of life, property and social institutions and it is difficult to imagine any definition of society that didn't regard violence as something generally to be avoided. A purely instrumental view of violence simply will not do. On the other hand, pacifism, the belief that violence is never justified, that war is always the worst choice whatever the situation, is also incompatible with the idea of a society of states; sometimes the only way in which the normative features of international society can be preserved is through force. What this suggests is the need for discrimination. A normative framework for the use of force is going to have to provide guidance on the circumstances in which force might be justified, and the circumstances in which it will not be justified. Such a framework actually exists within Western political and religious thought and has been important in establishing the approach to this subject in international society, and that framework focuses on the notion of a 'Just War'. This notion began life in a theological context in the middle ages and was then transferred, much adapted to a more secular age in the long sixteenth century – it went into abeyance for a substantial part of the history of international society, clearly being incompatible with the notion of war as *ultima ratio regnum* but the twentieth century has seen a revival, and in the process has stimulated a compelling account of the nature of the society of states as an expression of the rights of political communities. The first half of this chapter traces the history of the notion, and the second half looks at the relationship between Just War and the rights of political communities.

The Just War tradition: Origins and principles

All societies have some way of deciding when force is justified or not; a society without the intellectual resources that would enable it to discriminate between legitimate and illegitimate uses of force could hardly survive long as a society – and by the same token, no society could survive for long without legitimating some use of force under some circumstances. In the Islamic world the key notion is 'Jihad' and in the Christian, European tradition it is the 'Just War'; if the modern society of states had developed from the world of medieval Islam – unlikely given the difficulty Islam has in separating religion and politics, but not impossible – we would today be examining the concept of Jihad and considering its contemporary application. This is still a worthwhile enterprise, and Jihad has indeed been studied quite extensively of late, but in the context of this book, or at least this Chapter, it is the notion of a Just War that is central – the modern society of states developed out of the medieval world which produced the Just War tradition, and thinking about inter-state violence has been shaped by it as a result.

In fact, there are precursors of the Just War tradition in the Classical world – Cicero in particular had some thoughts on the matter that are of interest here – but it was Christian philosophers and theologians who developed the concept, and they did so out of need. A key figure is St Augustine (354–430 AD) because he was the supreme thinker of the first period in which Christians actually had to exercise power in what was quickly becoming the post-Roman world. Early Christianity seems to have been essentially pacifist, respectful of the powers that be unless asked to do something contrary to their core beliefs, such as offering sacrifice to the Emperor, and committed to non-violence. This stance was viable while Christian communities were small and Christians were debarred from taking office under the Empire, but by the middle and late fourth century Christianity had become the majority religion, and individual Christians held office, including the Imperial office itself, and this in a world where barbarian tribes – Goths, Visigoths, Vandals – threatened the basic social structure of the Empire. In these circumstances, pacifism moved from being the Christian norm to a stance that individual Christians might still adopt, but which could not be sustained by those exercising authority – a status pacifism still holds in our world today. Augustine, as the Bishop of a community in North Africa faced with schismatic Christians and barbarian invaders, was an office holder who had to come to terms with the problem of violence and he did so by setting out the proposition that although violence was undesirable and should not be resorted to readily, it was sometimes necessary in pursuit of justice, in self-defence, and to protect the weak. A Christian had to be prepared to pick up and wield the sword if ordered to do so by a legitimate authority.

Augustine did not set out in detail the conditions under which a war might be just, but it seems that he did actually coin the term 'Just War' (in Chapter 7, Book XIX of *The City of God*) and certainly many of the later ideas in the tradition can be found in embryo in Augustine. For an elaborated account, however, it is necessary to turn to the Christian theologian St Thomas Aquinas (1225–1274) who presents an account of the Just War as an element of a wider account of 'Natural Law'. Aquinas was a Christian theologian, but he was also an Aristotelian of a sort – like most of the scholars of his period he read Aristotle as a supporter of authoritarian government, but while this is misleading, he did take from Aristotle the key points that human beings are political and social beings, designed to live in society, and that they have natural intellectual capacities that help them to work out the principles appropriate to social life. His account of the Just War combines Christian revelation with those principles of natural law that can be discerned via human reason. His starting point is not actually war, but peace; peace – which is understood to encompass not simply the absence of war, but the presence of order, tranquillity, concord and community – is a necessity if people are to live the good life, to flourish as human beings, which is what God wills, but also what Greeks such as Aristotle meant by *eudemonia*, usually inadequately translated as happiness. Attaining peace in this full sense of the term, or preserving it, or regaining it if lost, is something that can require the exercise of force, and justly so (Finnis, 1996).

Following on from this central proposition are three preconditions for the justice of a war, each of which requires exegesis; proper authority, right intention, and a just cause. Proper authority establishes the principle that war is something that can only be justly waged by a legitimate public authority – private war cannot be just. This is an important principle in Aquinas's age because this was a time when the public authorities did not actually have a monopoly of the means to conduct war; even quite minor landowners maintained small private armies, and the great magnates had quite substantial forces at their command. Asserting that only public authorities have the right to wage war is another way of saying that these local forces should not be judges in their own cause; if they find themselves in dispute with their neighbour they should refer this dispute to the proper authorities and allow them to decide the matter. In our age we are very familiar with this principle – modern legal systems allow individuals to defend themselves if attacked but not to use force to pursue any other kind of claim, and the requirement of 'proper authority' simply applies this principle in a wider context. Of course, there is an issue as to who are the 'proper authorities' in the modern world when it comes to international relations; some argue that only the UN Security Council may properly authorise the use of force, others argue that the Council does not actually have the capacity to resolve disputes in an authoritative way, even though the UN Charter says it does. But, either way, the principle is clear – if there is an effective public authority then private actors may not resort to force.

The principle of 'right intention' states that force should be resorted to with the intention of attaining, preserving or regaining a just peace. The problem with this criterion is, of course, that the intentions of actors are not always – indeed, are hardly ever – transparent. From the point of view of Aquinas and his contemporaries this was less of a problem, because although human beings may not be able to read each other's minds, God does have that capacity, and so the intentions of princes are in fact transparent in so far as the fate of their souls are concerned. God at least would be able to judge whether this criterion was being met. Clearly in our world things are a lot less certain; we are still able to infer people's intentions from their actions and their statements in support of their actions, but without the reliability that divine judgement conveys. Finally, the requirement of a 'just cause' is interesting in Aquinas, because it differs some-what from what we now take to be basic. Much commentary in our age assumes that self-defence is at the heart of the concept of a just cause, but as John Finnis points out in his commentary on Aquinas and the Just War, this is not actually the case. Aquinas actually takes for granted the proposition that actors are enti-tled to defend themselves, and spends no time defending this principle – instead a just cause relates, as does right intention, to the business of attaining, preserv-ing and regaining a just peace. A cause is just if it involves righting a wrong, and the wrong in question need not to have been suffered by the actor.

These three preconditions for a just war are specific to the topic, but there are other conditions which reflect general principles of ethics, applicable in all cir-cumstances and encapsulated by the 'golden rule', the principle of basic fairness, 'do as you would be done by'. This principle generates the propositions that violence should be the last resort, that it should only be employed if propor-tional to the offence and there is a reasonable prospect of a just result, and that any foreseeable side-effects should not be excessive. The same principle requires that the innocent be protected where possible, although incidental harm may be acceptable in some circumstances. In this regard the doctrine of 'double-effect' applies; this states that an otherwise legitimate act (by a proper authority, with right intention and in pursuit of a just cause) may have a result that one would otherwise wish to avoid – intention here is central, which is why 'double-effect' is a principle not much approved of by those who doubt the importance of right intention. Still, without some equivalent to the doctrine of double-effect the actual conduct of military operations would be impossible, since any forceful action is likely to have some adverse consequences for the innocent, unless it can somehow be arranged that fighting takes place in a desert. Consider an example of the sort of situation where this kind of reasoning is necessary; in the Second World War there were occasions where it was known that an attack on an indisputably legitimate target would be certain to cause the deaths of innocents – a classic example involves the bombing raid on a Gestapo prison in the centre of Amiens in occupied France in February 1944 where it was known that, however accurate the bombing, some civilians would be killed in addition to the enemy. How is the decision to go ahead to be characterised morally? An utilitarian would make a cost-benefit analysis weighing the benefits to be expected against the predicted cost, but Aquinas would see this as an example of 'double-effect', a legitimate act with unintended if predictable side-effects – these two approaches might produce the same answer, but they get there by very different routes.

There are two features of the Just War in Aquinas which are worth noting because they are different from the way in which the concept is sometimes used today. First, Aquinas makes no distinction between *ius ad bellam* and *ius in bello*, the conditions under which it is legitimate to go to war and the ways in which war may legitimately be waged. This distinction comes much later in the history of the notion when, as we will see below, the focus was on the conduct of war; for Aquinas, and through until at least the seventeenth century, all the conditions for a Just War go together, they must all be met for a war to be considered just. There is no sense in which a trade-off between the conditions is possible. But, second, asking for all the principles to be met is not an invitation to provide a check-list and engage in a box-ticking exercise; each of the conditions requires the exercise of practical judgement and reasoning specific to the condition in question. Thus, for example, whether violence is actually the last resort depends on knowledge of the diplomacy of a dispute – are there non-violent options that have a reasonable prospect of success – and is not something that can be determined by the application of moral reasoning alone; proportionality and the reasonable prospect of a just result also require the exercise of the kind of judgement that relies on military and strategic knowledge. The overall judgement that the use of force is appropriate is the product of practical reasoning applied to a number of different areas – a suitably Aristotelian understanding of moral reasoning (Brown, 2013a).

The Just War and the Society of States

In the long sixteenth century the combination of the Reformation on the one hand, and the revival of Roman statist thought on the other, brought about a general turn away from the thought of Aquinas and the Scholastics – for quintessentially modern thinkers such as Hobbes and Descartes, the Scholastics were regarded as obscurantist, and their doctrines subversive of civil peace, liable to undermine the new doctrine of sovereignty (Toulmin, 1992). Part of this general rejection of scholastic modes of thought involved a serious reworking of the idea of the Just War, and this reworking focused on a feature of Just War thinking that had always been present but which came to be seen in a new light in the seventeenth century; according to Aquinas and other scholastics, only one of the sides in a war could be just – how do we know which one? The classic answer to this question was that we should use our God-given judgement to do the best we can to decide this question, while acknowledging that God alone would know the truth.

The lawyers of the seventeenth century, Grotius and his successors, eventually, after much cogitation, came to a different conclusion – since we can't be sure which side in a war is just we should leave the matter to God, and treat both sides equally (Boucher, 2011a). This just about keeps alive the idea that war should only be fought by the proper authorities, with right intention and for a just cause, but it does so by removing the capacity to exercise judgement on these issues, and it is not surprising that over the next three centuries the very idea that we can, and should, make these judgements disappears. Instead, by the nineteenth century, the right to make war is simply assigned to sovereign rulers as a feature of their sovereignty, not something subject to external judgement, instead the laws of war simply focus on the conduct of war. It is at this point that the distinction between *in bello* and *ad bellam* starts to make sense, because the latter is no longer something about which international lawyers have anything to say once war is simply acknowledged as a legitimate instrument of state policy. *Ius in bello* on the other hand, gradually becomes an important focus of international law. The customary laws of war, a mixture of the 'golden rule' principles outlined above, along with some practical rules inherited from an idealised account of the age of chivalry, were gradually codified and regarded as binding on the 'civilised' world, and later still, universally. The Hague and Geneva Conventions and the various Protocols and specific treaties gradually established the rights of prisoners of war and non-combatants, and outlawed various weapons believed to be inhuman, such as chemical and biological weapons (Roberts and Guelff, 2000).

The Hague Conventions of 1899 and 1907 were signed before the First World War and set in train this process of codification, although the foundation of the Red Cross (now the International Committee of the Red Cross, the ICRC), which was a necessary adjunct to this codification, took place in 1863. The First World War, however, set in motion the process by which the *ius ad bellam* again became part of International Law; the post-1918 Covenant of the League of Nations and the later Charter of the United Nations were both attempts to undermine the idea that war was simply an instrument of state policy and to regulate the circumstances under which war could justly be declared. Still, this was done with reference to a much more restrictive notion of just cause to that which was established by Aquinas. As noted above, Aquinas took for granted that actors were entitled to defend themselves and focused on other causes that might be deemed just. The modern approach on the other hand, takes self-defence as absolutely central; the norm of non-aggression effectively argues that self-defence (or perhaps assisting others to defend themselves) is the only just reason for a resort to force.

Such a position is given plausibility by the destructiveness of modern warfare – indeed, the development of nuclear weapons has led some thinkers, even those within the Catholic natural law tradition, to argue that the possibility of a war being justly fought has effectively disappeared (Boyle, 2013). The Just War tradition is not, in principle, pacifist, but it becomes so if this position is taken to extremes. Consider, for example, the case of the Gulf War of 1990/91. Did Saddam Hussein's annexation by force of Kuwait constitute a just cause for a war to expel his forces from that UN member? Many Christian theologians thought so, but the Vatican newspaper as the official mouthpiece of the Pope, thought not, presumably on the principle that although it would be difficult to deny that Kuwait had the right to defend itself, once it had lost its independence no other international actor had the right to reverse this state of affairs. It seems fair to say that Aquinas would have regarded this argument as perverse.

Just War thinking played relatively little part of the discourse that surrounded the First and Second World Wars. In the First World War leading theologians and moral thinkers on both sides declared their cause to be just, and anti-war sentiment – which certainly did exist – was either pacifist in orientation, or based on the socialist principle of opposition to capitalist wars. In the Second World War things were slightly more complex. In Britain the general sentiment more or less took for granted that opposition to Nazism constituted a just cause and, once again, opposition to the war was largely confined to pacifists and, initially, those socialists who still supported the Soviet Union after the Ribbentrop-Molotov Pact – the latter, of course, dropped their opposition to the war once Hitler invaded the USSR. In Germany, open opposition to the war was, of course, impossible and those few individuals who as a matter of conscience opposed the war on pacifist or Just War grounds were murdered by the regime, and in the latter case received no support from the Catholic hierarchy in Germany (or in Rome).

Interestingly, in England the 20-year-old philosopher G.E.M. Anscombe, a Catholic convert, wrote a pamphlet in 1939 'The Justice of the Present War Examined' in which she argued an anti-war position on what she regarded as Just War grounds – she held that the intentions of the allies were not of the right sort, and that their conduct of the war would inevitably involve harm to innocents. Miss Anscombe was consistent in her beliefs – later as a young Oxford don she opposed the award of an honorary degree to former US President Harry S. Truman on the grounds that he was a war criminal because of his decision to use the A Bomb on Japanese cities (Anscombe, 1981). Anscombe was an important moral philosopher, one of the figures most responsible for the modern revival of 'virtue ethics', and someone who held absolutist views on many issues, for example defending traditional Catholic doctrine in opposition to contraception and the legalisation of abortion. Her position on the Just War was equally absolutist, and in practice, her version of the Just War came close to a pacifist position, it being virtually impossible for any actual war to meet the standards she demanded; in any event her position in 1939 was unsupported by mainstream theologians or moral theorists. Indeed, the very language of the Just War tradition was little used in Britain, where at that time Catholicism was very much a minority religion. The one major figure who did employ Just War categories was the Anglican Bishop of Chichester, George Bell, who was one of the few voices raised in opposition to the area bombing of German cities, using his membership of the House of Lords to bring up the issue. Again, he received little support from his colleagues; the Archbishop of York replied to him in the House of Lords, 'it is a lesser evil to bomb the war-loving Germans than to sacrifice the lives of our fellow countrymen..., or to delay the delivery of many now held in slavery'; a sentiment that was widespread in public opinion.

Just War thinking revived somewhat during the Cold War; this was a conflict where individuals found it easier to find merit in both sides than had been the case during the Second World War, and the issue of nuclear weapons and their destructive power gave a degree of urgency to the search for a morally sound basis for evaluating war and the threat of war. Paul Ramsey, a Methodist theologian and ethicist in the US was one of the first non-Catholic thinkers to return to the Just War tradition and reclaim it for a wider Western intellectual public, and, as noted above, Catholic theologians also gave much attention to the problem of nuclear weapons and the apparent impossibility of using them in a discriminatory manner (Ramsay, 1961). In fact, virtually everyone within the tradition agreed that the use of nuclear weapons would be wrong – the issue became whether it was legitimate to threaten to use a weapon that it would not actually be legitimate to use. The theory of nuclear deterrence rests on the proposition that such threats can keep the peace, especially if both sides have weapons that are not vulnerable to destruction in a pre-emptive strike, but at one time or another most people who have considered the matter have had the thought that Mutually Assured Destruction is, indeed, a 'MAD' strategy. When the Second Cold War broke out in the 1980s after a period of détente, there was a great deal of soul-searching on this issue and a group of Catholic natural lawyers, John Finnis, Joseph Boyle and Germain Grisez produced a substantial text, *Nuclear Deterrence, Morality and Realism* (1987) which argued from Just War principles that unilateral nuclear disarmament was the right thing to do, even if the consequences were to be the Soviet conquest of Western Europe. Interestingly, Robert Goodin came to more or less exactly the same conclusion but from a utilitarian perspective that is as far removed from the natural law perspective as it is possible to be (Goodin, 1985).

The Cold War ended in the 1980s, although controversy remains as to how close the world came to destruction in this period – it has subsequently come to light that a realistic NATO exercise, codenamed Able Archer 83, in September 1983 almost convinced the Soviet leadership that NATO were about to attack and missiles were readied for a counter-strike before the true nature of the exercise was realised. Meanwhile, although American and Russian nuclear arsenals have been reduced (Scott, 2011), the threat that one day nuclear weapons will be used by one of the eight or nine countries that now possess them has not gone away, and it is somewhat surprising that interest in this topic has now died down to quite the extent it has.

Although nuclear weapons and the Cold War more generally stimulated some interest in Just War thinking, it was the American involvement in the Vietnam War which really began the process of reviving the tradition. This involvement developed through the 1960s from a relatively small commitment to the engagement of American armies of over half a million soldiers, which meant a very high proportion of the American people were directly or indirectly affected by the conflict. Many people in the US – probably never a majority, but a sizeable minority – believed the war to be misconceived and immoral, and took part in the very large anti-war movement that formed, especially at America's universities whose students were vulnerable to being conscripted. Some thinkers who responded to this situation opposed the war as pacifists, but others sought instead to discriminate between Vietnam which they took to be an immoral war, and other wars where they were unwilling to make this judgement – the Second World War being one such, but also more recent conflicts such as the Arab-Israeli 'Six-Day War' of 1967, where the predominant interpretation was that Israel had rightfully responded to threats from her neighbours. Once this sort of discrimination was called for it was natural that the Just War tradition should come into focus – here, precisely, was an approach to the morality of war that was based on discrimination unlike the different varieties of absolutism represented by pacifist and political realism. The result was that political and social philosophers who were not Catholic, or for that matter in many cases Christian, thinkers turned to the tradition for a degree of guidance, and in so doing brought it back into contemporary discourse, where it remains to this day. The most important of the philosophers who took this step was Michael Walzer, and in so doing he not only revitalised the Just War tradition, he also provided one of the best contemporary defences of the notion of a society of states.

Michael Walzer, the Just War and international society

Michael Walzer is a political philosopher whose first book, based on his PhD thesis, examined seventeenth-century puritanism in the English Revolution (*The Revolution of the Saints: A Study in the Origins of Revolutionary Politics*, 1965), and he is a democratic socialist, who has been associated with the magazine *Dissent* since the 1950s, and was its co-editor for 30 years. On the face of it, this makes him an unlikely figure to revive the Just War tradition, much less contribute to the theorising of the society of states, but, as noted above, the Vietnam War stimulated thought on the morality of war from anyone involved in active politics and the anti-war movement, as Walzer was.

The first product of this new emphasis to his work was a self-explanatory collection of essays, *Obligations: Essays on Disobedience, War and Citizenship* (1970), but by far the most substantial work this new engagement stimulated was *Just and Unjust Wars* (hereafter *J&UJW*), which appeared after the end of the Vietnam War and draws comparatively few of its examples from Vietnam, but which is clearly still steeped in the political concerns of the era (Walzer, 1976/2006). *J&UJW* is a modern classic which has been hugely influential and is still in print nearly 40 years later; it is an essential text on academic courses on the Just War tradition, and also has earned a wider readership by virtue of its accessible style. The book's subtitle, *A Moral Argument with Historical Illustrations*, provides a clue to its continuing appeal – although dealing with weighty matters, the book is intensely readable and poses moral dilemmas which are readily comprehensible to specialist and non-specialist readers alike. Walzer's opposition to America's Vietnam War quite naturally ruled out the adoption of a political realist, Clausewitzian understanding of war as simply an act of policy. However, unlike some other members of the anti-war movement, he did not adopt a pacifist stance, that is opposing all wars, nor did he espouse the ultra-radical position of only supporting so-called revolutionary wars, or wars of national liberation. His support for Israel in the Six-Day War of 1967, which he understood as a war of legitimate self-defence, ruled out both of these latter positions. Instead, he found himself seeking a way of distinguishing those circumstances where inter-state violence might be legitimate and those where it would not be, and this in turn led him to the notion of the Just War. As we have seen, previously the Just War tradition had been understood largely in Christian, more specifically Roman Catholic, terms; Walzer had a long-standing interest in religion and politics, as highlighted by his first book, but as someone heavily influenced by his Jewish heritage he approached that tradition from the outside and the result of his work was to secularise the argument. He takes the categories of Just War thinking and removes them from their theological context, setting aside those aspects of the tradition that could not be so easily secularised. The end result is an account of the Just War that is employable by those of all religions, and none – but, as will be argued later, some things are lost in the process.

One feature Walzer takes from the modern version of the tradition and reworks is the distinction between *ius ad bellam*, the justice of resort to war and *ius in bello*, which deals with right conduct in war. After dealing with realist approaches to war in Part 1 of *J&UJW*, in Part 2 he sets out 'The Theory of Aggression' which presents his version of *ius ad bellam*. The key proposition here is that states have moral standing and are entitled to protect themselves from outside interference, that is, from aggression. States have moral standing as political communities which have rights; these rights rest on the rights of individuals, their capacity to shape their lives and choose their own form of government. Because Walzer's statism is sometimes misinterpreted as unconditional, it is important to stress that this moral standing is understood as conditional:

> The moral standing of any particular state depends on the reality of the common life it protects and the extent to which the sacrifices required by that protection are willingly accepted and thought worthwhile. If no common life exists, or if the state doesn't defend the common life that does exist, its own defence may have no moral justification. (*J&UJW*, p. 54)

Unlike the English School writers examined in Chapter 2 of this book, Walzer's account of international society rests on an analogy between the rights of states and the rights of individuals. From this analogy he derives what he calls the 'Legalist Paradigm' which both sets out his current understanding of *ius ad bellam* in contemporary international law, and, with one or two amendments, provides a morally defensible position which allows us to identify which wars are justified. The Legalist Paradigm has six components:

1. There exists an international society of independent states.
2. This international society has a law that establishes the rights of its members – above all, the rights of territorial integrity and political sovereignty.
3. Any use of force or imminent threat of force by one state against the political sovereignty or territorial integrity of another constitutes aggression and is a criminal act.
4. Aggression justifies two kinds of violent response; a war of self-defence by the victim and a war of law enforcement by the victim and any other member of international society.
5. Nothing but aggression can justify war.
6. Once the aggressor state has been militarily repulsed it can also be punished.

With one or two limited exceptions to which we will next turn, Walzer holds that the only 'just cause' that can be recognized under modern conditions is self-defence, and all members of the society of states may defend themselves from external assault on their autonomy and territory. The Legalist Paradigm is seen as a morally defensible position by Walzer, if suitably amended: he argues that two such amendments are necessary.

First, a doctrine of *justified pre-emption* is required. Aggression is always wrong, but aggression cannot be defined simply in terms of being the first to resort to violence; in some circumstances, where a threat is immediate it may be legitimate to strike first rather than wait for a blow that is certain to be delivered. Pre-emption is recognised as a necessary concept in the laws of war, and, it should be noted, is distinct from *prevention* which involves acting on a potential threat before it actually emerges; this has become an issue in the twenty-first century, as the Bush Administration's post-9/11 National Security Doctrine has been accused of blurring the distinction between pre-emption and prevention (Chatterjee, 2013). In Walzer's account pre-emption really does means pre-emption; he has in mind the Six-Day War where Israel initiated the use of force, but (allegedly) with the belief that it was itself about to be attacked. This is a controversial judgement, but in any event, he does not develop this argument at length. More central to his concerns is the need for a doctrine of *permissible intervention*, that is to say a doctrine which lays out the circumstances under which intervention does not constitute aggression, circumstances in which the norm of non-intervention, central to the society of states, may be justly breached. Or, put differently, when the norm of non-intervention does not serve the purposes for which it was created, to preserve the integrity of political communities, and so intervention is justified, though not necessarily required.

Three such circumstances are identified by Walzer: First, when a set of boundaries contain two political communities, one of which is already engaged in a large-scale military struggle for independence; second, when a foreign power has already intervened, and so the case is one of counter-intervention; and third, and most significant, 'when the violation of human rights within a set of boundaries is so terrible that it makes talk of community or self-determination or "arduous struggle" seem cynical and irrelevant, *that is, in cases of enslavement or massacre*' (*J&UJW*, p. 90 (emphasis added)). The third set of circumstances is the most interesting because this addresses an issue where those critics of the society of states approach have most difficulty accepting its key norms. The moral basis of international society rests on the norm of non-intervention; in Chapter 2 the different varieties of the English School under examination held that international society existed in order to promote the good life – either, on the solidarist view, one universal notion of the good, or, for pluralists, different conceptions of the good – and that the norm of non-intervention worked to this end. Walzer is putting flesh on this argument by maintaining that the 'good' that non-intervention maintains is the right of political communities to govern themselves; self-determination is not the same thing as political freedom and it is communal autonomy that is central to Walzer's account of the society of states, and not the form of government chosen by the community. His position is that we should assume that this form of government is chosen by the community unless we have good reason to think otherwise. Point three above sets out when we might have such good reasons.

Supporters of the notion of humanitarian intervention will find his account of those good reasons very limited. Walzer's essential position is that political freedom – which, of course, he values – is not something that can be given to people, it can only be taken by them, a position he takes from J.S. Mill who expressed similar sentiments in a short paper 150 years ago. People are expected to engage in 'arduous struggle' against oppressive regimes (Mill's phrase) if they desire freedom – it is only when this is patently impossible that outsiders have any standing in the matter (Mill in Brown et al., 2002). Slavery and massacre are the examples Walzer offers in the text – and liberal, cosmopolitan critics of the society of states will argue that this is far too restrictive, that intervention should be at least considered if human rights are seriously violated at levels that are less than terrible. There is more to be said about this, but first, it would be helpful to present a summary of the rest of Walzer's argument.

In the second half of the book, on what he calls the 'War Convention', Walzer addresses *ius in bello* issues; the core position here relates to the distinction between, and different rights of, combatants and non-combatants. He takes the view that the justice of a war does not affect who might legitimately be killed in it; soldiers are targets whether fighting a war of self-defence or not, and non-combatants should not be targets in any circumstances, although, controversially, he does allows for the possibility that a 'supreme emergency' might justify a waiver of this rule were this to be the only way to prevent a great moral disaster. The example he gives here is actually quite restrictive; imagine, he suggests, if the bombing campaign against German cities in the Second World War had been the only way to prevent a Nazi victory. His argument is that the latter would have been a disastrous outcome not simply for the Allies, but for the world as a whole, and in those circumstances anything that was necessary to prevent this outcome would be justified. In fact, he argues, there was only a short period during the war when such reasoning might have been plausible – once the USA and USSR were engaged alongside Britain other means of achieving victory were available and area bombing became illegitimate – but the principle holds, and, as he acknowledges, has wider implications for the conduct of war.

For those who reject consequentialist reasoning of any kind, such as G.E.M. Anscombe, whose position was discussed above, this position is abominable; justice should be done, even though the heavens fall. For Walzer, such a position makes little sense – it is usually held by people with strong religious convictions who are convinced that the heavens will not actually fall, that God will find a way to prevent the worse from happening, or, at least, will give comfort to the souls of those who die as a result of rejecting consequentialist logic. Such thinkers will reject the idea that a supreme emergency might change the rules, although they usually adopt something like the doctrine of the double-effect to mitigate their absolutism. Walzer rejects this doctrine as double-think rather than double effect, a refusal to acknowledge what has to be done. Diplomatists and statespersons who have to do the best they can in a world characterised by moral ambiguity are likely to be sympathetic to Walzer's position. His earlier essay on 'Political Action: The Problem of Dirty Hands' argues that there are times when, all things considered, it can be right to do something that is morally wrong, with the important proviso that those who dirty their hands in this way must acknowledge and bear the guilt that attaches to their acts (Walzer, 1973, 2007).

As this discussion illustrates, Walzer's account of the Just War departs from the tradition in quite radical ways; he does so by making self-defence in effect the only cause for war, by accepting a firm division between *ius ad bellam* and *ius in bello* and, most of all, by removing the religious basis of Just War thinking. Figures such as James Turner Johnson, the most important modern historian of the Just War tradition, Paul Ramsey, Oliver O'Donovan and, later, Jean Bethke Elshtain are much more in tune with the world of Thomas Aquinas and its theological presuppositions. Walzer is, however, the most influential modern proponent of Just War thinking, perhaps precisely because he is somewhat removed from the tradition; most of his readers are similarly distanced from the world of Natural Law theology, and find his secular version, with its many historical illustrations, case-studies, and common-sense style of arguing very congenial.

Although *J&UJW* is, on the face of it, a book about war and violence, part of its longevity in political philosophical circles rests not on this overt agenda, but on the account of the rights of political communities that Walzer offers in order to justify his basic position. To recap, he argues that in defending the right of political communities to resist aggression, he is actually defending the rights of the individuals who make up these communities – political communities are worth defending because of the shared understandings and common life they promote, and, crucially, this may be true even if their institutions of government are non-democratic. Autonomy is to be valued in its own terms, and not simply if it leads to democratic self-government. As a social democrat, Walzer naturally hopes that communities will choose democracy, but outsiders are obliged to assume that whatever form of government exists reflects the wishes of the people concerned; even if pro-democracy movements are suppressed, as long as the society has not collapsed into civil war and insurrection it has to be presumed that there is a 'fit' between government and people. Short of such a collapse, the only real circumstances in which outsiders would be entitled (although not obliged) to intervene would be, as we have seen, in the case of genocide or mass enslavement – in such circumstances the fit between governed and governors has clearly broken down, but otherwise the presumption of *international* legitimacy must hold, whatever we think of the internal politics of the country in question.

This position is compatible with actual international practice – the UN is supposed to be composed of peace-loving peoples, but many of its members are not democracies or, for that matter, particularly peace-loving – but has attracted intense hostility from liberal, cosmopolitan political philosophers, such as

Charles Beitz, David Luban and Gerald Doppelt who carried out a prolonged controversy with Walzer in the pages of the journal *Philosophy and Public Affairs* (collected in Charles Beitz et al. (eds) *International Ethics*, 1985). These critics suggest, with some justice, that Walzer's defence of the moral standing of states is actually a defence of the moral standing of political *communities* and that most really-existing states do not map on to such communities. Even where they do, there is no reason to believe that authoritarian, non-democratic governments are there because that is the way the community wishes to be governed. Walzer's response is that outsiders are not in a position to make that kind of judgement because they do not participate in the common life in question; at one level, this makes good sense – rushing to judgement on other people's lives is never a good idea – but it seems rather far-fetched to suggest that foreigners are *always* disqualified from making judgements of this kind, even if they have studied the society in question at length, or have lived in it for some time. Still, while Walzer's critics very effectively reveal the loose ends of his arguments, they find it difficult to articulate a consistent position of their own. In practice, they often fall back on a pragmatic defence of the position that Walzer argues for from principle – Luban, for example, may argue that in principle any state with a better human rights record may intervene in the politics of oppressive regimes, but he knows he cannot offer this as a practical position in today's world. And it is the latter kind of engagement with real-world politics that Walzer strives for, here and elsewhere.

Before moving on from *J&UJW*, it should be noted that Walzer has somewhat modified his position in the circumstances of the 1990s and 2000s – in 'The politics of rescue' of 1995 (anthologised in *Arguing about War*, 2005) he widens the range of situations in which intervention might be justifiable, and anticipates a longer engagement with post-intervention politics than was envisaged in his earlier work. His basic position, however, remains unchanged. On the basis of his account of the moral standing of states, and his later works *Spheres of Justice* and *Interpretation and Social Criticism* Walzer is sometimes seen as a 'communitarian' writer – but his relationship to Communitarianism is actually complex and complicated (Walzer, 1983, 1993). At one level he is actually a liberal who does not support the ontological critique of liberal individualism offered by, for example, Charles Taylor or Alasdair McIntyre, but he is certainly critical of liberal universalism and the cosmopolitan version of global civil society. In *Thick and Thin: Moral Argument at Home and Abroad* he sets out his position on such issues – essentially, any kind of global understanding of words like 'justice' or 'freedom' has to start from the premise that individual societies will understand these core terms in different ways, even if there are 'family resemblances' that can be discerned (1995). He is perhaps best seen as a 'liberal nationalist' – a position which has had relatively few occupants in the twentieth century, but which would be perfectly familiar to nineteenth-century readers of J.S. Mill – who wishes to correct what he understands as the faults of modern liberalism, but not to replace it altogether. As noted above, his defence of the rights of political communities is conditional on such communities defending the rights of individuals, but whereas many modern liberals claim to know from first principles what those latter rights are, Walzer believes that outsiders are not well placed to make that determination.

This perspective is restated in Walzer's major work of the 1980s, *Spheres of Justice* (1983). In this book Walzer engages with the thought of John Rawls and his followers. Rawls and Walzer are both essentially social democrats with a commitment to equality and social justice, but whereas Rawls – at least in *A Theory of Justice* – strives to establish a single set of criteria against which to judge the institutions of any society, Walzer approaches things differently. He sees each separate society as establishing its own conception of justice; he is an egalitarian, but his egalitarianism requires that each social good (e.g. member-ship of the community, security and welfare goods, free time, education) should be distributed not according to some overall abstract theory, but in accordance with its own particular nature. No one sphere of justice should be allowed to dominate other spheres. Equality has to be understood as a complex term. The relationship with Rawls is an interesting one – as will be apparent in the next chapter, Rawls and Walzer actually have quite similar ideas on the nature of the society of states, at least by comparison with those cosmopolitan liberal critics of both men, even if they approach the issue of social justice from different directions.

Conclusion

The prevalence of war poses a challenge to the very notion of the society of states, but the Just War tradition has provided some language with which the use of force can be reconciled with the existence of a norm-governed international soci-ety. It would be a mistake to think that this resolves the problem – the norms that the Just War tradition mandates are rarely followed in full, and even such legally well-established principles of inter-state conduct as the ban on chemical weapons are flouted often with at least short-term impunity – but it does at least provide an appropriate normative framework without which any notion of a normatively defensible international society would make little sense. Violence constitutes but one challenge to the idea of a society of states; equally problematic, but from another direction, is the issue of humanitarianism and human rights – how can a society based on individual states provide the context for the rights of individu-als which modern society demands should be respected. This is the subject of the next chapter.

Further Reading

The most important historian of the Just War tradition is James Turner Johnson – of his many books (1985), (1986) and (2001) are the most useful for the tradition – see also Cian O'Driscoll (2008). The Catholic Natural Lawyer John Finnis is a reliable guide to the thought of St Thomas Aquinas, see Finnis (1996), (1998), (2011a) and (2011b). Still on the tradition, David Boucher's book and associated article (2011a) and (2012) place the Just War tradition squarely in the Natural Law tradition. For the Medieval reception of Just War theory see Whetham (2009). Two new collections on the Just War are very valuable, one by Caron Gentry and Amy Eckhart (2014), the other by Anthony Lang, Cian O'Driscoll and John Williams (2013), they supplant that of Jean Bethke Elshtain (1992). Useful general studies of the Just War include Alex Bellamy (2006), A.J. Coates (2012), Oliver O'Donovan (2003) and Brian Orend (2006). The theologian Nigel Biggar (2013) presents 'a defence of war' that is wholly in keeping with the Just War tradition, unlike the various statements by the United States Conference of Catholic Bishops www.usccb.org/issues-and-action/human-life-and-dignity/war-and-peace/nuclear-weapons/. A relatively recent development (albeit with a long pre-history) is the notion of *ius post bellum* – see e.g. the recent collection edited by Carsten Stahn, Jennifer Easterday and Jens Iverson (2014) and the Jus Post Bellum Project at Leiden University http://juspostbellum.com/publications.aspx.

In the last decade or two, a new group of Just War theorists have come to prominence, using some of the same terminology as the tradition but in the context of an individualist approach to human rights and warfare. This work will be discussed in Chapter 9 below; for a flavour see Jeff McMahan (2009). Both old and new Just War thinking is discussed in the Stanford Encyclopaedia of Philosophy entry for War http://plato.stanford.edu/entries/war/ and in the invaluable Just War Theory Com maintained by Mark Rigstad at Oakland University www.justwartheory.com. The latter is an extraordinary archive of new and old material on all aspects of the Just War – anyone wishing to write on the Just War should check into this website.

Most of Michael Walzer's relevant works are referenced in the text. David Miller (1995) contains critical essays on his work – some very critical, see Brian Barry's squid – and a reply by Walzer. Collections referenced in the introduction by Beitz (1985), Pogge and Horton (2007) and Pogge and Moellendorf (2008) contain extracts from Walzer and his critics. Walzer's own collections (2005) and (2007) are both very good value; the first of these *Arguing About War* contains most but not all of his writings on war. He remains associated with the journal *Dissent* and his occasional pieces published there are always worth reading www.dissentmagazine.org. A recent online interview of Walzer by Nancy Rosenblum is very revealing of his approach to politics and war www.youtube.com/watch?v=TvpnmmLoO38.

4

HUMAN RIGHTS, HUMANITARIANISM AND THE SOCIETY OF STATES

War poses one kind of challenge to international society, but, perhaps counter-intuitively, humanitarianism poses another, especially if to be humanitarian is translated into support for human rights, as it so frequently is nowadays. War seems to violate the idea that international society is norm-governed, but, as we have seen, that notion can just about be preserved by understanding the role of force in the context of the Just War tradition. Humanitarianism poses a different kind of problem; if the essence of an international society is that it is composed of individual states is it not possible that these individual societies will have different conceptions of what it means to behave in a humane manner? Some solidarist English School writers assume this problem away by understanding individual states to be the guarantors of human rights, local agents of the common good, as the phrase has it, but a cursory survey of human rights problems in the contemporary world undermines such confidence. It is clear that North American and Western European societies have different conceptions of, for example, Gay, Lesbian, Bisexual and Transgender rights than do African, Middle Eastern, and many East European societies. European countries have decided that the death penalty is inherently inhumane, but the United States, China, and most Middle Eastern and African countries would disagree. And so on. Is this diversity, which is supported by the norms of international society, incompatible with the notion of human rights? If so, the society of states may well be difficult to defend as a morally acceptable world order – but in fact the notion of an international society has proved quite capable of accommodating *some* notions of humanitarianism and *some* accounts of human rights. Which notions will be discussed below, as will be the writings of a great liberal theorist of justice and rights, John Rawls, who, as with Michael Walzer, rather by accident has produced one of the most important contemporary defences of the idea of international society, which he called a *society of peoples*. But before approaching this body of work, some preliminary definitions and clarifications are necessary.

Rights, human rights, humanitarianism: Basic ideas, terminology and history

The simplest way to think of a *right* is an entitlement that a person has, created by a system of law. What kind of entitlement? The American jurist Wesley Hofeld set out a classification early in the twentieth century which is still much used; he distinguished between rights (or claim-rights), privileges (or liberty-rights), powers and immunities (Jones, 1994). Claim-rights are the most basic rights – the only true rights, Hofeld believed; the classic example of a claim-right is a right generated by a contract and accompanied by correlative duties. Liberty-rights occur when I have the right to do something in the sense that I have no obligation not to do it – here there is no correlative duty. The other two meanings of the term are secondary; sometimes a right involves the exercise of a power, for example, to have the right to vote means to be empowered to vote, to be enfranchised; finally, a right sometimes means an immunity, the essence of which is that others are disbarred from making claims against one – for example to be legally insane, or under age, is to be immune from criminal prosecution.

These various kinds of entitlements all make sense in the context of a functioning legal system, one in which contracts exist and are enforceable thus creating claim-rights and where liberties are guaranteed by law – thus, for example, the liberty right of freedom of speech is exercisable ultimately only if mechanisms exist in order to prevent people from denying this liberty. An international legal order exists which creates claim-rights for states via treaties and which, in principle, supports various liberty rights – but enforcement mechanisms are weak, and it is states rather than individuals who are the subject of the contracts in question and who possess the liberties.

By way of contrast, a *human right* is, by definition, an entitlement that a person has simply by virtue of being human. It is therefore, again by definition, not created by any particular legal system, although it may be recognised by such a system and given the force of law thereby (Boucher, 2011c). It is important to get this right, because much of the literature of the international human rights movement obscures these points, and treats human rights as though they were the same kind of entitlement as the rights created by a domestic legal system. It is interesting that the founding document of the post-1945 human rights movement, the Universal Declaration of Human Rights passed by the UN General Assembly in 1948 does not make this mistake, although it is sometimes read as though it did. The Universal Declaration is clear that the rights it enumerates are *recognised* and *proclaimed* rather than created. This point will be returned to below.

The third term that needs to be clarified is *humanitarianism*. The basic frame of reference here is beneficence, an informal sentiment that expresses concern for basic human dignity, a generosity of spirit which argues that no one should be required to live below a bare minimum standard or be treated in ways that are obviously unjust. Humanitarianism is based on charity in the broad sense of the term – it may, or may not involve a sense of formal obligation. As will become apparent, the relationship between humanitarianism and human rights has become an important issue in contemporary politics – here it is sufficient to say that there no necessary connection between the two notions; human dignity can be served through treating individuals as rights-bearers, but this is not the only way in which it is possible for human beings to live decent lives. One final point here – humanitarianism should not be confused with humanism. Humanism was a movement in the seventeenth century that refocused attention away from God and towards humanity, and it still has that connotation today (for example, in the British Humanist Association); humanists may be humanitarians, but not all humanitarians are humanist in this sense of the term.

The origins of both the idea of rights (claim-rights and liberty-rights) and human rights can be found in the Middle Ages. Rights and liberties were established then through formal contracts between rulers and ruled (usually, in fact, between rulers and aristocrats, but sometimes with a wider frame of reference) – *Magna Carta*, the 'Great Charter' of 1215 is a famous English example. Human rights had a more complex origin; the medieval notion of *ius naturale* is the starting point here, but 'natural right' initially referred to a state of affairs [as in the phrase 'it is right that such and such'] and was bound up with the idea of natural law, the same source from which the notion of a Just War originated. This law was based on what God wills for humankind but also on what we can discern about the human condition using our God-given intellect and powers of reasoning (Finnis, 2011a, b). Gradually, in late medieval/early modern times the meaning of natural right changes and becomes a personal entitlement [as in the phrase 'having a right to something']; a natural right in this sense is still based on God's will, but in some contexts may be buttressed by legal rights as established by Charter or, in those countries where quasi-independent legislatures exist, by law.

By the eighteenth century, during the Enlightenment, the notion of a natural right in this sense came to be thought of in terms of what we now call human rights. The language, however, was only partially secularised. Consider, for example, the United States' Declaration of Independence, which famously begins, 'We hold these truths to be self-evident, that all men are created equal, that they are endowed by their Creator with certain unalienable Rights, that among these are Life, Liberty and the pursuit of Happiness'. The Creator has an important role in this Declaration, but here the reference point is the rather abstract God of the Deists; revelation no longer has a role to play. The American and French Revolutionaries may have believed in human rights, but they incorporated these rights into positive law. In the United States the First Ten Amendments to the Constitution establish the US Bill of Rights, and in France the emphasis in the 'Declaration of the Rights of Man and the Citizen' is on both 'Man' and 'Citizen'.

This change of terminology did not go unchallenged. Edmund Burke in the *Reflections on the Revolution in France* attacks the French conception of the rights of man as abstract and subject to the vagaries of popular power – he supports a notion of natural right which is grounded in custom and law (Burke, 2009). The rights of Englishmen, established over the centuries and handed down through the generations are to be preferred to the rights of man, the product of the minds of disaffected intellectuals. Burke's near contemporary Jeremy Bentham, on the other hand, objects to the idea of rights altogether, describing them as 'nonsense on stilts'; he challenges their ontological status, asking where these 'rights' come from, and argues that the assertion of rights interferes with public policy, which he famously believed should be guided by the 'greatest happiness' principle. Rights simply interfered with the 'felicific calculus', which should be employed to judge the value of laws (Bentham, 2000). And, to complete the circle of critics, socialists and Marxists regarded the focus on rights to be a not-particularly-covert way of defending private property. Still, in spite of all of these critics, the idea of rights has been popular with most people for the last 200 years, and still is; philosophical problems are for philosophers, ordinary folk are more likely to see the benefits of constraining state power than they are to see the various difficulties that certainly exist with the notion of rights.

Humanitarianism in the nineteenth century

Rights language may have been popular in domestic European societies but was little used in the society of states until around the time of the Second World War; humanitarianism, on the other hand, has a history that dates back to the nineteenth century – indeed many of the key issues of contemporary humanitarianism were prefigured in that period. As we have seen in earlier chapters, the notion of an international society rests on the idea of sovereignty and the associated norm of non-intervention, but most writers on the notion acknowledge that there are some circumstances where these norms may be challenged; situations which constitute 'gross violations of human dignity', or 'outrage the opinions of mankind' constitute the basis for interventions and, as David Trim and Brendan Simms have documented such interventions go back to the beginnings of the society of states (Simms and Trim, 2011). In the nineteenth century 'humanitarian interventions' became somewhat more frequent although, as Gary Bass and Martha Finnemore have documented they usually took place to protect Christians and or Europeans and the victims of European imperialism could not expect similar protection (Finnemore, 2003; Bass, 2008).

But humanitarian interventions were not the only way in which the humanitarian impulse was expressed in the nineteenth century. Other explicitly humanitarian campaigns took place, and provide interesting prototypes for the different kinds of humanitarian operations that take place today. The first campaign of this kind was based in Britain and was directed towards ending the slave trade, and abolishing slavery in the British Empire (Hochschild, 2005). In the eighteenth century Britain was at the centre of the slave trade and profited greatly thereby, but this grim business gradually attracted critics, and a head of steam built up for ending Britain's involvement. This was one of the first examples of a humanitarian campaign based in what came later to be called civil society, an archetypal political campaign directed at the organs of state in Britain initially but later with a wider reach; the anti-slavery movement in Britain had close links with the anti-slavery campaign in the United States in the 1840s and 1850s, and later with an international campaign against slavery wherever it existed and was legally tolerated.

The anti-slavery movement was very successful, succeeding in ending British involvement in the slave trade in 1807, and ending slavery itself in the British Empire in 1833 – but the matter did not end there. British diplomacy was directed towards getting other countries to agree to abolish the slave trade, and for 50 years after 1815 and the end of the Napoleonic Wars the main international task of the Royal Navy was to enforce the ban on the trade on the open seas. Chaim Kaufmann and Robert Pape have demonstrated that this was not a costless action; it actually harmed British commercial interests, and the costs of naval operations against the slave trade amounted to around 2 per cent of GDP p.a. for 40 years, a figure that is substantially higher than the current target for international aid of 0.7 per cent GDP, a target which, in any event is rarely met (Kaufmann and Pape, 1999). It is interesting that Kaufmann and Pape also document the fact that this very costly moral action was not actually driven by concerns for the slaves as such, and was certainly not driven by anti-racist sentiment. The abolitionists were primarily concerned with what they believed would be God's judgement on Britain for its involvement with an activity which denied the dignity of His creatures. The British political elite, on the other hand, agreed to adopt the anti-slavery agenda as a relatively low cost way of meeting the political aspirations of a rising middle class, largely non-conformist section of society, which would need to be appeased if the privileges of the aristocracy were to be preserved.

This position was characteristic of many nineteenth-century humanitarian campaigns, which were selective vis-à-vis who counts as human and which were not incompatible with racist attitudes. It raises a question which will be repeated often in the twentieth and twenty-first centuries, namely the importance of motive in the pursuit of humanitarian ends. We have seen in Chapter 3 that for the natural lawyers who originated the idea of a Just War intentions were of crucial importance – but we have also seen that secular accounts of the Just War are less interested in intentions and motives, and more interested in outcomes. Similar issues arise in this case – ending the slave trade and abolishing slavery was, surely, a good thing; does it really matter *why* the slave trade was ended?

Humanitarians in this period were not necessarily anti-imperialist, and had few compunctions about interfering with other people's customs and mores when they believed them to be inhumane. In the late nineteenth century and early twentieth one of the most extensive and long-lasting humanitarian campaigns was directed against the rule of King Leopold of the Belgians in the Congo, where levels of exploitation reached heights of inhumanity seen nowhere else in the period (Hochschild, 1999). Leopold ran the Congo as a personal estate employing slavery and mutilation to extract its natural resources but, interestingly, his critics rarely argued for the removal of European rule; instead they pushed either for the Belgian state to take responsibility, or for the Congo to be incorporated in the British Empire on the principle that British rule would abolish the inhuman techniques employed by Leopold. There is a more general point here; when colonialism was discussed meetings of the Socialist International in the 1900s opinion was divided as to the fate of the colonies under socialism – some, including the British Fabians, argued that that independence would simply throw the colonies into a world for which they were ill-prepared, and the humanitarian approach would be to continue to govern these territories but in their own interests as opposed to those of European capitalism, and in the meantime preparing them for self-rule (Porter, 2007).

The anti-slavery movement was a prototype for a *political* humanitarianism; its activities were directed towards state policy, which it aimed to change though political campaigns – as such it was a forerunner for many modern international humanitarian organisations. There is, however, an alternative model which developed in the nineteenth century, an approach to humanitarianism which explicitly stressed the need to *exclude* politics from its activities – this is the model provided by the International Committee for the Red Cross (ICRC). The Red Cross was founded in 1863 after the experiences of Henri Dunant at the Battle of Solferino in 1859 (Dunant, 1986). The Red Cross's initial mandate concerned the treatment of battle casualties and prisoners of war but it now has a wider – and unique – status in public international law as the guardian of International Humanitarian Law (IHL), most importantly of the Geneva Conventions (Forsythe, 1978). In order to fulfil its role and gain access its basic principles stress impartiality, neutrality and independence – it deliberately and consistently avoids taking sides or political positions.

This limited, focused mandate can sometimes seem perverse to outsiders. For example, in the Second World War the Red Cross was aware of the existence of Nazi extermination camps but did not share this knowledge with the world at large, fearing that this would compromise its independence and neutrality, a decision which led to a great deal of soul-searching after the war (Favez, 1999). However, the basic point, that because of its neutrality the ICRC is able to operate in places where other humanitarian organisations cannot, is valid. It is interesting to consider whether this position is going to be sustainable in circumstances very different from the inter-state conflict for which the ICRC was initially designed. Even the Nazis – or at least the German Army – actually wanted the ICRC to be able to operate to act on behalf of their own soldiers held prisoner in Western Camps, but the Soviet Union which had not signed the Geneva Conventions did not allow the ICRC to operate. In Afghanistan today the Red Crescent (the local version of the Red Cross) is the only organisation that does not employ armed guards to protect its personnel, relying instead on their reputation as neutrals; recently, however, Red Crescent operations have been attacked and some of their staff killed, so whether this can continue is an open issue.[1]

The anti-slavery campaign and the Red Cross represent two approaches to humanitarianism, which co-existed relatively comfortably in the nineteenth century and for much of the twentieth; political humanitarian campaigns have been waged in the sphere of civil society, while institutionalised humanitarianism remained largely apolitical on the ICRC model. Neither approach is incompatible with the assumptions of the society of states, but in the late twentieth century tensions between them began to emerge – this will be the subject of the next chapter; the next section of this chapter is concerned with the reawakening of the idea of human rights in the face of Nazi and Soviet atrocities.

The post-1945 development of the human rights regime

Prior to 1914 there was a widespread assumption that the kind of rights laid out in various British constitutional documents and in the US Bill of Rights or the French Declaration of the Rights of Man and the Citizen were either already enjoyed in most civilised states, or soon would be. In Europe torture had been abolished everywhere, and most countries had constitutions which gave reasonable guarantees that the rule of law would be upheld, Tzarist Russia being a conspicuous exception to that generalisation. In the colonies and in the non-European world in general there was further to go, but the belief in progress, the belief that all societies were moving in the same direction towards a world where the rights of individuals would be generally respected was widely held,

---

[1] www.icrc.org/eng/resources/documents/update/2013/07-23-afghanistan-activities-january-july-2013.htm

and not just in the main centres of liberalism, in Western Europe and North America. The aftermath of the 1914–18 war, the Great Depression and the rise of the dictators was, accordingly, a great shock to the system – democracies failed in much of Europe, a terrible tyranny was established in Germany, in some ways the most advanced European state, Russia performed the difficult feat of producing a regime worse even than that of the Tzars, and judicial torture, imprisonment without trial and the suppression of basic freedoms was widespread.

These deplorable developments actually led to a restatement of the idea of human rights in the rhetoric of the Western Allies in the Second World War. President Franklin Roosevelt's famous four freedom's speech is perhaps the best example:

In the future days, which we seek to make secure, we look forward to a world founded upon four essential human freedoms.

The first is freedom of speech and expression – everywhere in the world.

The second is freedom of every person to worship God in his own way – everywhere in the world.

The third is freedom from want – which, translated into world terms, means economic understandings which will secure to every nation a healthy peacetime life for its inhabitants – everywhere in the world.

The fourth is freedom from fear – which, translated into world terms, means a world-wide reduction of armaments to such a point and in such a thorough fashion that no nation will be in a position to commit an act of physical aggression against any neighbour – anywhere in the world. (Address to Congress, January 6th 1941)

The repeated theme 'everywhere in the world' is central to the argument of the address – what FDR is articulating is the notion of *human* rights not simply rights that are the product of one legal system. It is also interesting, given later debates on the status of economic rights, that his third freedom is given the same status as the first two, more classically liberal, freedoms.

The Preamble of the United Nations Charter gives some support to the notion that human rights are to be respected claiming that it 'reaffirmed faith in fundamental human rights, and dignity and worth of the human person' but the Charter itself is resolutely statist. Article 2(7) makes this absolutely clear:

Nothing contained in the present Charter shall authorize the United Nations to intervene in matters which are essentially within the domestic jurisdiction of any state or shall require the Members to submit such matters to settlement under the present Charter; but this principle shall not prejudice the application of enforcement measures under Chapter VII.

Chapter VII concerns threats to the peace and acts of aggression, and, in effect, the UN Charter far from generating a new world in which human rights are central actually endorsed a very strict reading of the norm of non-intervention – and the universal reach of the Charter makes it clear that this norm is not simply for European states but for all the world (even though, in practice, European colonialism still existed and the majority of UN members were European or from the Americas). Still, a Division of Human Rights was set up within the Secretariat, and UNESCO, the new world cultural body, established a committee of philosophers with the task of preparing a feasibility study on the framing of a charter of rights, and eventually a Commission on Human Rights – chaired by the former First Lady Eleanor Roosevelt – was established, tasked to draft an International Bill of Rights.

The Committee and the Commission were designed to reflect all manner of global ethical stances, with representatives from all the main religions and from philosophies such as Confucianism; in fact they managed to converge on a basic list of rights fairly quickly, but, as Jacques Maritain, a French Catholic philosopher remarked, 'Yes, we agree about the rights, but on condition no one asks us why'. At the time, no one did, but in time they would. In the end, it was decided that instead of a full-scale Bill of Rights with treaty status the international human rights regime would be launched by a Declaration by the United Nations General Assembly, and so the *Universal Declaration of Human Rights* was adopted on 10 December 1948. The 30 articles of the *UDHR* contain traditional 'political rights' (freedom of speech, association etc.), 'economic rights' (adequate standard of living, rest and leisure), 'family rights' (motherhood, educational choice) and some vague aspirations (for example, Article 28. Everyone is entitled to a social and international order in which the rights and freedoms set forth in this Declaration can be fully realized).

The *UDHR* was adopted by 48 votes to 0 but with 8 abstentions (6 Soviet bloc countries, South Africa and Saudi Arabia). The Soviet Bloc abstained ostensibly on the basis that they could not accept Article 13 (2) on freedom of movement between states and Saudi Arabia objected to Article 18 on the right to change one's religion – but in fact in both cases the governing structure and social mores of these countries was incompatible with many other articles of the *UDHR*. The South African abstention was more precisely focused on objections to those statements which asserted racial equality – it is worth noting that there was racial discrimination in many other countries which, nonetheless, signed up to the Declaration. These abstentions are interesting because they prefigure many of the later debates over human rights – in particular the Saudi objection prefigures later discussions of culture, multiculturalism and human rights, and the Soviet stance paves the way for later critiques that the UDHR stresses political at the expense of economic rights. It is also worth noting that the UDHR as well as employing gendered language unselfconsciously gives strong support to the family as an institution and to a traditional conception of gender roles – the influence, perhaps, of the European Christian Democrats, who were important in preparing the draft of the Charter.

Although the UDHR has only 30 articles it forms the basis for the later development of the human rights regime. In 1966 *The International Covenant on Civil and Political Rights* and *International Covenant on Economic, Social and Cultural Rights* were signed, and to these should be added specific conventions including those concerning *Racial Discrimination* (1965), women (*CEDAW* 1979), *Torture* (1984) and the *Rights of the Child* (1989). It should be said that while these documents take the form of international treaties they are essentially aspirational – thus, for example, none of the signatories of the *Convention on the Rights of the Child* actually provide all the rights set out therein; they have signed up to the Convention as an indication of general support for the principles it enshrines rather than with the intention of immediately acting on them. It is often remarked that the US and to a lesser extent the UK are unwilling to sign such documents – the US, for example, is one of only three states not to ratify the *Convention of the Rights of the Child*; this stems from the approach to law adopted in both countries and a reluctance to sign treaties that one has no intention of following. In addition to these general treaties, the international human rights regime also includes local conventions such as the *European Convention for the Protection of Human Rights and Fundamental Freedoms* (1950), or the *African Charter on Human and Peoples' Rights (The Banjul Charter)* (1986) although these are not, strictly speaking 'human rights' conventions; thus, the European Convention creates positive legal rights only for Europeans whose governments have ratified the convention, and for other residents in those states. In short, the international human rights regime has expanded from the brevity of the Universal Declaration of 1948 to the 1,600 pages of the current version of the standard textbook on the regime (Alston and Goodman, 2012).

The first decades of the International Human Rights Regime coincided with the Cold War and decolonisation; in this period there is little sense that rights are incompatible with state sovereignty or the core principles of the society of states; rights are claimed *through* not *against* the state, and the foundational documents listed above are international treaties signed by states and binding on states. Individuals might be the supposed beneficiaries of these treaties but they are not the actors who made them, and it is noteworthy that while rights remain central to liberal theories of justice, the most important modern theorist of justice, John Rawls, produces an account of the international dimension of rights and justice that is compatible with the society of states – 'the Law of Peoples'. In the next chapter we will see how human rights and humanitarianism have broken out of a state-centric framework, but here we will examine Rawls's position, which remains within that framework.

John Rawls, 'The Law of Peoples' and international society

In Chapter 3 we saw how Michael Walzer reworked the traditional notion of the Just War to produce one of the most compelling modern readings of the society of states. In this chapter a similar achievement by the political philosopher John Rawls (1921–2002) will be documented, a major work in the liberal discourse on justice which distinguishes between international and domestic society, and defends both the conventional norms of international society and a minimalist account of human rights – but at the same time introduces a new distinction between 'well-ordered societies' and others, a distinction with profound implications for international political theory.

It should be said at the outset that Rawls did not initially intend or desire to produce a theory of international society (nor for that matter did Walzer); instead, Rawls's first attempt to understand the international came as more or less an aside in his masterpiece *A Theory of Justice*, an aside produced in order to provide a context for the circumstances under which conscription might be considered to be just (Rawls, 1970). He built on this aside, and on some changes to his overall system introduced in *Political Liberalism* in an essay 'The law of peoples' in a collection of Amnesty International Lectures edited by Stephen Shute and Susan Hurley *On Human Rights* (1994) and then expanded somewhat this essay into a novella-length book *The Law of Peoples* (1999). The rather convoluted evolution of this latter text means that it cannot be approached directly as a free-standing work – instead quite a lot of background material on John Rawls and the liberal theory of justice will be needed before we can make sense of *The Law of Peoples*. Fortunately this will be worth the effort, not just because it is fascinating in its own terms – which it is – but also because many of the works on global distributive justice which will be examined in Chapter 10 of this book owe a great deal to Rawls's framework – even if they usually reject the explicitly international dimension of his thinking.

A Theory of Justice is Rawls's masterwork, and widely regarded as the most important work in liberal political theory since that of John Stuart Mill more than a century earlier. What is distinctive about Rawls's work in a twentieth-century context is that he actually attempted in a long and detailed book to tell us what a just society would look like, rather than, for example, simply analysing how the word 'justice' is used; in its ambition *A Theory of Justice* is a rather old-fashioned book, and none the worse for that. Rawls aims to provide an account of the basic institutions of society, and locates justice there rather than directly in individual behaviour. It is constructivist in so far as what is 'just' is not discovered, but constructed, that is determined by accessing individuals' views under ideal conditions and it is contractarian in so far as it builds on the notion of a 'social contract' as the basis for legitimacy. Finally, *A Theory of Justice* sets out universal principles of justice, valid for all societies, and operates at the level of what Rawls terms 'ideal theory'; ideal theory assumes that all the relevant actors will be compliant with whatever principles of justice are chosen and that circumstances more generally will be such that justice can actually be achieved, so that, for example, the society will not be so grindingly poor that survival will be the only goal anyone acknowledges.

So, what is Rawls's basic model? First, his is an account of justice in a society, and a society for the purposes of the argument is assumed to be a *self-contained co-operative scheme for mutual advantage*: the idea is that members of a society gain by social co-operation, that is, the 'goods' produced collectively are greater than the sum of the goods the members of society could produce as individuals – that is why individuals are prepared to enter society, it is assumed. Under what terms would potential co-operators agree to join such a social scheme prior to its formation (where they would be in what Rawls terms the *original position*)? The justice of the basic institutions of society is determined by the answer to this question, and the answer takes the form of a (fictional) social contract which will cover the rights of individuals and also the disposition of the 'goods' created by their co-operation. The choice of the terms of this contract will be made from behind what Rawls calls the *veil of ignorance*; the idea here is that while potential contractors know that they all value certain *primary goods* (that all rational persons behind the veil can be assumed to want, whatever else they want), they are otherwise ignorant about their own attributes (e.g. their race, intelligence, gender). The veil of ignorance is important because Rawls knows that individuals will make choices that benefit themselves if they are not constrained in some way – thus intelligent people will always think it right that society rewards intelligence, white people may think white people are superior to black or brown people and so on. The veil of ignorance is a thought experiment that is designed to get beyond this self-centredness; the assumption is that individuals behind a veil of ignorance will be risk-adverse and will not, for example, choose a system based on slavery if there is the possibility that they themselves will be slaves. Whether we can think about our choices in such an abstracted way is, of course, debateable.

In any event Rawls says that the choices people would make under this procedure would constitute *'justice as fairness'*. He assumes first that people would choose a system with the *most extensive equal political liberties available*, ruling out slavery or other forms of structural inequality. This is straightforward but the second principle which concerns the distribution of economic and social goods is more difficult. He considers two very basic distributive principles – strict egalitarianism and utilitarianism – and rejects them both; an egalitarian distribution of the gains from co-operation would mean passing up a potential overall increase in the production of goods that differential rewards could bring, and utilitarianism, rewarding the most productive, is insufficiently respectful of the rights of individuals. Instead, economic and social goods are to be distributed according to (i) fair equality of opportunity and (ii) what he calls the *difference principle* which states that inequalities are just if and only if they work to the advantage of the *least* advantaged.

In *A Theory of Justice* these were universal principles, with the implication that only societies committed to these principles (that is, 'liberal' societies) could be just. In his later work, *Political Liberalism* he revises this position. There is no need for agreement on a what he calls a 'comprehensive metaphysical doctrine' (such as liberalism) for a society based on the principles of justice to be stable as long as there is an *overlapping consensus* of support for various just principles, arrived at by *public reason* (that is to say, via public debates that do not rely on reference to a comprehensive metaphysical doctrine). This is a complex position which, fortunately, we don't need to go into in depth here – the basic idea is that in deciding a contested issue the goal is to reach a consensus that can be defended using arguments that rely on reason alone. Thus, to take an example of great significance in US politics, arguments about the law as it affects abortion cannot be cast in terms which rely on religion for their force. It is characteristic of contemporary American liberalism that so much effort is put into determining what kinds of argument are legitimate – part of the bitterness of contemporary US debate derives from this procedure; dissenters from the liberal consensus feel, correctly, that their arguments are not being heard.

The international dimension of Rawls's thought

For Rawls, societies are assumed for the purposes of his theory to be bounded, self-contained and self-sufficient: individuals enter them by birth and leave by death. Of course, Rawls understands that this is not an accurate account of the world but is simply a theoretical assumption which follows necessarily from his contractualism; a social contract needs contractors and Rawls assumes, plausibly enough, that a global contract between individuals would be impossible (although others differ on this point as we will see). Relations between societies are to be determined by a *second contract*, made by representatives of just societies in a *second original position* (that is, not knowing salient facts about the societies they represent, such as size, endowments). They would agree, he says, to political principles analogous to political liberty, that is the traditional principles and practices of international society and international law: non-aggression, non-intervention and so on, but *not* to principles of global distributive or social justice. There would be no international *difference principle*. The reason he argues thus is because, employing his definition of a society, there is no world or international society – a society is a co-operative scheme for mutual advantage and no such arrangement exists internationally. This means there is no international surplus to distribute, which in turn means that there is no basis for global social justice.

This is a very conventional account of international society – although in his original version it is an international society of 'just' societies, which constitutes a big shift away from the pluralist model of a society of states based on an ethic of co-existence. And, whereas Michael Walzer argues that we should assume that states are legitimate unless there is some good reason not to make that assumption, Rawls lays down strict conditions for legitimacy, at least in the realm of ideal theory – effectively, in the first version of his international thought, states are legitimate if and only if they are liberal states. But, in spite of this restriction, his initial model was very heavily criticised by other liberal theorists who believed the refusal to address the problem of international inequalities was simply perverse, given that inequality on a global scale is at least as significant as inequality within any given society. Rawls, however, held his ground and responded by developing an account of *The Law of Peoples* which elaborates and refines his earlier account, additionally theorising relations between Liberal and non-Liberal peoples and offering some thoughts on *non-ideal theory* and international relations.

The first thing that needs to be explained about *The Law of Peoples* is why Rawls uses the term 'peoples' rather than say, societies or states? His answer is provided by his definition of a 'people'; for purposes of ideal theory, a people have (i) a political structure, a 'reasonably just constitutional democracy' in the case of liberal states, (ii) 'common sympathies' and (iii) a 'moral nature', which requires them to be *reasonable* as well as *rational* in the pursuit of their interests – to be reasonable, for Rawls, is to take account of the interests of others when pursuing one's own interests, while to be rational is simply to engage in a cost-benefit calculation which is entirely self-centred. States clearly have political structures, and their populations may share common sympathies (although they may not) but they do not have a moral nature – Rawls understands the state to be a 'cold monster' of calculation. As well as distinguishing a people from a state, Rawls's definition also leads to the conclusion that there is no *global* people; global political institutions of a rudimentary kind may exist, but the peoples of the world do not share common sympathies and do not have a moral nature. Even if one understands why Rawls uses the term peoples and derivatives such as the law or society of peoples, it must be admitted that this terminology is a source of confusion, and the effect Rawls is looking for is undermined by the constant need to translate back into ordinary language if his formulations are to have any impact on the way we think about the world.

Returning to the *Law of Peoples*, Rawls maintains that representatives of liberal peoples are obliged to create a 'law of peoples', which establishes a 'Confederation of Peoples'. This is based on a set of principles the most important of which involve a commitment to the rule of law and to the abolition of violence within the confederation. Readers of Immanuel Kant's *Eternal Peace* may think they recognise this proposition, that the confederation of peoples sounds rather like Kant's 'pacific union' with liberal peoples substituted for republican states. This is not quite right; Kant argues that only republican states can be members of his federation, but Rawls extends membership beyond the category of liberal peoples. He maintains that another category of peoples who he rather tentatively describes as 'decent' peoples also qualify for membership; decent peoples are defined as those that respect basic human rights, have some kind of system for consultation or representation, and respect the law of peoples, even though they are based on a non-liberal comprehensive doctrine (for example, a privileged religion) which means that they do not provide the full package of liberal rights (for example, by restricting some positions to believers). Rawls argues that decent peoples are entitled to equal membership of the society of peoples alongside liberal peoples; in a second original position they would choose the same rules as liberal peoples and, in a sense they are co-owners of the law of peoples.

No doubt aware that the notion of 'decent' peoples would attract criticism, Rawls provides a fictional example, the *well-ordered hierarchical society,* which he terms Kazanistan. In Kazanistan the Islamic religion has a privileged position, and certain leading posts in society are not available to non-Muslims; non-Muslims play a part in the polity but via group representation, and there is no political equality. On the other hand, other religions are tolerated and may be practised, and their adherents are encouraged to take part in the civic culture of the society. 'Jihad' is interpreted in a spiritual and moral and not a military sense, and Kazanistan has no aggressive intent towards the rest of the world. It is fair to say that very few people are satisfied by the category or this example. Liberals argue that the existence of a privileged religion undermines even the limited range of human rights available in such a society, while non-liberals are inclined to see decent societies as a watered down version of a liberal society. Still, the idea that such decent societies might exist does have some resonance in the real world – arguably constitutional democracies do behave differently towards each other than they behave towards undemocratic regimes, but equally they make distinctions between the latter; undemocratic but 'well-ordered' regimes where the rule of law more or less holds (Singapore comes to mind) are treated with more respect than simple dictatorships. Liberal theorists often approach the world with a mind-set that says that all non-liberal states are by definition inferior to liberal states, Rawls does at least provide some language to allow us to modify such a binary classification.

Liberal and decent societies are both suitable members of a Confederation of Peoples and subject to the Law of Peoples – but these entities exist in the realm of ideal theory, they describe what Rawls calls a *realistic utopia* that is to say a world that does not exist but could, a world in which everyone complies with the demands of morality. *Non-ideal theory* deals with the world as it is and with relations between liberal and decent peoples and states that are neither liberal nor decent. Rawls talks about two such societies (actually three, but his account of *benevolent despotisms* is so cursory as to be not worth dwelling on). *Outlaw states* are states that do not respect the rights of their peoples, and do not obey the law of peoples; they engage in rational but not reasonable behaviour – see above – and are prepared to resort to force to achieve their ends. Liberal and decent peoples must protect themselves from outlaw states, and in extreme conditions (unfortunately not specified in detail by Rawls) may intervene in their domestic affairs. *Burdened societies* are societies that do not have the human capital, the political culture or, perhaps, the material resources, to be well-ordered. They must be helped to this status by liberal and decent societies, by the promotion of human rights and, possibly, material transfers. (Rawls assumes that in most cases material transfers will not be needed.) This, it should be noted, is *not* a cosmopolitan principle; there is no assumption that all well-ordered societies will be wealthy or that there may not be inequalities between individuals in different societies. The 'duty of assistance' that Rawls describes is designed to bring burdened societies to the point where they can become full members of the society of peoples.

Rawls in *The Law of Peoples* restates the basics of international society in terms of contemporary political theory, adding in Kantian thoughts on the relationship between peace, stability and liberal political institutions. He provides criteria for distinguishing between different kinds of non-liberal polities, acknowledging that a stable international order cannot be composed only of liberal societies, and identifying which non-liberal polities it is desirable to tolerate, thereby addressing some of the issues raised by 'cultural relativists'. He defends a universal account of human rights, but on a minimal basis, acknowledging that some 'decent peoples' may not respect the full package of rights. This adds up to an impressive modern defence of a modified version of the conventional idea of a society of states.

Still, there are many problems with the way Rawls sets up his framework and with the answers he gives. What is the relationship between 'peoples' and 'states' and by extension, between the 'law of peoples' and 'international law'? The aim is to create a 'realistic utopia' – but can the category of 'peoples' be the basis for such a utopia? In some respects this is a similar set of problems to those posed by the work of Michael Walzer – Walzer focuses on the rights of political communities, but we are really interested in the rights of states since states actually exist whether they are composed of political communities or not. Similarly, we are interested in relations between states and so find ourselves trying to translate 'peoples' into states, whether Rawls wants us to or not. Rawls gives some assistance here by using terms such as 'reasonably just' or 'reasonably liberal' when referring to actually-existing liberal societies, thereby allowing us to apply his ideas to those states that do not fully meet his demanding conditions for being considered a 'people' but this does not get rid of the issue. Some of the problems with decent peoples have been rehearsed already. A key issue is whether his account of minimal human rights is coherent. Is it too minimalist, giving up too much that is important? Or actually not minimalist enough to do the work he wants it to do? Are there in fact any 'decent, well-ordered, non-liberal societies'? Michael Doyle has suggested that Bahrain, Kuwait, Oman, Qatar, the UAE, and perhaps Bhutan are possible decent peoples, and a recent doctoral thesis has added Singapore, Samoa and possibly Brunei to the list (Doyle, 2006; Förster, 2012). Given that all of these candidates are small somewhat anomalous states this may suggest that the category of decent peoples is actually not of great significance, certainly not as significant as Rawls or his critics suggest.

If anything, there is even more of a problem with non-ideal theory. Rawls acknowledges that the categories he identifies here are tentative and sketchy and that is indeed the case. 'Outlaw' states are defined as violating human rights at home and acting aggressively abroad, but there is actually no reason to think that these two behavioural traits actually go together; some very oppressive regimes have quietist foreign policies, and some liberal polities have rather bad records when it comes to the use of force. Also, Rawls doesn't consider the possibility that some states might be both outlaws and burdened, in which case should liberal and decent peoples try to undermine them first and then give them assistance? And where, for a rather important example, does the People's Republic of China fit into the schema? In fairness to Rawls, he does invite us to try to do better when it comes to non-ideal theory, which suggests that he recognises that his own analysis is not as clear as he would like it to be.

Perhaps, in fact, the problems with the way Rawls sets up his theory actually reflect the first principles from which he is operating. As noted above, Rawls remains committed to a world of separate states and an ethical framework that assumes that separation. There is some justice to the charge, made by Allen Buchanan, that he is providing a set of rules for a 'vanished Westphalian world', or, to put the charge in a slightly different way, that Rawls is the last in a long line of political theorists who assume that domestic politics and international politics have to be theorised in radically different ways (Buchanan, 2000). The tradition of understanding international relations in terms of a society of states runs parallel to the tradition of understanding the moral basis of domestic politics as encapsulated by the idea of a social contract – Rawls is, perhaps, the culminating figure of both traditions, the theorist who takes both ideas, the social contract and the society of states, to the point where it is clear that they are no longer adequate. That, certainly, would be the view of those who have developed an account of global politics that is based precisely on the blurring of distinctions that Rawls believes continue to be central to a theoretical understanding of our world and its possibilities. In the second half of this book that account of global politics will be elaborated, but the next chapter will set out in more detail the reasons why the old idea of a society of states perhaps no longer cuts the mustard.

Further Reading

On rights in general there are many good books; Jones (1994) and Ivison (2008) are good routes into this literature, as is Leif Wenar's essay on 'Rights' in the Stanford Encyclopaedia http://plato.stanford.edu/entries/rights/. Andrew Vincent (2010) is a substantial contribution to the literature as well as an excellent textbook. Philip Alston and Ryan Goodman *International Human Rights* (2012) is the latest edition of the primary source collection on the subject – other books present human rights law and materials on the politics of human rights, (see e.g. Haas, 2013) but this Behemoth, currently 1,632 pages, is indispensable. At the other end of the scale, Brown (1997) and Donnelly (2006) provide short overviews of the issues. Tim Dunne and Nicholas Wheeler's collection (1999) is now a little dated but still provides some good framing essays – the present author's piece in this collection, a critique of human rights from a broadly neo-Hegelian perspective, is still widely cited, largely because until recently it has been rare to find any critiques of human rights at all. As we will see in the next two chapters, this is no longer true.

Vincent (1986) approaches human rights from a 'solidarist' English School perspective – indeed this was a key text in framing the solidarism/pluralism distinction. Donnelly (1989) is equally wide-ranging. Evans (1998) re-appraises human rights as a tool of US foreign policy. There are many approaches to human rights that stress gender or culture – these will be addressed in Chapter 6 of this book. In Chapter 5 new meanings of humanitarianism will be discussed; in the meantime, Michael Barnett (2011) provides an excellent overview.

The 'Rawls Industry' is enormous, well summarised by Leif Wenar again in the Stanford Encyclopaedia http://plato.stanford.edu/entries/rawls/. Samuel Freeman (2007) provides an excellent book-length account of his work, and a great many contemporary political philosophers work 'in the shadow of Rawls' even if not endorsing all of his positions. Jon Mandle and David Reidy (2013) is a Companion to Rawls that collects a lot of these authors between its covers. Rawls's *The Law of Peoples* was initially ill received – see e.g. Charles Beitz (2000) and Allen Buchanan (2000) – with only a few positive reviews, including Chris Brown (2002b). More recently his international theory has received more serious attention – see Rex Martin and David Reidy's (2006) collection. The most controversial aspect of *The Law of Peoples* is probably his refusal to recognise a principle of international distributive justice – the literature reflecting this controversy will be discussed in Chapter 10.

5

CHALLENGES TO THE SOCIETY
OF STATES

The English School writers discussed in Chapter 2 consciously set out to produce versions of the society of states fit for purpose in the twenty-first century. The work of Michael Walzer and John Rawls, presented in Chapters 3 and 4 respectively, is not motivated by the same ambition – neither writer saw himself as producing a theory of international society – but still, their accounts of the rights of political communities and the law of peoples can actually be seen as narratives within the tradition of the society of states. Each of these very different accounts attempts to provide an intellectually coherent and morally acceptable version of international society, but in each case critics have argued that they are producing 'rules for a vanished, Westphalian world' to generalise Allen Buchanan's critique of Rawls. Assuming for the purposes of this argument that this is a just indictment, what are the features of the modern world which have caused the Westphalian world to vanish? In this chapter two features are singled out for particular attention, the changing nature of international law, and the dramatic changes that have taken place in the international human rights regime. In both cases the changes in question have taken place essentially in the last quarter century, and this points to the importance of the end of the Cold War; between 1945 and 1989 the society of states was locked into a conflict between two power blocs, thereby preventing change from taking place, or at least slowing down dramatically the rate of change. The end of the Cold War unfroze the system in the same way that it unfroze a number of particular stalemates in, for example, the Balkans and the Horn of Africa – this could be a painful process, and was in both of those locations, but it also unlocked the possibility of a new kind of world politics, a possibility that will be examined in the second half of this book. But first, the challenges to the old order need to be examined in some detail.

International Law and the Society of States

International Law is now and always has been one of the pillars of the society of states (Reus-Smit, 2004). As was argued in Chapter 2, the establishment of an international legal order was one of the factors that explains why the international order was able to understand itself as a 'society', a norm-governed social arrangement, rather than simply the expression of power and interest. Not all of the norms of international society were understood initially in legal terms, but International Law was a key institution nonetheless, and its significance became greater as international treaties came to equal custom as a source of law, that is, as states came to recognise the necessity to codify the rules under which they nominally conducted their relations – a modern example of this process is the Vienna Convention on Diplomatic Relations of 1961 which codified notions of diplomatic immunity that were centuries old. International Law very obviously did not preclude conflicts between states, although the laws of war did attempt to regulate them, but in the nineteenth and twentieth centuries attempts were made to find legal solutions to inter-state conflicts that could act as alternatives to war. International arbitration began to take off at the end of the nineteenth century, partly buoyed by the success of the *Alabama* arbitration, where a dispute between the UK and the US over the former's responsibility for a Confederate commerce raider, the *Alabama*, which could have led to war, was resolved in 1872 by arbitration. The willingness of the UK government to abide by the decision against the British position of a five-person panel, with representatives nominated by Italy, Switzerland and Brazil as well as the US and the UK, gave impetus to the international arbitration movement. In the twentieth century the informal movement towards the judicial settlement of disputes was buttressed by the establishment of permanent judicial bodies; the Permanent Court of International Justice was established in 1919 as part of the League of Nations system, and was retained, rebranded as the International Court of Justice (ICJ) as part of the United Nations System after 1945. The ICJ is based at The Hague, and has played an important role in the development of International Law, with 156 cases entered in the General List between the first, in 1947, and the present day (February, 2014).

All this is impressive, but there are two features of International Law and the ICJ which are central to its role in the society of states but which at the same time limit its ability to function as a legal system analogous to domestic law. In the first place, the ICJ is, in effect, a voluntary system for dispute settlement. There is no way in which states can be forced to employ the Court to resolve their disputes, and even if they do resort to the Court, its judgments are, in effect, unenforceable. In a famous case *Military and Paramilitary Activities in and Against Nicaragua (Nicaragua vs. the United States)* decided in 1986, the Court found that the US support for the *Contras* in the Nicaraguan Civil War constituted a series of wrongs done to Nicaragua, but the decision was simply ignored by the US, and there was effectively nothing that Nicaragua could do about it. Lest this be thought to be simply an example of American bad behaviour, it should be noticed that this case was unusual in that it actually got to the ICJ in the first place – in many similar examples, other states have simply refused to recognise the jurisdiction of the Court. The point is that the voluntary nature of the system is not some unfortunate by-product of a badly drafted Statute, it is absolutely central to the nature of International Law, which regulates the relations of states in the absence of an authoritative government or police system.

The second key feature of International Law, related to the first, is that it regulates, or attempts to regulate, the relations of states; individuals are the subject of International Law only if their relationship to a state was or is in some respect anomalous. Thus, a diplomat had a status under International Law because he (almost always he in the old order) actually represented a state, while pirates had such a, very different, status because they were the common enemies of humanity, *hostis humani generis*, and thus divorced from all states. Private International Law, or the Conflict of Laws as it is termed in Common Law systems, regulates disputes which might involve individuals, but more usually corporations, in different states, but Public International Law is a matter for states and, nowadays, international organisations. Disputes are between states rather than the individuals who lead or represent states.

These two features limit the role of International Law in the conduct of international relations, but they are central to the idea that the international order consists of a society of states as opposed to a world society of individuals. Thus it is that challenges to these features represent challenges to the society of states itself.

Twentieth-century emergence of international criminal law

There is nothing particularly innovative about the idea of criminal prosecutions of specific individuals for international offences such as piracy or war crimes, but until the twentieth century such proceedings were rare, took place in national courts, and did not involve heads of state or government, the latter being considered immune from prosecution by virtue of their office. They are still rare, but now international tribunals are a possibility and sovereign immunity is somewhat qualified (Cassese, 2001).

The change here began in principle, if not in practice, at the end of the First World War (Simpson, 2007). Whereas at the end of the wars with France a century earlier, the Emperor Napoleon had been exiled without trial, first to Elba and then, after Waterloo, to the rather more bracing climate of St Helena, the peacemakers at Versailles proposed that the German Kaiser should be brought to trial before a Tribunal composed of judges from the five victorious powers (the UK, the US, France, Italy and Japan) for 'a supreme offence against international morality and the sanctity of treaties' (*Treaty of Versailles*, Article 227). Reassuringly, Article 227 continues that the tribunal will be 'guided by the highest motives of international policy', but the government of the Netherlands, where the Kaiser had taken refuge in 1918, was unconvinced and refused to extradite him. Under Article 228 the German Government was required to hand over German military personnel wanted by the Allies for war crimes, but again this did not actually take place – Germany was not occupied and in practice refused to co-operate.

In 1945, at the end of the Second World War, things were very different. Germany was occupied and in no position to protect its nationals; moreover, the nature of the Nazi regime and its crimes was such that no country was willing to offer sanctuary (at least not openly – a number of Nazis were assisted by the Vatican to escape to privately sympathetic regimes in Latin America). On the other hand, even if the crimes of the vanquished were of a different order of magnitude to those of the defeated in 1918, the hands of the victors were also less clean; the Soviet Union had committed atrocious crimes against its own citizens and acts of aggression against Poland, Finland and the Baltic Republics, while the Allied policy of area bombing of German and Japanese cities was morally dubious. Still, by the Treaty of London in 1945 an International Military Tribunal was established at Nuremburg to try surviving Nazi civilian and military leaders on charges of crimes against peace, war crimes, and crimes against humanity (Article 6). Article 7 stated that 'The official position of defendants, whether as Heads of State or responsible officials in Government Departments, shall not be considered as freeing them from responsibility or mitigating punishment' thereby overriding the notion of 'sovereign immunity'.

Many lawyers were unhappy with the proceedings at Nuremburg, which in the trial of the major war criminals led to 12 death sentences (one, on Martin Bormann, *in absentia*). The charge of 'crimes against peace' was widely regarded as violating the principle *nulla crimen sine lege* (no crime without a pre-existing law), and the one-sidedness of the proceedings, not to mention the presence of Soviet judges whose commitment to judicial fairness was non-existent, led to the charge that this was 'Victor's Justice'. As against that, the trial produced a mountain of evidence documenting the crimes of the Nazi regime, evidence that might not have emerged so quickly had the leading figures of the regime simply been shot out of hand, as some had proposed, and at the end of the day few doubted the basic justice of the verdicts. Moreover, interestingly, although 12 of the accused were found guilty of crimes against peace, 11 of the 12 were also found guilty of either war crimes or crimes against humanity (the 12th was

Rudolf Hess, who was sentenced to life imprisonment). In fact, of the 11 defendants actually executed, 10 were found guilty of war crimes, which since that was the least legally controversial of the charges suggests that the Judges were conscious of the precariousness of the legal standing of the Tribunal (the 12th defendant, executed solely on the basis of crimes against humanity, was the anti-Semitic journalist Julius Streicher who had held no official position in the regime since 1940; he was a thoroughly odious man and seems to have been convicted on that basis).

Nuremburg was followed by a similar Tribunal in Tokyo, but the Cold War ended any possibility that these two *ad hoc* Tribunals would lead to a major change in international criminal law, and the idea of a permanent International Criminal Court, which had been floated in 1945, was put into cold storage. In 1989 at the end of the Cold War it was brought out again when Trinidad and Tobago requested that consideration be given to establishing an international criminal tribunal; their interest was in combatting drug trafficking, which is not the direction in which the debate proceeded but the International Law Commission ran with the ball and drew up a Draft Statute in 1994 and a draft Code of Crimes in 1996. The key conference that established the Statute of the International Criminal Court was held in Rome in June and July 1998, but before then the process was interrupted by the creation of two *ad hoc* Tribunals in response to the conflict in former Yugoslavia, and the genocide in Rwanda.

International Criminal Tribunals

First, some facts. The details of the wars in former Yugoslavia and the genocide in Rwanda will be discussed in Chapter 7, suffice it to say here that the atrocities that were committed in Bosnia and Rwanda shocked the conscience of the world and led to the UN Security Council establishing two International Criminal Tribunals as UN organs with restrictive and time-limited mandates, charged with applying rules of international humanitarian law which were 'beyond any doubt part of the customary law' (see UN Doc. S/25704 para. 34), in other words, grave breaches of the Geneva Convention, violations of the laws and customs of war, genocide and crimes against humanity. The International Criminal Tribunal for the Former Yugoslavia (ICTY) was established by the UN Security Council under UNSC Resolution 808 in 1993. The ICTY has indicted 161 persons, produced 69 convictions – a further 21 cases are before the Appeals Tribunal, and four cases, including those of Radovan Karadžić and Ratko Mladić are still before the court. The most famous defendant, Slobodan Milošević, former President of Serbia, died in custody of natural causes. The International Criminal Tribunal for Rwanda (ICTR) was established by UN Security Council Resolution 955 in 1994 with the same Prosecutor & Appellate judges as the

ICTY but with different trial judges. The ICTR has handled 75 cases with 47 convicted, a further 16 pending appeal and 12 acquitted; there are no open cases. Both Tribunals are now being wound down – a replacement body, the Mechanism for International Criminal Tribunals, is handling residual business.

There are two ways to look at these two Tribunals. On the one hand, they could be seen as appropriate responses to horrifying events, expressing the righteous desire that wrongdoers be brought to justice. On the other hand, they could be seen as wholly inadequate responses to atrocity, an attempt by the Security Council to compensate for its failure to respond to these crimes at the time. Both perspectives have a great deal of truth to them. It is certainly the case that the UN Security Council did virtually nothing to prevent or end the geno-cide in Rwanda, and although some action was taken in the case of Yugoslavia it was mostly a matter of too little, too late; it is not difficult to conclude from this that the Tribunals were designed to make the leading members of the Council feel better about this failure. Still, an important principle was estab-lished, and the two Tribunals contributed substantially to the process of ending impunity for such terrible crimes. The ICTY in particular, with its indictment of leaders such as Milošević and Karadžić, has sent an important message to those who might commit atrocity crimes in the future, although whether they will heed this warning is another matter.

The ICTY has been, on balance, a success, largely because of the economic strength of the European Union – the successor states of the former Yugoslavia have, for the most part, desired to join the EU, and the EU has made it clear that co-operating with the ICTY is a precondition for membership. Even so, 69 con-victions at a cost of over £2 billion seems a rather inadequate return for all the effort involved. Very few people would argue that the ICTR has been a success – again a small number of convictions have been achieved at a very high cost (over £1.5 billion). Part of the problem for the ICTR has been that the govern-ment of Rwanda has been very unwilling to co-operate – it would prefer to handle the important cases itself; also, the sheer scale of the genocide with tens of thousands of people participating in the murder of nearly a million is beyond the capacity of any court to handle. As against these criticisms, one positive factor that has come out of the Tribunals is, paradoxically, that their inadequa-cies as *ad hoc* tribunals – the slow speed with which they have operated, the possibility of inconsistent judgments, their cost – provided an impetus for the creation of a permanent body.

The International Criminal Court: Rome Conference

Between 15 June and 17 July 1998, a Conference of 160 states, 33 International Organisations and literally hundreds of NGOs met in Rome to work on a Statute for an International Criminal Court. The Agenda was driven by a group of around 60 states known as the caucus of the 'like-minded', chaired initially by Canada and including most EU members, a number of Latin American and African states, but only one of the Permanent Five members of the UN Security Council (the UK). Other groups representing, for example, the Non-Aligned Movement and the Islamic states also existed but the 'like-minded' by virtue of the breadth of their support, and their good links to the NGO movement, managed to dominate the drafting process and it was their draft that was presented for approval at the end of the Conference. A key feature of the final Statute was the absence of a Security Council veto on court proceedings, and the US, voicing its opposition to this feature in particular, forced a vote. The Statute was passed by 120 votes to 7 with 21 abstentions – the vote was unrecorded but the US, China and Israel announced that they had voted against and the other opponents were said to be Libya, Iraq, Qatar and Yemen; abstentions included India and a number of Arab countries (Schabas, 2007).

The International Criminal Court came into existence when 60 states ratified the Statute on 1 July 2002; to date 118 states have ratified, including the UK and France but no other nuclear power. Only two Middle Eastern states have ratified (Tunisia and Jordan) and many major Asian countries remain outside the Court, including India, Pakistan, Indonesia, Bangladesh and Malaysia. The first Prosecutor, appointed when the Court got underway in March 2003, was Luis Moreno Ocampo from Argentina; he was replaced in June 2012 by Mrs Fatou Bensouda from the Gambia – the latter appointment reflecting the African clientele of the Court to date. As of now 20 cases emerging out of eight 'situations' (all in Africa) have been investigated but only one trial has been brought to a conclusion with the conviction of Thomas Lubanga Dyilo, for crimes committed in the Democratic Republic of the Congo, in March 2012.

The Rome Statute gives the ICC jurisdiction (non-retroactive) over genocide, crimes against humanity, war crimes, and aggression – the latter crime was defined in 2010, and will be part of the ICC's jurisdiction from 2017 onwards – 'sovereign immunity' is no defence in these cases. Cases can be instigated by the Prosecutor, by state parties, or by the UN Security Council. Jurisdiction covers acts committed by the nationals of state parties, acts committed on their territories, whether by their nationals or not, and matters referred to the Court by the UN Security Council (thus, the nationals of non-state members may find themselves before the Court). The principle of complementarity applies – the ICC can act only if national courts are unwilling or unable to handle a case. The UN Security Council can defer investigations in the interests of peace and security, but only on a positive vote (that is, if none of the Permanent Five members of the Council exercise a veto).

Before looking more closely at the politics of international criminal law and the ICC, it may be helpful to look at one other issue, that of 'universal jurisdiction'. As noted above, there are particular circumstances where the ICC has jurisdiction over the nationals of non-state parties, but the idea of universal jurisdiction has much wider application. The notion is that there are some crimes that are sufficiently serious that any state can claim criminal jurisdiction over an accused person regardless of where the alleged crime was committed, and regardless of the accused's nationality, or country of residence. This has enormous implications and is highly controversial – thus, for example, Belgium's 1993 'law of universal jurisdiction' a flagship piece of legislation, was amended in 2003 after Belgium was defeated in a case at the International Court of Justice brought by the Democratic Republic of Congo. Probably the most famous case concerning universal jurisdiction – or at least something close to universal jurisdiction – was that which followed the arrest of former General Pinochet in London in 1998 on an extradition warrant from Spain for offences allegedly committed against Spanish nationals while he was Head of State in Chile. Chile objected to the arrest on the basis that no court other than one in Chile had the right to try Pinochet for acts performed while he was their head of state. Eventually, in 1999 the British House of Lords gave a ruling that was quite restrictive but still gave some support to the idea of universal jurisdiction. The ruling stated that torture in another country became a crime against UK law after the *International Convention Against Torture* of 1984 was incorporated into UK law in the *Criminal Justice Act* of 1988 so extradition was possible, albeit only on the basis of post-1988 acts allegedly committed by Pinochet. The House of Lords took the view that sovereign immunity was intended to protect a Head of State acting *properly* and torture was not proper behaviour for such a person. In the event, Pinochet was deported to Chile on health grounds, but a precedent had been set.

The juridification of world politics?

Take the ICTY and ICTR along with the ICC, other 'hybrid' national/international tribunals or courts (such as those established in Sierra Leone and Cambodia), add to the mix various regional tribunals and quasi-judicial bodies such as the WTO Dispute Settlement Panels and a picture begins to emerge of a world in which it is increasingly common to expect the legal regulation of political disputes – call this the 'juridification' (an ugly, but useful word) of world politics. Is this actually a realistic picture given the level of opposition to this trend in some of the most powerful countries in the world, including the US, Russia, China and India? And in any event, would higher levels of juridification actually be desirable?

A great deal of attention has been paid to US opposition to the move to juridification, partly because the US has been the driving force behind so many of other liberal post-1945 innovations in world politics and, indeed, was a leading force in the move to develop ICL in the 1990s, but also because of a widespread and not unrealistic belief that the future of institutions such as the ICC may well depend on US co-operation. The US opposed the terms of the Rome Statute from the outset; President Clinton signed the Statute on the last day possible, 31 December 2001, but without the intention to ratify, and later in 2001 President George W. Bush expressed his disapproval by 'unsigning' the Statute, a dubious, probably meaningless step. In 2002 Congress passed, and Bush signed the American Service-Members Protection Act, widely known as the Hague Invasion Act because it mandated the US President to use whatever force was necessary to 'rescue' US servicemen who might fall under the Court's jurisdiction.

As this last Act suggests, part of the US opposition to the ICC is pragmatic, a fear that because US servicemen are spread throughout the world they would be particularly vulnerable to vexatious prosecutions. This is not unreasonable, but since the US has a well-established system for investigating and punishing crimes committed by American service personnel the principle of complementarity would apply, and the ICC would not have jurisdiction – it was for this reason that the UK government was prepared to ratify the Statute. But the opposition to the ICC in the US is not simply pragmatic – there is also a principled case in favour of a more conventional, not to say traditional, approach to international legal obligations (Posner, 2009). American 'new sovereigntists' resist the development of ICL because they see it as inconsistent with the US constitution – essentially they take the view that the US and its citizens should only be bound by obligations they have specifically accepted through international treaties ratified by the US Senate, and the idea that US citizens could end up facing criminal charges under laws that have not been so approved is totally unacceptable. Customary international law as traditionally understood – that is laws that have developed over time and become widely accepted – is regarded as legitimate, but the attempt to argue that new norms can be quickly seen as 'customary' is strongly resisted. These writers in particular wish to resist international attempts to place US conduct of the War on Terror under the auspices of international criminal law.

In practice, US opposition to the ICC has been rather less absolute than the rhetoric might suggest – in the second Bush and both Obama Administrations the US has agreed to the UN Security Council referring issues to the ICC, for example over Darfur and, in 2011, Libya. In any event, American reservations are actually shared by many other countries including Russia, China and India. China in particular regards the movement towards juridification as restricting its recently won sovereignty, and generally as acting as an instrument of Western Hegemony. As noted above, the indictments issued by the ICC give some support to the argument that the ICC is a 'European Court trying Africans' – although the Africans in question were all referred to the Court by other African Governments.

Perhaps European rather than Western is indeed the appropriate word here; and not simply because the most important Western country is not party to the ICC. Juridification can actually be seen as an attempt to Europeanise world politics. In Europe since 1945 international relations have been legally regulated with the threat of force more or less abolished (at least in Western Europe), and many of the strongest proponents of the ICC and other similar bodies have wanted to repeat the trick on a world stage. Realists, of course, would argue that Europe has become a consumer rather than a provider of security since 1945 and juridification represents an attempt by 'Venus' to restrain 'Mars' as Robert Kagan nicely put it in his *Paradise and Power* (Kagan, 2004). More fundamentally, criminal law to be effective requires a high level of moral consensus, a level which Europe may have reached but which there is little evidence that the world has. It is interesting that one of the dilemmas of international criminal law is the clash between a universal desire to punish crimes against humanity, and a local desire to resolve conflicts as soon as possible and on terms acceptable to the participants – thus, sometimes an indictment by the ICC may make local peacekeeping more difficult by restricting the kind of deal that can be struck. Such a clash is also latent in domestic criminal proceedings, but in countries which have effective systems of criminal law it is not allowed to emerge; crimes such as murder, theft and fraud are offences against the state (the crown in the UK) rather than against the particular victims. But this is an arrangement that took a long time to become established, and the world as a whole is still, perhaps, at an earlier stage of the process – which is not to deny that the attempt to juridify international politics has already changed many aspects of the ways in which states go about their business. We will return to this issue in the final chapter of this book.

Human rights and the new humanitarianism

In the last chapter the emergence of the international human rights regime was briefly outlined, and the point made that in the early years of that regime there was little sense that human rights were incompatible with the notion of state sovereignty. The assumption was that rights would be claimed through rather than against the state – the foundational statements of the regime were international treaties in which states promised *to each other* that they would promote the rights outlined therein. In any event, the first years of the regime coincided with the Cold War and with the shake-up of the international system by decolonisation – the right to self-determination was centre stage in this era and promoted by both East and West (reluctantly and selectively in some cases) but other rights were hotly contested on ideological grounds. The West stressed the classic political rights which were routinely violated in the East, while the latter claimed that the economic rights that communism allegedly guaranteed were the most significant for ordinary people. Arguably both sides were in bad faith given the West's support for reliably anti-communist authoritarian regimes, and the East's actual failure to deliver either economic or political rights. In any event, the politics of human rights were deadlocked.

The situation began to change in the 1970s. Samuel Moyn argues persuasively that in that decade human rights developed into a utopian ideology that could be set against both Western capitalism and Eastern communism (Moyn, 2010). The Vietnam War and increasing economic difficulties had, at least temporarily, de-legitimised Western liberal democracy in the eyes of many, and the failures of Soviet communism and of the majority of post-colonial states undermined the possibility that these alternative models of politics could replace liberal democracy. Instead, for many well-intentioned people human rights became the new focus for their hopes, and, crucially, now human rights were defined not as something that could be achieved through the state, but as something to be achieved in opposition to the state. It was in this period that sovereignty and human rights came to be seen as pointing in different directions.

One sign of this latter shift was provided by the fate of the 'Third Basket' of Human Rights in the Helsinki Accords, which were signed in 1975 with the intention of stabilising affairs in Europe. In effect, the West agreed to recognise existing European borders, including those of East Germany, as a way of releasing tension, and, in what at the time looked like a sop to Western opinion, the Soviet Union and other Warsaw Pact countries agreed to recognise the package of human rights set out in the aforementioned Third Basket. This was widely seen as a meaningless gesture by many in the West, a sign that the Helsinki negotiations had been 'won' by the Soviets, but in fact the human rights provisions of the Accords proved to be of great importance. Throughout the Soviet Bloc dissidents set up Helsinki Monitoring Groups with the aim of holding their governments to the terms of the Accords. The rights these Groups were now demanding could no longer be characterised by the authorities as 'Western' since they were set out in documents to which those same authorities had attached their signatures. In fact, the Helsinki Monitoring Groups were harassed by the regimes and in some cases closed down with their members arrested – but the damage was done and the challenge to the legitimacy of the regimes of 'really-existing socialism' was a contributory factor to their collapse in the 1980s.

The 1970s also saw a growth in human rights advocacy groups in Western civil society. 'Helsinki Watch' was formed in the US in 1978 in support of the Helsinki Monitoring Groups in the Soviet Bloc, but gradually evolved into the most important civil society human rights group, taking the name Human Rights Watch in 1988. Amnesty International had been formed in 1961 to campaign on behalf of 'prisoners of conscience'; in the 1970s it extended its remit to cover campaigns against torture, political killings and, eventually, the death penalty – in the latter case opposing capital punishment even for non-political crimes. Originally Amnesty had refused to offer support to political prisoners who had employed violence; by the 1980s it had become a general human rights group, working *inter alia* on behalf of anyone facing the death penalty, even those convicted of violent, non-political crimes.

An equally significant development in the same period was the transformation that took place in the discourse of 'economic and social rights'. These rights do feature in the UDHR of 1948 and, of course, in the 1966 Covenant on Economic, Social and Cultural Rights, but until the late 1970s thinking on these rights was shaped by two factors that were not, as such, rights oriented. One was, yet again, the Cold War, and the story here was of Western resistance to the Soviet use of economic rights language to assert the superiority of communism over capitalism. The other was decolonisation, and the emergence of political pressure for a 'New International Economic Order', a movement that looked at the implications of economic inequality but without employing rights language, at least not in a very extensive way. By the late 1970s both of these factors were of declining importance. As noted above, communism had lost its sheen by then, the post-colonial states that had emerged from the wreckage of the old empires had proved fragile and largely incapable of meeting the demands put on them, and the NIEO was in the process of becoming irrelevant – with the rise of Thatcherism and Reaganism and the decline of social democracy, the chances that the developed world would respond to the demands for a NIEO declined sharply.

However, the playing out of these factors cleared a space for a different approach to economic rights, and here one book takes on considerable significance – Henry Shue's *Basic Rights: Subsistence, Affluence and US Foreign Policy* (1980). Shue's book is, for the most part, an account and critique of US food policy, the use of American grain reserves to buttress US foreign policy goals, but the initial chapter on the notion of basic rights has been highly influential. Basic rights he argues are 'everyone's minimum reasonable demand upon the rest of humanity' (p. 19) and can be divided into *Security Rights* – a basic right to physical security, i.e. 'not to be subjected to murder, torture, mayhem, rape or assault' (p. 20) and *Subsistence Rights* – the right to minimal economic security 'unpolluted air, unpolluted water, adequate food, adequate clothing, adequate shelter and minimum preventive public health care' (p. 23). These apparently simple statements herald a new way of looking at human rights. In the past, in so far as economic or social rights were analysed in depth at all, the understanding was that they related to standards that states were expected to provide for their citizens, and that citizens thus had a right to demand of 'their' state, in much the same way that the Helsinki Monitoring Groups were demanding that their states adhered to the political standards set out in the Helsinki Accords. Now, it is 'the rest of humanity' to whom everyone has a reasonable demand that certain basic standards are met.

It isn't clear whether making a demand on the rest of humanity can actually be worked into a coherent theory of rights – is not making a demand on every-one perilously close to making a demand on no-one? – but this hardly matters given the political attractiveness of this stance. Rights are not simply divorced from an increasingly unpopular agency, the state, they are widened so that they cover potentially everything that one might desire. Clearly we all want ade-quate shelter, adequate food, adequate clothing and so on, but now we are told that these things are not just desirable, we have a right to them. And in the late 1980s, the American international lawyer Thomas Franck completed the picture by adding an 'emerging' right to democratic government to the list – the notion of a right is not simply divorced from the state and claimed against the rest of humanity, the state itself is to be the subject of a right (Franck, 1992).

The implications of this new meaning of human rights for the society of states is clear and uncompromising – just as the state is no longer understood as the deliverer of human rights, so international society itself becomes an object of suspicion, its pluralism an obstacle to the achievement of genuine human rights. Moreover, this tendency is reinforced by shifts in the meaning of humanitarianism.

The new humanitarianism

To recapitulate some points made in the last chapter, nineteenth and early twentieth century humanitarianism was largely dominated by 'apolitical' notions, symbolised by ICRC's commitment to impartiality and neutrality, but it also encompassed civil society campaigns such as that against the slave trade and, later against colonial atrocities. The formation of the UN and the process of decolonisation threw up some challenges to this situation, and the end of the Cold War has transformed the meaning of humanitarianism.

The UN is a statist organisation, which, in principle, respects 'domestic juris-diction', on which see Article 2(7) of the UN Charter. However, it is also, in principle, judgmental when it comes to the use of force and that immediately raises an important hypothetical question – is the neutrality prized by the ICRC appro-priate when UN-sanctioned military operations are underway? Initially Switzerland, the home of the Red Cross, declined to become a full member of the UN pre-cisely because of this dilemma (it eventually joined in 2002). In any event, because of the Cold War, UN-sanctioned collective security operations under Chapter VII of the Charter were uncommon and 'Peacekeeping Operations' under Chapter VI become the accepted way of handling the humanitarian crises thrown up by decolonisation or the policing of cease-fire lines and truces. But keeping such operations apolitical proved very difficult. In the Congo crisis 1960–4, the UN force in the Congo (ONUC) whose mandate was to keep the peace eventually used force to end the secession of the province of Katanga – a decision that caused some Western backers of the Katangan regime to describe the UN force as a 'Red Army in Blue Berets' (O'Brien, 2011). Overblown rhetoric aside, the decision to use international troops to end a secession was indeed an incursion into internal politics of the host country and, arguably, went beyond ONUC's mandate. The key point is that sustaining impartiality in such circumstances was very difficult, a point reinforced by the fate of UNEF, the UN Emergency Force tasked with maintaining the truce between Israel and Egypt in the Sinai. When originally drawn up in 1957 the then UN Secretary General Dag Hammarskjold made sure that it was composed of troops from many neutral countries but by 1987 his successor had allowed it to be dominated by a few, essentially pro-Egyptian countries (particularly Yugoslavia and India). The result was that when Egypt asked the UN to pull out the force was immediately withdrawn, because Hammarskjold's plans for procrastination in such circumstances could no longer be put in effect.

The fate of UNEF and ONUC was of importance in the 1960s, but the key movement in the development of a new approach to humanitarianism came with the famine generated in 1968 by the Nigerian Civil War, also known as the Biafra Secession (1967–70). Initially the international community responded by a major partnership between UN agencies and NGOs – this was the first large-scale famine relief operation conducted by the ICRC, and only the second by Oxfam. Then Nigeria took the view that the best way to end the famine was to end the secession and refused to allow agencies to deliver food to 'Biafra'. Official agencies and ICRC accept this decision; in line with their commitment to impartiality and neutrality they could not operate against the wishes of the internationally recognised government. Other NGOs (including Oxfam) went in a different direction, participating in an airlift to Biafra, sometimes alongside those who were supplying the secessionist province, and Bernard Kouchner led a breakaway of doctors from the ICRC, which became *Médecins sans Frontières* (*MsF*) on the principle that a political stand had to be taken (Allen and Styan, 2000). As a matter of fact – and as Oxfam at least acknowledged – the aid provided to Biafra actually extended the war and, since the feared post-war genocide did not materialise, it could well be argued that the wrong decision was made, but the key point is that Biafra established the idea of a different kind of humanitarianism. This new, rights-based, humanitarianism took political stands and set itself against the primacy of the state – these new humanitarians considered (and consider) themselves entitled to override sovereignty if they believe the occasion demands it.

In the 1970s French IGOs developed the notion of *le droit d'ingérence*, which is the first explicit doctrinal elaboration of the idea of external humanitarian intervention as a legitimate response to state failure. *Le droit d'ingérence* does not translate easily into English – it conveys the notion of a *right* to intervene (or interfere) but could also be read as a *duty* to act. Either way, it is a controversial notion that is obviously open to be interpreted as justifying neo-imperial actions, and, predictably, was the subject of heated debate within the French Left. English-speaking humanitarians in the 1970s were less doctrinal in their thinking (notions such as Tony Blair's 'Doctrine of the International Community' and the idea of a 'Responsibility to Protect' were not developed until two or three decades later) but harboured similar thoughts to Kouchner and his colleagues in organisations such as *MsF*. Meanwhile, UN agencies continue to think of humanitarian action as requiring state approval – but it is noteworthy that in response to the crises that emerged in the 1980s, UNGA Resolution 43/131 (1988) was passed; this provided a legal basis for giving armed international protection to humanitarian actors in areas where no legitimate government could protect them.

These doctrinal developments took place during the Cold War, that is at a time when the international contest between the two blocs, East and West, acted both as a force for stability, preventing latent local conflicts from developing, and as an inhibitor on international action when conflicts did take place. As Nicholas Wheeler demonstrates in his classic *Saving Strangers*, interventions did take place in the 1970s in Bangladesh, Cambodia and Uganda, but they were not explicitly claimed by the interveners as 'humanitarian' because the notion that military action to relieve suffering could be seen in such terms had not been developed (Wheeler, 2000). But when the Cold War ended and latent conflicts re-emerged in e.g. the Horn of Africa and the Balkans, humanitarian action became both possible and necessary, and the 'new humanitarians' came into their own.

Rights-based humanitarianism

To recapitulate: the best representative of the older notion of humanitarianism is certainly the Red Cross, the ICRC; its fundamental principles, restated at its XX Congress in Vienna in 1965 stress Humanity, Impartiality, Neutrality, Independence, Voluntary Service, Unity, and Universality. These principles, as noted in Chapter 4, pose no threat to, indeed provide services for, the society of states. This version of humanitarianism looks to meet the immediate needs of suffering individuals and eschews the taking of political stands – but the new, rights-based, humanitarianism is no longer content simply to provide 'a bed for the night' (Rieff, 2002). Instead, the new humanitarians have taken sides, abandoned neutrality and actively involve themselves in political action. The multiple post-Cold War crises that developed in the 1990s have led in many cases to extensive external interventions in the name of humanitarianism by both states and non-state organisations. Some of these interventions will be examined in more detail in Chapters 7 and 8; here it suffices to identify some of the important ways in which they have raised challenges to the operation of the society of states.

First, these interventions have raised *Ethical and Normative* questions. The basic proposition that underpins the new humanitarianism is that the rights of individuals trump the rights of states and political communities, that the sovereignty norms that have dominated inter-state relations for several centuries have to give way to norms based on human rights. But can we be sure that these new norms represent genuinely universal values and that the new humanitarianism is not, in fact, a cover for a new imperialism? Earlier theorists of international society have argued that some humanitarian crises create a right on the part of outsiders to intervene, but do they actually have a duty to intervene, as some would suggest – as we'll see, the modern formulation of this duty is 'a responsibility to protect'? Can military means be justified for humanitarian ends? And how important are motives and intentions – the classic Natural Lawyers who developed Just War criteria were convinced that 'right intention' was central to legitimate action, but need we follow them in this respect, given that motives are always mixed and rarely transparent? T.S. Elliot in *Murder in the Cathedral* described 'doing the right thing for the wrong reason' as the greatest treason, but if an atrocity is actually ended, should we be too concerned about why those who ended it did so?

Then there are *legal* issues raided by the new humanitarianism. What is the legal basis for intervention by one state in the affairs of another? Are such interventions only legally permissible in response to a Chapter VII Resolution of the UN Security Council, as a strict reading of the UN Charter would suggest? If so, humanitarian concerns are at the mercy of the Permanent Five veto powers in the Council and, given the divisions between these powers, it is unlikely that legal sanction will always be related to need as opposed to political interests. Perhaps instead it could be argued that there is a customary right to intervene when mass atrocity crimes take place – but then the Charter of the UN was designed precisely to supersede customary laws on the use of force. In the case of the Kosovo conflict of 1999 a distinguished group of scholars and practitioners argued that the NATO intervention was 'illegal but legitimate' – but this formula does not find favour with the majority of international lawyers and is clearly open to abuse.

Finally, there are *political* and *practical* issues raised by the new humanitarianism. Clearly in the case of humanitarian action political will is crucial, but the factors that might generate such a will are contradictory and difficult to predict. The so-called 'CNN effect' produced by journalists in areas of conflict and crisis can easily generate the sentiment 'something must be done', but the same television cameras, when they document the effects of intervention, can have the reverse effect. On the one hand, they can show the effects of military intervention on the local civilian population – and there is always 'collateral damage' to show – while, on the other, they can show the effect of action on 'our boys', the 'body-bags' effect. Critics of any particular humanitarian action are always able to point to issues of selectivity – there are always political reasons why one humanitarian crisis invokes a sustained response while another does not and such political reasons can be used to delegitimise action, or to characterise it as imperialistic rather than humanitarian. And, purely as a practical matter, we might ask whether humanitarian interventions actually work, i.e. do they generally make matters better or worse? What sort of longer-term obligations do those who intervene for humanitarian reasons take on? Is state-building something that outsiders can actually perform?

All these issues are posed most starkly by military humanitarian interventions, but they arise in less dramatic forms whenever humanitarianism moves beyond the ICRC principles of neutrality and impartiality. Humanitarians who actively engage in attempting to solve political problems necessarily are undertaking interventions, even if they do not wear uniforms or carry guns. And in any event, not everyone who wears a uniform or carries a gun is necessarily intervening militarily. Many modern humanitarian actions involve the speedy movement of goods on a large scale, and the military are most adept at this; it is striking that in the case of both the 2004 Indian Ocean tsunami and Typhoon Haiyan in 2013, it was US Navy ships that were first on the scene to deliver relief supplies – modern aircraft carriers have a mobile lift capacity that no humanitarian organisation can come close to matching, and the military are equally able to mobilise long-haul transport aircraft very quickly on a scale that no civilian carrier can equal. Of course, the US Navy are not what most people have in mind when they think of a humanitarian organisation, but this simply raises again the issue of motives vs. outcomes. If the US Navy – or, as Stephen Hopgood has posited, Wal-Mart – can react to a crisis faster than any comparable civilian body, it seems counter-intuitive to suggest that they are not fulfilling a humanitarian role (Hopgood, 2008).

The expansion of the humanitarian sphere, combined with expanded notions of human rights has create a new 'humanitarian space', which by its very existence poses a challenge to the society of states, but which is itself challenged by the problems it generates. This is increasingly recognised and understood as problematic. David Rieff's polemic *A Bed for the Night* is the response of one journalist who lived through the many crises of the 1990s – and contributed to the new humanitarianism by his calls for action – and who has ended up as a defender of the older notion of what humanitarians can actually do (Rieff, 2002). From the academy and the work of mainstream figures who have a long track record of working in the field, Michael Barnett and Thomas Weiss in their collection *Humanitarianism in Question* (2008) and their later *Humanitarianism Contested*, (2011) by their very titles recognise the existence of a problem.

The problems thrown up by the new humanitarianism could lead to a return to the ICRC model of apolitical action, providing a bed for the night, but it could also lead in the other direction, to the defining of humanitarianism in much wider terms, shifting attention away from immediate crises towards even deeper causes, leading to an interest in global inequality and global social justice.

Could the problems caused by, for example, global warming be defined in humanitarian terms? Oxfam and Amnesty International certainly thinks so, judging by their websites, which might well be a source of surprise for the individuals who set up these organisations with much more limited briefs some decades ago.

Conclusion

The rapid development of international criminal law, and the new politics of humanitarianism and human rights, taken together, are indicators of a genuine change in the nature of world politics. Alongside the society of states, a global polity may be emerging – in the former, states and the organisations they have created are centre stage, in the latter they are joined by office-holders who are no longer protected by sovereign immunity, individuals who are deemed to have rights which are not dependent on states, and a myriad of civil society groups who are devoted to expanding the sphere of those rights. Something important is happening, but still the most important word in the last sentence is 'alongside'; the emerging global polity is not replacing the society of states, rather the two conceptions of world politics exist side by side. This is, predictably, a source of considerable tension. In the first part of the book the problems involved in understanding the world as an international society have been explored; in the second part, the problems of the emerging global polity will be the focus – and one of the most important of these problems is the fact that this emergent political focus has to share the world with the older society of states.

Further Reading

Jackson Maogoto (2004) and John Laughland (2008) provide general background to political crimes and the rise of international criminal law, Gerry Simpson (2007) brings the story up to date in a manner that is very palatable to international political theorists. Antonio Cassese (1999a), (1999b) and (2008) *inter alia* was the doyen of international criminal lawyers and a staunch, but sensible advocate of the ICC. The Canadian international lawyer Frederic Megret (2001), (2002) and (2005) is another strong advocate; Geoffrey Robertson (2012) is a less temperate supporter of ICL. A Symposium in the *American Journal of International Law* (1999) is

(Continued)

(Continued)

still the best source for a detailed account of the terms of the Rome Statute. Jason Ralph (2004) links the ICC to the English School. On the link between justice and peace Jack Snyder and Leslie Vinjamuri (2004) is thoughtful, and look out for an LSE PhD from Mark Kersten (2014).

Philip Allott (1999), (2001) and (2002) is an unclassifiable and very stimulating writer, cosmopolitan in outlook but critical of the sudden rise of international criminal law. American critics of the ICC are decidedly uncosmopolitan but raise very compelling points; see in particular Jack Goldsmith and Eric Posner (2005), Posner (2009), Jonathan Rabkin (2005) and the collection from the *National Interest* magazine edited by R. James Woolsey (2003). The notion that ICL is a European project designed to reduce the role of power politics in the world is discussed in Chapter 11; in the meantime, see Robert Kagan's polemic (2004) or, from the European end, Robert Cooper (2003).

Journals of particular interest to international political theorists who wish to keep up with legal thinking on international criminal law include the *American Journal of International Law, European Journal of International Law* and *The Journal of International Criminal Law* as well as numerous American college law journals. The ICC has an excellent website www.icc-cpi.int/en_menus/icc/Pages/default.aspx and a dedicated fan-club The Coalition for an International Criminal Court www.iccnow.org; the ICTR and the ICTY are also to be found online, though less informatively.

On humanitarianism and the new human rights regime in-text references to the work of Stephen Hopgood (2008) and (2013), Samuel Moyn (2010), Michael Barnett (2011) and Barnett and Thomas Weiss (2008) are crucial – Barnett and Weiss's 2008 collection is the best source for general meditations on the difference between the new and the old humanitarianism. Weiss (1999) is an excellent brief survey of humanitarianism old and new. David Rieff's journalism in the 1990s helped to define the new humanitarianism, but his critiques of what he helped to create (2002) and (2006) have been very influential. An indefatigable critic of the new humanitarianism is David Chandler, best represented by his (2005) book and by the journal he founded *The Journal of Intervention and Statebuilding.* Oliver Ramsbotham and Tom Woodhouse (1996) provide an account of the classical approach to humanitarianism. The second half of this book will try to show how the changing meanings of humanitarianism have influenced world politics over the last two decades, and further reading will be found there.

PART II

THE EMERGING GLOBAL POLITY

6

THE NEW HUMAN RIGHTS REGIME

Introduction: The new politics of identity and difference

In 1946 UNESCO set up an international committee of intellectuals to explore the notion of human rights; the committee took soundings from people they believed represented the various ethical and moral traditions, and their deliberations fed into the drafting of the Universal Declaration. As we have seen, the idea that human dignity is best defended by the language of rights has a distinctly Western origin, but the result of this consultative exercise was a degree of consensus that, seen in the context of the politics of human rights in the 1990s, was perhaps surprising. Partly this consensus was shaped by the conditions of the era and the tendency to consult only those Buddhist, Muslim, Hindu and Confucian scholars who were already oriented towards consensus, but it was also achieved by agreeing to 'bracket' some of the most important philosophical and ontological questions. The situation was perfectly summarised in a quote attributed to the French Catholic philosopher and ethicist Jacques Maritain; 'we agree about the rights but on condition that no one asks us why' (UNESCO, 1949).

For nearly 40 years after 1948 no one – or at least very few people – did. As we have seen in Chapter 5, until the 1970s human rights issues were bound up with the politics of the Cold War and decolonisation. The relative weight of political and civil as opposed to economic and social rights was a major issue and the small but growing number of human rights activists who could be found in civil society groups were mostly concerned with issues of compliance and enforcement. This was particularly the case with the various 'Helsinki Watch' groups that sprang up to monitor Soviet compliance (or, more accurately non-compliance) with the Helsinki Accords. The ontological status of human rights was the last thing on the minds of these groups – they were concerned to use the idea of human rights to extract political freedoms from the regimes of the Eastern Bloc, and they achieved leverage by focusing on the legal implications of the Accords which the Soviet Union and its satellites had signed rather than by raising philosophical questions about the origins of the notion of rights. Again as we have seen in Chapter 5, in the 1980s the issue of economic rights came to be redefined in terms of Basic Rights to security and subsistence and, as we will see in Chapter 10, the notion that a right could be understood, in Henry Shue's words, as 'everyone's minimum reasonable demand upon the rest of humanity' resonated with a new interest in notions of global social justice, with considerable implications for the ways in which we think about international political theory, but still, within this discourse as well, Maritain's question remained unasked. The promoters of the idea of basic rights and economic justice were Western liberals and social democrats who were, understandably, not concerned by the Western origins of rights, and the potential recipients of the benefits of a hypothetical system of global economic justice, though themselves neither Western nor, usually, liberal or social democratic, were not inclined to dismiss these benefits on philosophical grounds.

None of this is to suggest that there were no disputes about the nature of rights in the four decades after the Universal Declaration of Human Rights in 1948, but rather that the disputes that did take place during the Cold War and the era of decolonisation were situated within a particular framework in which certain key positions were taken for granted, even though the participants in these disputes did not always, or usually, recognise that this was the case. Soviet Communism and Western Liberal Capitalism looked very different on the surface, but both systems were based on a conception of politics which took the ownership of the means of production and the nature of the relations of production to be central, and both rested upon an understanding of the human animal as an autonomous, self-directing being whose personhood was central to political action. During the Cold War the West almost by definition saw itself as instantiating 'Western Values' but the pedigree of Soviet Communism was equally Western – no-one could deny the Karl Marx was a product of the Western Enlightenment, and Lenin, Trotsky and even Stalin and Mao Zedong were, in the context of their societies, Western modernisers. The Cold War was certainly a contest over the meaning of the West, a struggle over the meaning of the Enlightenment Project, but, seen from the outside, the two sides had a great deal in common.

In 1989 the Berlin Wall fell, and over the next two years first the Soviet empire in Eastern Europe, and then the Soviet Union itself, unravelled. The West had won the Cold War as surely as the Allies had won the Second World War, although on this occasion the equivalent of raising the Red Flag over the Reichstag in Berlin was the opening of a branch of McDonald's in Moscow.

The core questions surrounding the management of a modern economy had been answered; there appeared to be no substitute for some kind of market economy. There was plenty of room for dispute over second order questions such as determining the appropriate level of governmental involvement in the market, but the possibility that a modern economy could operate on the basis of commands from a central planning authority had been eliminated, a fact acknowledged even by most of the surviving communist countries and denied only by North Korea, at appalling cost to its people. China and Cuba joined North Korea in continuing to resist the 'liberal' part of liberal capitalism, but still, Western liberal democracy was given an enormous boost by the end of the Cold War, and waves of democratisation rolled over Latin America and Africa, albeit sometimes, in the latter case especially, with unfortunate results, as we will see in later chapters. Francis Fukuyama's rather misunderstood declaration of the 'End of History' may have over-stated the case, but it can still be argued that the end of the Cold War, the victory of the West, and the way in which that victory was won, constituted a world-historic moment – something very big happened in 1989 and attempts to deny this are unconvincing (Fukuyama, 1989).

The implications for human rights of 1989 are interesting, and perhaps counter-intuitive; one might have thought that a victory for liberal democracy would translate unambiguously into a victory for human rights, but in fact the ending of one kind of politics opened up space for another kind to develop, and the new post-1989 politics made it more difficult to leave Maritain's question unasked. With the contest over the meaning of the Enlightenment project more or less settled, and the previously dominant politics of economic organisation reduced to a limited contest over the management of a market economy, the space was cleared for a new kind of politics; instead of the politics of class and property, the 1990s saw the emergence, globally and locally, of a politics of identity and difference. The kind of assumptions about the nature of human beings that had previously been widely accepted were now scrutinised; the Western origin of the rights regime was now problematised and new questions concerning gender were raised. To put the matter succinctly, was the allegedly universal rights-holder of the post-1948 international human rights regime actually a Western man? In the following sections of this chapter the various dimensions of this question will be examined; first up will be the general 'cultural' critique of Western human rights thinking summarised by the notion of 'Asian Values'; then we will look at group rights, indigenous peoples and the general claim of a right to be different, and then the feminist critique of the human rights regime will be examined. In the second half of the chapter two possible ways out of the dilemmas previously set out will be scrutinised – the capabilities approach associated (in different versions) with Amartya Sen and Martha Nussbaum, and the notion of a human rights culture, best expressed by Richard Rorty.

Culture and the 'Asian Values' debate

A convenient entry-point to the new politics of identity and difference is pro-vided by the 1993 *UN World Conference on Human Rights* held in Vienna. The intention behind this conference was to collect what was widely thought of as the potential human rights dividend that the ending of the Cold War, and in particular the way the Cold War ended, was supposed to bring. This was to be an opportunity to revisit and strengthen the *Universal Declaration* of 1948; this time there would be no need to pander to the reservations of the Soviet Bloc, and the wave of democratisation that swept across Latin America and Africa had removed many of the most egregious examples of right-wing authoritarianism. Moreover, whereas the Bush Administration, which had presided over the dis-mantling of Soviet power, had shown very little interest in human rights, the new American Administration of Bill Clinton was emphasising human rights to a degree not seen since the Carter years. Clinton's new National Security Adviser, Anthony Lake, was an advocate of 'democracy promotion' as a goal of US policy – in part this reflected the newly articulated 'democratic peace' thesis, the proposition that liberal democracies do not go to war with each other (Doyle, 1983; Cox et al., 2000). The Democratic Peace thesis was controversial in the academy, but popular with liberal politicians; the argument that democ-racy was not just a good in itself but also conducive to peace was compelling. Given that, at least in the minds of human rights groups, democracy and rights go together, it seemed that all the stars were aligned for a successful Conference that would strengthen rights protection. In the event, things turned out rather differently.

Prior to the Vienna Conference in June 1993, regional conferences were held in order to collect opinions and clarify options. The Regional Meeting for Asia of the World Conference on Human Rights took place in March 1993 in Bangkok, and produced the 'Bangkok Declaration', a short statement which actually came to dominate the Conference in Vienna, and is now seen as foun-dational for the 'Asian Values' debate and the critique of human rights universalism (Bauer and Bell, 1999). The Declaration is actually a complex and at times contradictory document, the product – as all such Declarations are – of compromise and deliberate obfuscation. It begins by enthusiastically endorsing the idea of universal human rights, critiquing double standards and selectivity, and calling for the democratisation of the UN; it goes on to reject the idea of tying human rights to development assistance, to endorse national sovereignty and non-intervention and to stress that all countries have the right to deter-mine their own political system without the use of human rights as an instrument of political pressure. In general, the state is to be seen as the delivery mechanism for human rights. This endorsement of human rights within the context of the society of states and Westphalian political arrangements would not have been controversial in the first few decades post-1948, but in 1993 it represented a defence of an order that many human rights activists hoped was on the decline. Worst was to come.

Article 8 of the Declaration deserves to be quoted in full; the Ministers and Representatives of the Asian states represented at the Conference

> <u>Recognize</u> that while human rights are universal in nature, they must be considered in the context of a dynamic and evolving process of international norm-setting, bearing in mind the significance of national and regional particularities and various historical, cultural and religious backgrounds.

Whereas the state-centricity of much of the Bangkok Declaration simply represents a return to a pre-1970s understanding of human rights, this Article could be read as subversive of the very notion of universality, which, surely, is precisely to de-legitimise national and regional particularities if they diverge from universal values, whether they are rooted in historical, cultural or religious backgrounds or not. Still, the influence of the Bangkok Declaration can certainly be seen in the *Vienna Declaration and Programme of Action*, that the World Conference produced in June 1993. Article 5 of the Declaration reasserted the universality of human rights but adopted the language of Bangkok, albeit to slightly different effect; thus –

> While the significance of national and regional particularities and various historical, cultural and religious backgrounds must be borne in mind, it is the duty of States, regardless of their political, economic and cultural systems, to promote and protect all human rights and fundamental freedoms.

This very clearly represented a compromise, simultaneously recognising but downplaying the Bangkok position, but of greater significance for the human rights movement as a whole was the absence in the Vienna Declaration of the 'great leap forward' that the movement had hoped for – the creating of a UN Human Rights Commissioner though welcome in itself was no substitute for substantive progress. The Declaration is essentially an anodyne document, and it is understandable that the Bangkok Declaration had had more influence than the Conference it was supposed to lead up to.

What was going on at Bangkok? It is necessary to make a distinction between the political forces which made the Declaration possible and the underlying ideas which it represented. As to the former, the key point is that the 'Asians' who formulated the 'Asian Values' position represented a relatively small, but influential, sub-set of Asian states – key were Singapore, Indonesia and Malaysia – and it is interesting that neither India nor China were much involved in the debate (a point that will be returned to later). The key feature of this sub-set of Asian states is that they were all, to different degrees, both authoritarian and economically successful. Because of the former, they were concerned by the trend towards 'democracy promotion' in Western, especially American, thought;

because of the latter – their economic success – they felt themselves under less pressure to roll over in the face of Western influence. The motivation behind the stress in the Bangkok Declaration on the illegitimacy of using political pressure to promote human rights is easy to see, as is the utility of declaring that the form of rule in countries such as Singapore and Indonesia represented the 'historical, cultural and religious backgrounds' of those states.

Because of these considerations it is often argued that the very notion of Asian Values is no more than a smokescreen for the defence of authoritarian rule, but this is to miss the point. It may well be that some of the rulers who promoted the notion did so cynically, but they drew on arguments that were not inherently self-serving. The core case here is that the rights-holder privileged by the international human rights regime is a secular individual whereas the Asian world view privileges religion and the community. Thus, Confucian thinking, or so it was said, privileges family and age in a way inimical to the individualism that characterises Western thinking and the human rights regime. Islam shares with the West the notion of an individual with but one life to live – in contrast to the Hindu or Buddhist emphasis on the oneness of all life – but defines the highest purpose of the individual as submission to God.

These are positions that could be, and have been, elaborated at length but enough has been said here to give the gist of the argument, and perhaps enough to see that while there may be some truth to the general proposition that the contemporary human rights regime is individualistic and secular, it is a mistake to think that these are characteristics that can be described as inherently 'Western' or necessarily non-'Asian'. The key point is that both 'Asia' and the 'West' are contested categories, stereotypes that obscure more than they reveal. Consider the issue of religion and secularism; it is certainly true that in Western Europe today secularism has a firm hold, but it is equally true that in East and Central Europe and *a fortiori* in North America religious approaches to political and social issues are still central, as much as they are in Africa, Asia or the Middle East. There is certainly a tradition of Eastern mysticism, but there is also a tradition of Eastern rationalism, as Amartya Sen has spent a lot of time elaborating – and for that matter, there has been in the past, and may be again in the future, a strong tradition of Western, Christian mysticism (Sen, 2006b). The wider point is that within and between both West and East there are many divisions and many cross-cultural alliances – the Vatican and Islamic radicals come together at international conferences to resist the use of contraception to solve the problems of AIDS and global overpopulation, and to deny tolerance to homosexuality but many Catholics and Muslims use contraception and/or are gay. The kind of illiberal democracy practised in Singapore has admirers in the West and critics in Singapore itself.

In the 1990s the Asian Values controversy was of considerable significance, and it still has some value as a way of indicating that the 1948 version of the characteristics of a rights holder cannot be taken for granted in the way the framers of the Universal Declaration certainly did. In short, Asian Values advocates asked the question that Maritain identified as unasked in 1948. Still, in the twenty-first century the caravan has moved on and the Asian Values debate now seems somewhat outmoded. The 'Asians' behind the Asian Values argument were the so-called 'baby tigers', the small(ish) capitalist success stories of the 1980s and 90s – today in Asia we have the 'Emergent powers', India and China as contemporary success stories, and neither of these giants are interested in that particular controversy. Both are too big to be much concerned by the use of human rights for political pressure – irritated certainly, think of China over Tibet, but not really worried, because they know they are far too important players in world politics for critics to take any serious action against them. India is a democracy at home, with a constitution that protects a decidedly Western list of human rights even though it is often critical of the global civil rights movement; China most certainly does not protect human rights, but it has never defended its position in terms of Asian values – its attitude is rather that these are purely internal matters and no-one else's business. The Asian Values debate died because the important Asians weren't interested in keeping it alive. But still, as we will see, some of the issues raised in Bangkok remain relevant.

Self-determination and the right to be different

The Bangkok Declaration stressed the importance of sovereignty and self-determination and in so doing they were merely echoing the *International Covenant on Civil and Political Rights* of 1966, Article 1.1 of which states that 'All peoples have the right of self-determination. By virtue of that right they freely determine their political status and freely pursue their economic, social and cultural development.' Leaving aside for the moment the problem of defining a 'people', this Article poses an obvious question – does the right of self-determination imply a right to be different? If not, how can such a right be meaningful, but if so, what level of difference is compatible with the universality demanded of the human rights regime? Some kinds of difference are clearly not important in this context; if, for example, there is indeed as some have argued, a right to democratic governance, no-one is going to be particularly concerned about whether this right is met through a parliamentary or a presidential system or via a uni-cameral or bi-cameral legislature. We could all agree that these are the sorts of questions that 'peoples' could and should freely determine.

Other kinds of difference are less easily reconciled with universal formulations. Consider the case of indigenous peoples. In 1948 much of the world's surface was still governed by imperialism and the rights of indigenous peoples was of little concern to the drafters of the UDHR, but by the 1980s indigenous peoples throughout the world were organising and asserting their rights wherever they were able to do so – most forcefully in relatively wealthy liberal-democratic countries such as Australia, Canada, New Zealand, the USA and the Scandinavian democracies, but also in countries such as India, Brazil and Indonesia (Crawford, 1988). Some of this self-assertion concerned rights to land, as in New Zealand where Maoris successfully campaigned for the terms of the Treaty of Waitangi of 1840 to be honoured, but other issues concerned self-government and the applicability of universal standards. Should indigenous peoples be obliged to conform to the majority standards of the wider society when these standards conflict with their way of life? By definition, indigenous peoples did not ask to become a minority in lands which they once owned and their claim to self-determination involves a right to determine their own political status, independent of the majority society. They have asserted their right to be different – and in this case, being different may not be easily reconciled with universal standards; it may, for example, involve government by a patriarchal council of (male) elders.

The claim here is that there exist group or collective rights, which are not simply an aggregation of individual rights. In the case of indigenous peoples, the claim is that a collective wrong was perpetrated when these peoples were subjected to the rule of outsiders and that the only adequate response to this collective wrong is the recognition of a collective right. On this basis, peoples of, for example, a North American First Nation, are entitled to govern themselves even if the principles they choose to employ are inconsistent with the standards of the majority society, and even if they contradict universal principles established internationally. This presents a genuine dilemma, especially if, as sometimes happens, an individual member of a First Nation tries to claim his or her rights as a member of the wider society against the tribe. There is the possibility of a genuine clash here between the individual rights-holder who is the sovereign figure of the international human rights regime, and the community which claims to be doing no more than exercising its right to self-determination (Kymlicka, 1995).

In fact, the problem the international human rights regime faces in dealing with indigenous peoples is no more than one manifestation of a much wider problem that exists when any group claims that its practices are legitimate expressions of its identity as a group, irrespective of whether the practices in question contravene majority standards or universal human rights standards. Consider, for example, the fact that many European countries nowadays have standards of animal welfare which require that the animal be rendered unconscious before slaughter – does respect for the Muslim and Jewish faiths require that special exceptions be made to allow the practice of halal and shechita (kosher) butchery in which the conscious animal is killed by cutting its throat and draining its blood? Different countries have come up with different answers to this question; such practices are given a special exemption from the law in the UK, but not in much of Scandinavia or Poland – most recently, in February

2014, Denmark outlawed the practice, announcing that 'animal rights come before religion'. A similar, but even more emotionally charged, issue concerns infant male circumcision, again practised for religious reasons by Jews and Muslims; in May 2012 a German Court ruled that the practice amounted to grievous bodily harm and was therefore illegal – a very acrimonious debate followed before the Bundestag passed an Act in December 2012 which authorised the right of parents to have their male infants circumcised by a trained practitioner, but it is doubtful if the issue will go away.

Although these two examples of cultural practice deviating from what some see as the norm generate a lot of heat, in practice they are not too difficult to deal with; a case can be made that halal butchery is as humane as what passes for humane killing in a modern slaughterhouse, and the practice of infant circumcision, although mainly justified on religious ground in Europe, is regarded as contributing to health and hygiene in the USA. Allowing these practices to continue is generally regarded as good public policy – liberal democratic polities are usually prepared to make exceptions to general rules when religious belief is involved and when, as in these cases, no great harm is done. But the implications of such tolerance are clearly subversive of universal standards. If a particular cultural or religious practice is to be regarded as legitimate on the basis that it is a long-standing expression of authentic belief then the floodgates are opened to all kinds of difference, many of which will be much less benign than the two examples given above. For example, there can be no doubt that the caste system in India is culturally authentic – it has existed for thousands of years – yet it clearly stands against the principle of human equality built into the international human rights regime, and has inflicted (and still inflicts) great suffering on those it considers 'untouchable', the Dalits at the bottom of the system. Again, female genital mutilation is not, in fact, a requirement of any major religious system and is certainly a very harmful practice, but it is well established in many cultures and cannot be described as inauthentic.

Because of the way in which arguments on relatively benign practices such as halal butchery can constitute the thin end of a very thick wedge, some militant liberals have argued against allowing exceptions to general rules on religious or other grounds. Brian Barry, a very militant liberal in this respect, famously argued that Muslims and Jews who did not wish to eat meat from humanely slaughtered animals should become vegetarians – he also argued that Sikhs who did not wish to abandon their turbans for crash helmets should instead abandon their motor-cycles (Barry, 2000). These were, to put it mildly, controversial positions and even those sympathetic to the claims of universalism were usually unwilling to take matters quite that far. In effect, Barry treats religious belief and deeply engrained cultural beliefs as secondary characteristics of human beings, analogous to what analytical political philosophers call 'expensive tastes'. The idea behind expensive tastes is that whereas generally people's preferences and personal projects should be respected by liberals, there is an implicit assumption that such projects will not be unreasonable; if, for example, my personal project is to amass the finest wine cellar possible, regardless of cost, society is under no obligation to finance or make possible this expensive taste, even though it is indeed the authentic expression of my deepest desires. This is a life-style choice, which others are under no obligation to respect or facilitate. The problem with this analogy is that whereas secularly minded liberals may regard religion as a life-style choice – and in some Western societies religious belief may indeed by understood in this way – for many believers their religion is part of their identity, not something that they have chosen.

In a world where the politics of identity are increasingly important, the liberal universalism which underlies the international human rights regime is increasingly under threat, and the standard arguments in favour of universal values which went more or less unchallenged during the immediate decades post-1948 now need to be supplemented by other perspectives. Fortunately for the future of the regime such perspectives do exist, but before moving to consider them another, even more basic, challenge to the sovereignty of the liberal rights-holder needs to be investigated.

Feminist critiques of the international human rights regime

Eleanor Roosevelt, widow of FDR, was one of the leading feminists of her era as well as chair of the drafting committee for the *Universal Declaration of Human Rights*, but still the UDHR contains a great deal of what a later generation would regard as sexist language and gendered presuppositions. The masculine pronoun is used throughout to describe the rights-holder, who is assumed to be a male head of the family, which in turn is seen as the 'natural and fundamental group-unit of society' (Article 16.3). All this was pretty much standard for the period, and remained so in the mid-1960s when the International Covenants were drafted. However, soon thereafter the influence of the Women's movement was felt in the international human rights regime as elsewhere in society, or at least Western society, and a decade or so later, in 1979, the *Universal Convention on the Elimination of all forms of Discrimination against Women* (CEDAW) was signed. Since then there have been a range of other legal and political measures designed to recognise different aspects of the rights of women, culminating in the 1990s with the 4th *UN World Conference on Women* and the *Beijing Declaration*, along with more specific acts such as the recognition of rape as a war crime in the statutes of the International Criminal Tribunals for Rwanda and Former Yugoslavia in 1993 and the International Criminal Court in 1998, and the appointment of Special Rapporteur on Violence against Women in 1994.

Gender has now been mainstreamed as an issue within the international human rights regime – although it would be wrong to suggest that the high level of official recognition attributed to gender issues has actually changed behaviour to any great degree. Most countries have now ratified CEDAW – although not the United States, always tardy when it comes to the ratification of international treaties because of the role of the Senate in the ratification process – but, equally, many countries have entered extensive reservations at the time of ratification and even where they have not, non-compliance is still an issue. There are now numerous bodies designed to prevent violence towards women, but such violence continues especially in wartime, and the number of recent occasions when even UN troops have perpetrated rape and engaged in sex trafficking in war zones is truly deplorable and depressing. Still, very slowly progress has been made.

Or perhaps this is the wrong way of looking at gender and human rights? The assumption behind CEDAW and similar legal initiatives is that in documents such as the UDHR and the 1966 Covenants rights language is only contingently masculine – that this language and the social assumptions it expressed simply represented the linguistic conventions and the mind-set of that particular age and that a more enlightened age (i.e. ours) is capable of corrective action. But some more radical feminists have argued that the rights-bearers of the international human rights regime are not simply contingently masculine but that their masculinity represents accurately the world the regime is designed to operate within. This position is perfectly summarised by Catherine MacKinnon's dictum that 'human rights principles are based on experience, but not that of women' (MacKinnon, 1993: 83). Developing this thought leads to a much more wide-ranging critique of the notion of human rights than liberal feminists have delivered, one comparable to – though not necessarily compatible with – that delivered by cultural critics of the rights regime.

MacKinnon's point is that human rights as classically understood are based on the requirements of active citizenship operating within the public sphere; active citizenship requires free speech, freedom of assembly and freedom of association if it is to be effective and these freedoms require protection from those who would prevent them from being enjoyed. Historically this public sphere has been the preserve of men – as Jean Bethke Elshtain points out, originally the citizen was simultaneously a soldier defending the *polis* – and is to be contrasted to the private sphere which has been the characteristic source of women's experiences (Elshtain, 1982). Rights protect the activity of the citizen in the public sphere, but have not, until very recently, been extended into the private sphere; in the public sphere rights protect the citizen, but in the private sphere women have no protection from the citizen. Unequal property rights of men and women were until recently the norm in most jurisdictions; the right of the husband to chastise his wife was a form of domestic violence that the law condoned, the crime of rape within marriage was unrecognised, the assumption being that, in a revealing phrase, men were entitled to their 'conjugal rights'. This state of affairs was justified by notions such as the sanctity of the family and the importance of excluding the state from 'private' life. Some countries have now amended legislation to remove the worst of these abuses, but the process is incomplete, and by no means universal.

Given this history, it is understandable that it should be thought difficult to extend rights thinking to cover the rights of women. CEDAW is designed to remove discrimination against women, explicitly on the model of the *International Convention on the Elimination of All Forms of Racial Discrimination* of 1969, but the analogy between discrimination on grounds of race and discrimination on the basis of gender is imperfect at best. It may well be that, in the very long run, if all forms of discrimination against women in the public sphere are eliminated then this will impact indirectly on the private sphere, but this is a very indirect way to approach the kind of abuse that women are subjected to in the home.

In any event, the notion of non-discrimination resonates differently in different parts of the world; Article 16 of CEDAW sets out the model of a free, independent, empowered woman based on non-discrimination and for all that this is an incomplete response to the problem of women's rights it does at least connect with notions of politics current in the West where rights language is well established. But in many places rights language has no such resonance – there, *empowerment* rather than non-discrimination may be central. Interesting on this is Radhika Coomaramaswamy, a Sri Lankan human rights advocate who was the UN's Special Rapporteur on Violence against Women from 1994 to 2003 and later an Under-Secretary General of the UN. Her essay '"To Bellow Like a Cow"; Women, Ethnicity and the Discourse of Rights', in a seminal collection on the *Human Rights of Women* edited by Rebecca Cook draws on her experience of rights advocacy in the Indian sub-continent and argues that while the language of rights may actually be written into the Indian Constitution it does not have a great deal of purchase at the level of Indian society, where deep-seated practices need to be challenged and where Indian women who deliver this challenge do not draw much sustenance from ideas of non-discrimination (Cook, 1994). Their need is to be empowered and rights language in this context is not empowering because the wider society does not instinctively think about politics in terms of rights.

Coomaramaswamy is a critical supporter of the notion of human rights and her argument is unusual in so far as it brings together the cultural and the gendered critique of rights. On the face of it this ought not to be difficult – the argument is that the typical rights-holder, but atypical human being, is a Western man and both gender and culture are obvious reference points here. Still, there is a problem here, summarised by Susan Moller Okin's dictum that 'most cultures have as one of their principal aims the control of women by men' (Okin, 1999). This may seem a rather stark assessment, but it certainly is the case that 'culturalists' often refer to the importance of various personal, sexual and reproductive practices that they wish to preserve from the levelling impact of universal standard-setting, and such practices rarely operate to the advantage of women – although it is important not to over-emphasise the liberality of the West in this context. Ann Norton in a somewhat scathing review of Okin's position, and that of Martha Nussbaum which we will come to later, points to the importance of not comparing the role of gender in non-Western societies with an idealised account of gender equality in the West (Norton, 2001).

The complex relationship between gender and culture is well illustrated by the somewhat tortured debates that have accompanied the ending of NATO's involvement in Afghanistan. It goes without saying that NATO did not intervene in Afghanistan to protect women's rights, although some of the statements by the Bush Administration in 2001, issued to generate support for the action, gave that impression, but it cannot be denied that the influence of NATO on the lives of women has been generally positive – the compulsory wearing of the burkha has been abolished, likewise restrictions on employment and education and women are no longer executed for adultery in football stadiums. There is a serious danger that these advances will be reversed if in the future some kind of agreement is reached with the Taliban. Many figures within the left in Europe and North America who opposed the intervention in the first place and now wish it to end as soon as possible, including many human rights activists, are conflicted by this issue; on this occasion an anti-imperialist stance is likely to result in a reactionary version of patriarchy.

Defending and redefining rights: Pragmatism and human capabilities

Summarising what has gone before in this chapter, it is clear that the role of human rights in global politics can no longer be seen in quite the way it was two decades or more ago. Jacques Maritain's question has been asked, and the 'why' issue can no longer be swept under the carpet. Arguably, this has been an unavoidable development. In the history of Western thought on rights – and, as we have seen, rights are indeed a Western notion – central figures such as John Locke were clear that rights ultimately made sense on the basis that they were God-given; even the American Founding Fathers expressed a similar thought, although for most of them the 'God' they had in mind was very different from the God of traditional Christian belief. In our twenty-first century world of many faiths and none, this is no longer an answer that works, but there is no obvious alternative foundation for rights, at least not one that can attract universal support.

And yet, the first half of Maritain's quote still holds to a remarkable extent. We don't all agree on all the possible rights that could be attributed to human beings, but many of us agree on most of them; the language of rights is still very widely employed and still has the power to move people to action – think, for example, of the crowds who took to the streets during the so-called 'Arab Spring'. As has become apparent in the years since 2011, many different aspirations were encapsulated by the demands of the protesters in Cairo, Tunis, Tripoli and Damascus, but the notion of rights obviously had great rhetorical power even if different groups had different outcomes in mind. The key point is that it would be a mistake to abandon the idea of rights – instead we should look to refine and perhaps redefine them, to try to reshape rights into a form that makes sense in the 2010s. Two strategies here suggest themselves; one, pragmatism, involves dropping the foundational claims made for rights and understanding them in much more overtly political terms, the other, the human capabilities approach, involves shifting the key term from rights to capabilities, with a view to establishing a firmer base for the notion.

A central figure for the pragmatic approach to human rights is Richard Rorty (Rorty, 1994, 1998, 1999). Rorty understood himself as falling within the tradition of American pragmatism represented by such figures as Charles Pierce, William James and John Dewey, but in his philosophical writings he also identified with 'Continental' philosophers such as Heidegger and Wittgenstein; Rorty was a philosophical radical, an opponent of 'correspondence' theories of truth, and the idea that some unshakeable foundations for knowledge are available (Rorty, 1989). But, rather unusually for a philosopher with these views, his politics were quite conventionally liberal – he described himself once, semi-seriously, as a 'post-modern bourgeois liberal' (Rorty, 1990) – as such he was keen to defend a conventional account of human rights and to promote the values of solidarity, albeit in 'ironic' terms, that is to say while always keeping open the possibility that he might be mistaken. Clearly he cannot defend human rights as representing a deep truth about the human condition, which is how most human rights advocates want to see them – instead he understands human rights as a culture.

In his clearest articulation of this position (appropriately to be found in an *Amnesty International* sponsored collection of essays – as it happens the same 1994 collection that contained the first version of Rawls's 'Law of Peoples' and the Catherine MacKinnon essay referenced above) he argues that rights act to 'summarise our culturally-influenced intuitions about the right thing to do in various situations'; such summarising generalisations increase 'the predictability, and thus the power and efficiency, of our institutions, thereby heightening the sense of shared moral identity which brings us together in a moral community' (Rorty, 1994: 117). This formulation relies on being able to identify the referent object of 'our' and 'us' and for Rorty 'we' are the Americans and Europeans who, over the last two centuries, have created a 'human rights culture' – in fact, during this period the role of the human rights culture has been to oppose prejudices of one kind or another and thereby expand the scope of the 'we'. This achievement is both based on and reinforced by *'security'* ('conditions of life sufficiently risk-free as to make one's difference from others inessential to one's self respect, one's sense of worth' (p. 128)) and *'sympathy'*, the ability to put one's self in another's shoes, to perceive the Other as a fellow human-being. These two requirements are mutually supporting. The scope of the moral community is continually open to question and never fixed once and for all; prejudice is never conquered once and for all, and what counts as prejudice is never a closed issue.

Of course, many people are not part of the 'we' that is expanding its moral horizon in this way, and do not want to be part of that world – Rorty's argument is that it is pointless to tell such people that they are wrong or irrational. Such language would imply that the expanding moral universe of the human rights culture is based on firm foundations, universal moral standards, and that is simply wrong. There are no general moral standards that apply here, there is no 'human nature' in which rights can be grounded. People who reject the human rights culture may be deprived of the security and sympathy on which the culture rests; they are in need of an environment in which they can reflect on these matters in relative safety. Such reflection, to be effective, must take the form of an education in the sentiments, a 'sentimental education', rather than an education in human rights law or moral philosophy. The ability to perceive people who are different from oneself in some apparently relevant aspect – skin colour, gender, religion, sexual orientation – as nonetheless worthy of respect will not be something that is generated by reading a text in moral philosophy; a work of fiction is much more likely to generate empathy than a philosophical argument.

Rorty's vision here seems sociologically well grounded. Consider, for example, the way in which gay, lesbian , bi-sexual and transsexual (GLBT) rights have come to be accepted as part of the culture in Western Europe and North America over the last three or four decades. First, it should be noted that although increasingly large majorities within those societies see GLBT rights as uncontroversial, within many other parts of the world this is very definitely not the case; it would be obtuse to suggest that there is something foundational about these rights, that it was somehow an accident that they were not mentioned specifically in the UDHR or the 1966 Covenants – instead they are a classic example of the way in which the rights culture has developed. Once, in the very recent past, prejudice against gay sex was not considered a prejudice at all, but rather something natural – now, in some parts of the world, this has changed and the scope of the moral community has been enlarged. Second, it should be noted that although changes in the law have been important in the recognition of GLTB rights, it is in the realm of popular culture that the most potent engines for change have been located. The 'sentimental education' provided in the United States by mainstream and popular TV shows such as *Ellen, Will and Grace*

and *Modern Family* surely have a great deal to do with the widespread acceptance of gay rights in even quite conservative American households, households
unlikely to be in contact with overt GLTB advocacy groups or philosophical
tracts on equality.

The area of rights and sexual orientation also provides an illustration of
Rorty's point that there is no pre-given direction to the development of a rights
culture, no progressive narrative working itself out in history. In the late 1960s
in Britain and the US there was a movement towards the recognition of children
as sexual beings. Radical and 'hippie' groups took up this cause, rock musicians
boasted of their under-age sexual conquests, and a group devoted to the promotion of understanding of sexual relations between adults and children, the
Paedophile Information Exchange (PIE) was, briefly, affiliated to the National
Council on Civil Liberties (now known as Liberty). This was, however, very
emphatically a road not taken – in the aftermath of the recent Jimmy Savile
affair in the UK a number of figures from the rock and pop world have found
themselves deeply embarrassed, and in some cases in court, as a result of these
indiscretions, and Liberty has gone out of its way to express regret at ever having given credibility to the PIE and those of its officers who are still active in
public life as Labour politicians have been obliged to distance themselves from
decisions taken decades ago. This is one area where there is much less tolerance
than there was three decades ago; in this case the sentimental education which
paedophiles attempted with reference to the love between men and boys in
Classical Greece was an abysmal failure.

A more difficult question for Rorty's position is posed by more extreme situations, where the stakes are somewhat higher. In a thoughtful critique of Rorty,
*Solidarity in the Conversation of Mankind: The Ungroundable Liberalism of Richard
Rorty* (1995), the political theorist Norman Geras questioned the extent to
which an 'ironic' sensibility will actually produce solidarity in extreme conditions. Referencing studies of the Holocaust, he points out that those individuals
who risked their lives to rescue Jews were generally motivated by religious
belief, or by their political commitments, usually communist or socialist. In
such extreme circumstances an ironic commitment to a human rights culture
bolstered by edifying fiction is unlikely to cut the mustard. To which Rorty
would no doubt reply that it is one thing to say that a foundational commitment is needed, another thing to provide the basis for such a commitment.

In summary, the details of Rorty's argument may well go to places that human
rights advocates often do not want to go, but the pragmatism of which he is the
best modern representative is certainly a feature of a great deal of recent human
rights thinking, even among those who are not *au fait* with the philosophical
arguments involved. It is quite common for human rights advocates to admit that
rights are convenient fictions, and to acknowledge that they are not fixed, but
develop over time. Rorty provides a sophisticated defence of such positions. His
approach involves abandoning the search for foundations and admitting that

human rights are indeed culture-bound and can be defended in such terms. Others look to find an alternative way out of the dilemmas set out in the first part of this chapter by approaching rights from a different direction altogether; this strategy is exemplified by the 'human capabilities approach' associated with the economist Amartya Sen and the classicist Martha Nussbaum – since Nussbaum has worked this approach most extensively in the direction of providing a theory of human rights hers will be the work examined in detail here.

The context for this approach was provided by the work of Sen and Nussbaum in the late 1980s at the World Institute for Development Economics Research (WIDER), associated with the UN University in Helsinki. The aim of this work, initially summarised in a collection they edited entitled *The Quality of Life* (1993), was to produce a more sensitive account of the meaning of 'development' than that characteristically used by economists which focused on economic indicators such as growth in the gross domestic product. Part of this work involved an emphasis on women's issues, reflected in the collection Nussbaum edited with Jonathan Glover in 1995, *Women, Culture and Development* – development, it was plausibly asserted, should not neglect issues such as differential male-female rates of illiteracy or violence against women. Earlier in a seminal article in the *New York Review of Books* in 1990, Sen had pointed out that '100 Million Women are Missing', a figure he derived by studying different sex ratios. At birth boys out-number girls at a ratio of 1.05 to 1 throughout the world, but in adulthood in Western Europe and North America there are 105 women for every 100 men while in India, Bangladesh, Pakistan and Southern China there are only 93 women for every 100 men. Less this be thought of as simply an effect of poverty it should be noted that the figure in Sub-Saharan Africa is 102 women to 100 men. To summarise a complicated argument, Sen concludes that the difference lies in the lack of economic empowerment of women in those areas where the difference is most stark – these women have no independent source of income and are unable to ensure that they and their daughters are properly fed and looked after.

Nussbaum widens the argument to look at culture more generally, coming to the conclusion that has already been noted above, namely that 'culture' is frequently a short-hand terms for practices that harm or disadvantage women. However, in her interaction with development specialists at WIDER she came across a set of attitudes which she summarised as 'relativism' – an unwillingness to judge cultural practices as 'good' or 'bad' – and what she saw as an unnecessary sensitivity to the charge of Western ethnocentrism when it came to human rights advocacy. Whereas from a Rortyan perspective the correct response to this situation would be to acknowledge the ethnocentrism but to press home the value of the human rights culture anyway, Nussbaum sought instead to challenge this relativism by trying to develop a conception of human dignity not susceptible of being described as 'Western', to which people of different perspectives can subscribe without the feeling that they are in some way betraying their own culture in the interests of another.

As a classicist, unsurprisingly, she went back to the source for this going beyond the Medieval origins of Natural Law thinking and drawing on a Classical Greek, more specifically Aristotelian notion of the virtues in order to paint a picture of human flourishing that actually had substantive content but which, she hoped, could not be described as specifically 'Western'. In the aforementioned *Quality of Life* collection she offered this set of human characteristics as genuinely universal:

> Everyone has some attitude, and corresponding behaviour, towards her own death; her bodily appetites and their management; her property and its use; the distribution of social goods; telling the truth; being kind to others; cultivating a sense of play and delight, and so on. No matter where one lives one cannot escape these questions, so long as one is living a human life. (p. 245)

There are, she suggests, many ways of living a human life, but there are also social arrangements that do not allow for these characteristics to be developed, and we are entitled to describe such social arrangements as unsatisfactory without being liable to charges of ethnocentrism. People who are not allowed to develop a capacity to respond to these questions adequately are being oppressed, and we need not be reluctant to say so. The key term here is capacities – what is important is that people have certain capabilities not that they exercise them in a particular way; the charge against the standard notion of a 'rights-holder' is that it values a particular (Western) take on political and social life, the claim of the capabilities approach is that what is crucial is the ability to live a human life, not the way that life is lived.

In this early formulation Nussbaum stuck quite closely to her Greek sources, and the stress on capabilities as opposed to rights resonated with Sen's work on capabilities and development, although Sen's source was Marx rather than Aristotle – but perhaps this is a false opposition, since the early Marx at least was very heavily influenced by Greek thought. More recently, however, Nussbaum's formulations have become much more elaborate and also much closer to more conventional liberal thinking. Her account of the 'central human capabilities' presented in *Women and Human Development* (2000), the more popular text *Creating Capabilities: The Human Development Approach* (2011) and in the version discussed in a 'Symposium on Martha Nussbaum's Political Philosophy' in *Ethics* (2000) sets out an elaborate list covering Life, Bodily Health, Bodily Integrity, Senses, Imagination and Thought, Emotions, Practical Reasons, Affiliation, Other Species, Play, and Control Over One's Political and Material Environment. Some of these capabilities seem rather general (e.g. Life: Being able to live to the end of a human life of normal length; not dying prematurely, or before one's life is so reduced as to be not worth living) while others are quite specific (e.g. Affiliation: Having the social bases of self-respect and non-humiliation; being able to be treated as a dignified being whose worth is equal to that of others. This entails provisions of non-discrimination on the basis of race, sex, sexual orientation, ethnicity, caste, religion, national origin).

What is the ontological basis for this list? Greek thinkers would have had little hesitation in identifying the virtues as linked to a human nature that was biologically based – but Greek biology did not meet modern scientific standards and contained a number of features that are unacceptable today, such as the category of 'natural slaves', or the somewhat pejorative account of women's capacities. But if not 'human nature' where does the list come from? Nussbaum stresses the contributions that many people have made to refining her list of capabilities and she explicitly endorses the Rawlsian idea of an 'overlapping consensus' as the basis for this account of the central human capabilities, explicitly linking her thinking to a cosmopolitan liberal framework. Unfortunately there is no evidence that such an overlapping consensus exists, at least not for some of the items on her list. As noted above, GLBT rights are not acknowledged in many countries, and the idea that non-discrimination on the basis of sexual orientation is now generally accepted does not stand up to close scrutiny.

The list of human central capabilities is, of course, intended to be a critical device designed to set standards that ought to be met even if they aren't at the moment, and in this respect it performs the same aspirational task as the 1966 Human Rights Covenants and the various Conventions on the elimination of discrimination of one kind or another or on the rights of children or indigenous groups. But if it is to perform this task more effectively than they do it has to make good its claim to be rooted in something beyond the preferences of a particular society, which is the case made against human rights notions by culturalist critics. Unfortunately, the more detail that Nussbaum has poured into the notion of human capabilities, the less plausible is the claim that there is something going on here that cannot be linked to a particular culture and a particular way of life. It may well be, as Nussbaum claims, that some activists have found the rhetorical move from rights to capabilities valuable – she draws many examples from feminist groups in India with which she is in contact – and if so then from a human rights perspective that is a positive good, but it seems unlikely that in the longer run the problems associated with human rights will be solved in this way. Moreover, the extent to which Nussbaum is in fact articulating the views of Indian women is open to doubt – the aforementioned review by Anne Norton challenges Nussbaum on the basis that she ignores many post-colonial voices that do not support her position (Norton, 2001).

Conclusion

It may be that the difficulties that the human rights regime experiences when dealing with the problematic of difference is deep-seated within a particular way of looking at the world that is characteristic not just of modern liberalism, but of the West over the last half-millennium. The problem here is well examined by the Bulgarian literary theorist Tsvetan Todorov in his book *The Conquest of America*

(1984). Rather counter-intuitively for a literary theorist, this book is actually about the conquest of America post-1492, when Europeans came face to face with people who were genuinely different in so far as they could not be fitted into one or other of the categories that Medieval and Classical Europeans possessed for characterising strangers – these people were neither Christian, Jew nor Muslim, indeed they weren't even pagan as that term had usually been understood. Todorov contrasts two attitudes to this situation: for the Conquistadors, the 'Indians' are *different* and *inferior* thus available for imperial exploitation, slavery and the like – this is not an unusual perspective; the view that 'we' are normal and others are deviant is very common. For Las Casas and other missionaries, the Indians are not inferior but *equal* – they share our humanity as the children of God – but this equality removes *difference* – they have been incorporated into our frame of reference. Todorov's point is that, crucially, the category of *different* but *equal* isn't filled, indeed seems not to be available.

The best of liberal, Enlightenment and Post-Enlightenment thought down-plays the Christianity, but follows the line of Las Casas; that is it is anti-racist and fundamentally committed to equality, but at the expense of denying differ-ence. The rationality and reasonableness liberal thought stands by is defined in ahistorical terms. Richard Rorty grasps that this is so and looks to redefine the liberal underpinnings of the human rights movement in cultural and ironic terms, but, as we have seen, with only limited success. There are fundamental issues here about the nature of contemporary liberal thought and the global political theory which it produces, issues which these concluding comments are, for the time being, simply signalling – the bigger picture will be returned to in the concluding chapter of this book.

Further Reading

Identity politics is an area that is difficult to navigate; Kwame Anthony Appiah (2005) and (2007) is a reliable guide as is Amartya Sen (2006a) and (2006b). William Connolly (1992) establishes that 'identity' is always based on 'difference'. Various attempts have been made to reconcile human rights and cultural diversity – see e.g. collections by Lynda Bell, Andrew Nathan and Ilan Peleg (2001), Simon Caney and Peter Jones (2001), Robert Patman (2000), Ian Shapiro and Will Kymlicka (1997), and individual contributions from Jack Donnelley (1989) and (2007), Alison Renteln (1990) and Will Kymlicka (1995). Brian Barry (2000) will have none of it in his defence of equality and Charvet (2008) is equally firm, though rather more tactful.

The 'Asian Values' debate is now receding into the past partly as a result of the rise of India and China; still there are some contributions to this debate that are still worth engaging with – Joanne Bauer and Daniel Bell's (1999) collection is one such, and Bell's two books (2000) and (2007) have certainly outlasted the Asian Values debate. James Crawford's collection on the rights of peoples (1988) is seminal as is Gene Lyons and James Mayall (2003). The best way to get a sense of group rights is to follow through a particular example – Maori rights as established by the Treaty of Waitangi are very well represented online, with www.justice.govt.nz/tribunals/waitangi-tribunal as the best starting point. James Tully (1995) brings a historian of thought's contribution to the problems generated by the imposition of Western political forms on non-Western peoples.

On gender and human rights two collections from the 1990s are still valuable starting points, Rebecca Cook (1994) and Julie Peters and Andrea Wolper (1995). Human rights are a major concern of most general studies of gender and IR – see e.g. Kimberly Hutchings (2000) and most recently Jill Steans (2013). Jean Bethke Elshtain's monograph (1982) establishes a key distinction between public and private – her later contributions are discussed in Chapter 9 but this distinction is key to the work of Catherine MacKinnon (1989), (1993) and, most compellingly (2006) – her 1993 Lecture, referenced in the text of this chapter, needs to be understood in the wider context of her work. Susan Moller Okin (1999) establishes the idea that women's rights and multiculturalism are often at odds, a position taken up by Martha Nussbaum, see below. Anne Norton's critique of this position (2001) in a review essay is an important piece in its own right.

Richard Rorty's works are referenced in the text. Matthew Festenstein and Simon Thompson (2001) is a good collection of critical essays on his work, each with a response from the man himself. Harry Bauer and Elisabetta Brighi's (2008) collection on pragmatism and IR contains many references to Rorty's work, while Molly Cochran's *Cambridge Companion to John Dewey* (2010) takes us back to an even more influential pragmatist. Norman Geras's specific response to Rorty (1995) is worth reading in its own right as is his monograph on the 'contract of mutual indifference' (1999).

Martha Nussbaum's many works are mostly referenced in the text; of particular interest is her monograph on Greek thought *The Fragility of Goodness* (2001) – this was written before she developed the Capabilities approach and it is interesting to trace the way in which the influence of Greek thought has slowly faded from her writings on capabilities. The *Ethics* Symposium (2000) is a source of critical material on capabilities; Anne Norton's review (2001) has been mentioned already, see also Anne Phillips (2001). Amartya Sen's rather different approach to capabilities can be found summarised in Sen (2005) and infuses Sen (2009).

7

INTERVENTION: THE 1990s LEARNING CURVE

If the discourse of human rights was changed by the end of the Cold War, both the discourse and the practical politics of intervention were even more radically reshaped by the collapse of the Soviet Union and the debris left behind by that collapse. For a decade after 1989 the international community was faced with a sequence of humanitarian crises that could be traced, directly or indirectly, to the end of the Cold War and that are now readily identifiable by shorthand geographical/political terms. 'Iraq', 'Somalia', 'Bosnia', 'Rwanda', 'Kosovo' – these are shorthand expressions for some of the various crises which the international community was forced to confront in the 1990s, and generally failed to deal with in a satisfactory manner. A decade later, in the new century, the game changed again, partly because of the changed political environment produced by 9/11 and the 'War on Terror', partly because the experience of the 1990s changed the nature of the debate on intervention – in the 2000s, a new notion emerged, that of a 'responsibility to protect' and although this notion was by no means universally accepted it has increasingly framed debates on intervention since it was first promulgated in 2001 and given some institutional form in 2005. The next chapters will be shaped by the interaction between the responsibility to protect and the war on terror, but neither notion, and in particular the former, can be fully grasped without some understanding of intervention in the 1990s – in a strong sense, we are still living in a world shaped by the successes, and more frequent failures, of that decade.

The legacies of the Cold War

The most obvious legacy of the Cold War was that it brought about an end to authoritarian governments in the old Soviet Bloc and gave an impetus to democratisation more generally; it also, equally obviously, brought about an end to superpower confrontation via proxies. Although it would be churlish to deny that these consequences were on the whole highly positive, each of these desirable movements produced side-effects which were much less desirable and in some cases posed serious problems for the international community. Again, the end of the Cold War meant that the international community had now the opportunity to respond to these problems in a way that simply wasn't available in the era of superpower conflict. These legacies interacted with each other in unpredictable ways to produce the practical exercises in conflict management and mismanagement that the 1990s witnessed. Each needs to be examined further before actual cases are discussed.

The last of the aforementioned legacies is, from the perspective of International Political Theory, the most interesting because it focuses on the way in which issues of intervention came out of the seminar room into the real world and how, as a result of this change of location, arguments changed and positions shifted. While the Cold War was a reality, the possibilities for intervention on humanitarian grounds were very limited; the rough and ready balance that existed between East and West made it difficult for either to intervene outside of their respective spheres of interest. As a result, the academic discourse on humanitarian intervention took place at one level removed from actual global politics. As we have seen, Michael Walzer, in this respect representing a strand of communitarian thought, set the bar for intervention on humanitarian ground at a very high level – the presumed fit between government and people could only be said to have broken down under conditions of genocide or mass enslavement; non-intervention was the general rule, even in cases of quite severe human rights violation (Walzer, 1976/2006). His cosmopolitan critics such as Charles Beitz were much more willing to argue against the norm of non-intervention, which they saw as defensible only on pragmatic grounds; they saw no principled reason why states should be allowed to violate human rights norms, although they acknowledged that intervention would often make a bad situation worse (Beitz, 1979).

This was an interesting academic debate, but that was what it was, an academic debate – but after 1989 the issue moved out of the seminar room and into the real world. Now when a crisis emerged where human rights violations on a large scale were taking place – and, as we will see, such crises were partly stimulated by the end of the Cold War – the major players in world politics no longer had their hands tied; there was now no rival superpower to stop those with the power to act from acting. But the result of this apparent freedom was that some of the positions worked out in the seminar room no longer seemed so attractive to their academic adherents. In large part this was because humanitarian intervention in the 1990s was a field where power politics and ethical theorising interacted in ways that had not been predicted a decade or more before. Of course, it always had been apparent that intervention would be an act of the powerful directed at the less powerful, even if it was motivated by humanitarianism, but this aspect of global politics became much more salient once interventions actually took place. In effect, for many writers the issue changed and what became crucial was no longer their take on the norm of non-intervention but rather their attitude towards the power of the United States, which in practice was the state with the greatest capacity to actually carry out a humanitarian intervention. Michael Walzer – who could best be described as a critical patriot – shifted his position somewhat towards the interventionist camp, his 'politics of rescue' paper being less anti-interventionist than his formulations in *Just and Unjust Wars* (Walzer, 1995). Meanwhile those cosmopolitan or solidarist writers who were in principle pro-intervention but in practice very suspicious of US power, continued to offer theoretical support for interventions but only under conditions that are usually quite difficult to achieve, such as unanimity in the UN Security Council (Wheeler, 2000; Chesterman, 2001).

These shifts were important because, as noted above, the end of the Cold War inadvertently created conditions which cried out for interventions of one sort or another. Partly this was because in some areas the ending of authoritarian governance allowed for the re-emergence of problems and attitudes that had been latent for generations, and actually provided encouragement to those who wished to exploit these tensions. The classic case here concerned – and indeed still concerns – the territories of former Yugoslavia. The ending of authoritarian rule and the push this ending gave to movements of democratisation also created potential problems in those areas where democracy was simply equated with majority rule, with no, or too little, thought being given to the protection of minorities – such was the case in former Yugoslavia, but the most tragic example of the unintended side-effects of an illiberal democratisation was the genocide in Rwanda in 1994 which was directly connected to the end of authoritarian rule in that country and the misuse by the majority Hutu population of the opportunity that majoritarian democracy presented (Prunier, 1995). In these cases a process that was in principle benign had unfortunate side-effects, but in other areas nothing remotely benign was on offer. The best example here comes from the Horn of Africa where for thirty years or more superpower conflict had kept in power, but under a degree of control, heavily armed authoritarian governments; when the Cold War ended the superpowers withdrew but the arms remained and in this case there was no move to democratisation, but rather a collapse into civil war and anarchy, fuelled by the vast amount of firepower that the superpowers had endowed their protégés with.

In the rest of this chapter these cases will be reviewed, not so much in terms of the empirical details of the conflicts, which have been examined at length elsewhere, but in terms of the dilemmas they threw up for the international community, and the solutions, or in many cases non-solutions, they generated. Before getting on with this task there is one last piece of contextualisation that is necessary, and that is a brief examination of the first genuine post-Cold War crisis, that generated by the invasion of Kuwait by Saddam Hussein's Iraq in August 1990 (Freedman, 1993). The Gulf War of 1990/91 was not a humanitarian crisis in the same sense as the iconic humanitarian crises of the 1990s – rather it was a conventional act of aggression carried out by one UN member against another, and responded to by a UN-sanctioned war to reverse this act of aggression. At the end of the war, in the very exceptional circumstances that followed the defeat of Iraq and its expulsion from Kuwait, there was a humanitarian action in the form of the establishment of a 'safe-area' for the Kurds of Northern Iraq enforced by Anglo-American airpower, but although this did create a precedent that was employed, unsuccessfully, in Bosnia, it was not this action but the wider conflict that prefigured much of the politics of the 1990s.

In spite of the obviousness of Iraq's aggression and the fact that the UN Security Council explicitly sanctioned a military response, in the eyes of many it was the United States and the coalition that supported American arms who were the imperialist aggressors. This was the first example of the phenomenon noted above, the fear of overweening US power, a fear enhanced by the way in which that power was used, namely by an overwhelming campaign of 'shock and awe' (the phrase comes from Iraq 2003, but is equally appropriate here) based on the employment of technology to the full, especially airpower, and with extreme casualty aversion. The kind of superiority the Coalition possessed in 1991 would have been desired by military commanders throughout history and few nationals of the countries involved in the Coalition would have welcomed more of their soldiers getting killed, but still the sense that there was something vaguely unfair about a contest that was so one-sided was pervasive – this was a sense that recurred almost every time US power was actually deployed in the 1990s, no matter how good the cause. US President George H.W. Bush spoke at this time of a 'new world order' emerging and for some this translated into the 'new world' giving the orders. Such sentiments persisted throughout the crises of the 1990s.

International political theory and the break-up of former Yugoslavia

For all the fears of American power, initially the Bush Administration was very reluctant to become involved in the various crises that accompanied the break-up of the Socialist Federal Republic of Yugoslavia (SFRY) after 1990 – famously, and rather tactlessly, Bush's Secretary of State James Baker (allegedly) announced that 'we don't have a dog in that fight', and signalled that this was Europe's problem. And, again initially, 'Europe' was happy to pick up the challenge; the end of the Cold War meant in principle the end of the division of Europe and the possibility that Europe could indeed solve its own problems without the assistance (or interference) of the United States. This was a sentiment that was particularly strong in the new unified Germany, where the absorption of the German Democratic Republic into the German Federal Republic in 1990 led to the hope that Germany could now once again exert the kind of influence on European politics that might be expected of the largest European power – although this influence would now be exercised within the European Community and based on the 'soft power' generated by the Federal Republic's strong economy rather than the military power wielded by former incarnations of the German state. This was to be the 'hour of Europe' and Yugoslavia was to be where the new Europe came into its own (Gow, 1997).

So, what was the nature of the Yugoslav problem? Yugoslavia – the land of the 'South Slavs' – was a country, which after the adoption of the 1974 Constitution, consisted of six Republics (Bosnia and Herzegovina, Croatia, Macedonia, Montenegro, Serbia, Slovenia) and two autonomous provinces (Kosovo, with an Albanian majority population, and Vojvodina, predominantly Hungarian, both in Serbia) with similar powers to Republics. After the death of Tito in 1980, the Federal leadership was collective, and the Presidency rotated amongst the Republics, but in practice within this complicated structure actual power rested with the all-Yugoslavia 'Communist' party (technically a federation of six communist parties). Yugoslavia was a communist country but independent of the Soviet Bloc and a leading member of the Non-Aligned Movement. Partly because of this status it enjoyed closer relations with Western Europe than the other East/Central European communist countries, and its Adriatic coast was a popular tourist destination; because of this interaction, power and wealth within the Federation were located in different places – Serbia was politically dominant and the Yugoslav National Army (YNA) was Serb dominated, but Slovenia and Croatia were the centres of wealth.

Although the majority of citizens of the SFRY were of similar ethnicity and spoke the same or very similar languages – Croats, Serbs, Montenegrins and Bosnians all speak 'Serbo-Croat' with minor local differences – Communist rule papered over a number of differences which had been important in the past, and became important again in the 1980s and 1990s. When the Emperor Diocletian divided the Roman Empire in 285 AD into East And West, the dividing line ran though the lands that became the SFRY, and once the divided Empire became the basis for the distinction between Roman Catholic and Greek Orthodox Christianity, divisions were created that still have resonance today. Croats and Slovenes are Catholic in culture, employing the Latin alphabet,

Serbs and Montenegrins are Eastern Orthodox and employ the Cyrillic script. To add to the complications, the largest group of Bosnians are of Muslim descent, the descendants of medieval converts, and the Kosovars are of Albanian ethnicity, and also mainly Muslim. There are Serb minorities in Croatia and Bosnia, and Croat minorities in Bosnia.

To what extent were these divisions actually crucial to the conflicts of the 1990s? It became a commonplace for those Western politicians who did not want to get involved in the affairs of former Yugoslavia to describe its woes as essentially tribal and based on historic enmities. Certainly such enmities did exist – as recently as the Second World War conflicts between pro-German Croats in the Fascist Ustache movement, Bosniak Muslims recruited by the SS and Serb 'Chetniks', Royalist and anti-German, were fierce and brutal; only the Communist Partisans, led by the Croat Tito, offered the semblance of a pan-Yugoslav movement, although they spent more time fighting the Chetniks and the Ustache than the Germans. Still, it is worth remembering that many Yugoslavs thought of themselves as just that, Yugoslavs; intermarriage between different groups was quite common especially among the educated and city-dwellers – the old identities were kept alive among the less educated rural populations (Glenny, 1996; Campbell, 1998).

More to the point than historical enmities were the strategies adopted by political entrepreneurs once the system began to collapse in the 1980s and the pressures to democratise became stronger. Under the communist regime the kind of civil society groups that contributed to political identities in Western Europe were not allowed to flourish, and when former communist leaders began to transform themselves into 'democratic' politicians, they mobilised support on the basis of the only kinds of identities that the old regime had not been able to stifle, religious and historical. It was according to this logic that Slobodan Milošević, the Serbian communist leader garnered support in Serbia by ending autonomy for Kosovo and Vojvodina, and Franjo Tudjman employed Second World War Croatian nationalist symbol in his successful mobilisation of support in Croatia, in spite of himself having been, as a very young man, an anti-Ustache partisan. In Bosnia, Alija Izetbegovic had not been a communist but rather an explicitly Muslim political philosopher, persecuted for his beliefs, and when the system democratised in 1989 he formed a party, the Party of Democratic Action which was overwhelmingly Muslim in its appeal.

Thus it was that the new democratic politics of Yugoslavia came into existence in a context that stressed disunity, and in Croatia, Slovenia and Bosnia-Herzegovina fear of Serbian nationalism and Serb control of the YNA led to increasing demands for autonomy for the Republics, until 1991 when Serbia blocked a Croatian from rotating into office as President of the Collective Presidency and in response Croatia and Slovenia declared independence, to be followed in March 1992 by Bosnia and Herzegovina, the latter on the basis of a 99 per cent majority for independence in a plebiscite in which the Serbs of

Bosnia abstained and the Croats voted tactically. The Serbian-led YNA responded initially by invading Slovenia, but soon withdrew from what was effectively the only mono-ethnic Yugoslav Republic; in Croatia, the largely Serbian province of Krayina successfully resisted Croat government control, while in Bosnia-Herzegovina the stage was set for a three-way civil war. Meanwhile, in Kosovo the majority Albanian population, denied self-government, embarked on a policy of passive resistance to Serbian control.

This then was the multi-layered crisis that first Europe and then the wider international community found itself obliged to respond to – obliged initially because the new Republics demanded recognition of their independent status and membership of bodies such as the UN and the Council of Europe and this demand could not be ignored. Later a response would be needed to the wars that were being fought in Croatia and Bosnia, but initially recognition was the big issue, and this was an issue that was fraught with difficulties partly because the various European countries understood the politics of the situation in different ways, but also because the principles that should be applied to requests for recognition were very unclear and potentially self-contradictory.

Post-1945 decisions on the deconstruction of the old European empires had taken place on the basis of the legal principle of *uti possidetis juris* which holds that newly formed states should be formed within the borders of the colonies out of which they emerged. This principle was developed in Latin America in the nineteenth century, was designed as a pragmatic solution to border disputes, and is still strongly supported on that basis in the African Union; paradoxically, in a world where all borders are arbitrary the best policy is to treat them as sacrosanct – any alternative formula is a recipe for endless conflict. The problem with *uti possidetis juris* is that it contradicts the principle of national self-determination, unless, that is, the boundaries of the self-identifying national community are the same as the pre-existing administrative unit. Of the republics of the SFRY only in Slovenia was this coincidence of principles more or less the case, and it is no accident that Slovenia was the only republic to achieve independence without serious resistance from the Serb-dominated centre; the YNA initially attempted to prevent it from breaking away but very soon cut its losses in order to concentrate on those republics where there was a substantial Serb minority.

Here, then, was one element of the dilemma facing Europe and the world – should recognition of the new states be based on *uti possidetis* and the old administrative boundaries, or on the principle of national self-determination which would require border changes? The parties themselves were, predictably, inconsistent on this issue; Croatia argued for *uti possidetis*, but also wished to incorporate the Croat majority areas of Bosnia within Croatia, while the Serbs argued that the principle of national determination meant that Serb majority areas in Croatia and Bosnia-Herzegovina should be allowed to join Serbia, but at the same time denied the rights to self-determination of Kosovo's majority

Albanian population. The situation was further complicated because of the different attitudes to the fate of the SFRY adopted by the most important European countries. Russia was generally supportive of Serb nationalism, although Boris Yeltsin, the new Russian President was personally hostile to Milošević because of the latter's support for the attempted coup by the communist old guard in Moscow in August 1991; France and Britain were initially sympathetic to the Serbs for historical reasons, but more generally favoured the continuation in a loose form of the SFRY on the grounds that this would be the least disruptive outcome; German sympathies, on the other hand, were with Croatia and Slovenia, also for historical reasons, which the Serbs believed related to the Second World War, but which the Germans argued had much more to do with the close relationship between the Catholic 'South Slavs' and the old Hapsburg Empire.

In any event, the Europeans were divided in their approach, but they all agreed on the importance of not allowing these divisions to take concrete form; everyone involved remembered that Balkan conflicts led directly to war in 1914, and everyone was determined not to allow something similar to happen in the 1990s. The result of this determination might have been positive if it had lead to steady, constructive consensus-building; instead, the way things developed the result was a determination to act in unison even if that meant doing the wrong thing. This attitude was illustrated more or less immediately in late 1991 and early 1992. In September 1991 the European Community convened a Conference on Yugoslavia at the Hague, under the Chairmanship of Lord Carrington, a former British Foreign Secretary and NATO Secretary General. The Conference set out a number of principles upon which the decision to recognise a breakaway republic would be based, including that there would be no border changes without agreement, minority rights would be guaranteed and irresolvable differences between the republics would be referred to arbitration. These were eminently sensible principles – but they were immediately ignored. In January 1992 Croatia and Slovenia were recognised by the EC without any guarantees being built into their constitutions; this was under German pressure which Britain and France went along with in accordance with the aforementioned principle that it was better to do the wrong thing together rather than pursue individual conceptions of the right thing to do.

After Croatia and Slovenia came Bosnia-Herzegovina and in May 1992 all three countries were accepted as new members of the United Nations. What is interesting, and illustrative of the normative confusion that ran through the decision-making of outsiders in this period, is that even the countries that drove the process of recognition were not actually prepared to follow through its logic. Thus, UN Security Council Resolution 713 passed in September 1991 applied an arms embargo to the territory of the former Yugoslavia and this remained in place even after the breakaway republics were recognised, in spite of the fact that it was of obvious benefit to the Serbs, given that it preserved the advantage in military power possessed by the Serb-dominated former national army. In effect, the international community refused to distinguish between the governments it had just recognised and the groups in Croatia and Bosnia who were in revolt against these governments. Similarly, in January 1993 a mediation effort sponsored by the EC and the UN produced the so-called Vance-Owen Plan which envisaged the division of Bosnia-Herzegovina into ten provinces, each effectively self-governing, again over-riding the interests of the recognised government in Sarajevo. In April 1994 a 'contact group' of France, Russia, the UK and the US was established to oversee policy – once again, the desire was to ensure that the major powers co-ordinated their positions, if necessary, although this was obviously not spelled out, at the expense of the locals.

Humanitarian war in former Yugoslavia

The fighting in Croatia and Bosnia-Herzegovina inevitably led to civilian casualties, refugees and the disruption of normal food production and distribution; the EC and the UN provided what humanitarian relief they could, and in February 1992 in UN Security Council Resolution 743 established a UN Protection Force (UNPROFOR) to provide protection for the relief effort, initially in Croatia, but extended to Bosnia-Herzegovina in June and to the new republic of Macedonia in December. The humanitarian effort saw itself as non-political, delivering aid to those in need, of whom there were many, but one of the principles that the Yugoslav and other crises of the 1990s established is that in a war zone it is more or less impossible for humanitarian aid to be given without political consequences. To put things bluntly, if you attempt to feed people who someone else wishes to starve, you are engaging in politics however much you may want to avoid doing so. Even more to the point, in these conflicts, as in many other 'New Wars' in this period, the creation of civilian distress was not an unfortunate by-product of a conventional war but, on the contrary, a deliberate strategy designed to bring about ethnic cleansing, driving populations of the wrong sort away from their current homes (Kaldor, 1999). In so far as humanitarian actors were able to prevent this from happening they were frustrating the plans of the aggressors.

The result was that UNPROFOR frequently found itself attack, usually, but not always from Serbian forces. A sequence of international responses to this situation followed; mandatory sanctions against the new Federal Republic of Yugoslavia (previously Serbia & Montenegro) were introduced by UN Security Council Resolution 757 in May 1992, and a 'No Fly Zone' was established in Bosnia-Herzegovina enforced by NATO in October 1992 as a way of neutralising at least one aspect of the advantage to the Serbs of the aforementioned arms embargo. In April and May 1993 'safe areas' were designated in Bosnia-Herzegovina under the protection of UNPROFOR whose mandate was extended for this purpose, and which could now call on NATO air-power for this task under a dual-key arrangement, with both UNPROFOR and NATO having a key. In effect, the international community increasingly found itself engaged in a conflict with Serbia and Serb forces in Croatia and Bosnia-Herzegovina – however, predictably, things were not that simple.

As the conflict intensified some voices were heard in Europe and, especially, in the United States, calling for the pretence of neutrality to be dropped, for the arms embargo to be ended and for air-power to be used against the Serbs – the policy of 'lift and strike' as it became known in the US. This was opposed quite vehemently by the UK government, which argued that the international community should avoid taking sides in what it described as a long-standing tribal conflict. Brendan Simms has with some justice described this as Britain's 'unfinest hour', however there was one aspect of the British position that captured a genuine dilemma (Simms, 2001). At its height UNPROFOR had some 39,000 personnel of whom some 3,500 were British and 4,500 French; in the event of the international community overly taking sides these troops, who were widely dispersed and not in battle formations, would in effect become hostages. The use of military force for humanitarian relief became in effect a hindrance to their use for the more traditional aim of compellance (Rose, 1999).

It was also the case that many of the troops who made up UNPROFOR lacked the kind of 'attitude' that made for effective war-fighting. This was an advantage for the role of peacekeeping, where the ability to keep one's temper under difficult circumstances is crucial, but the disadvantage of the 'soldier as social worker' model was illustrated in July 1995 with the fall of the 'safe area' of Srebrenica. The Dutch battalion supposedly protecting Srebrenica did not prevent Bosnians based there from carrying out military actions but, more important, offered no resistance to the Serb forces led by Ratko Mladić who took the town, and indeed allowed them to confiscate some of their equipment, which was subsequently used to fool Bosniak men into surrendering – the result was a massacre, with perhaps 8,000 Bosniak men and boys killed. The Dutch, it should be said, were let down by lack of support from UNPROFOR's commanders, although that hardly excuses the willingness of the departing Dutch commander to accept a gift of flowers for his wife from Mladić (Blom et al., 2002).

Srebrenica preceded and partly caused a turning point in the conflict. In August 1995 Croat and Bosnian forces, surreptitiously armed by the US and supported by NATO land- and air-power, launched a successful campaign against the Serbs, resulting in the withdrawal of the latter from some of their conquests, and the expulsion of the Serbs from Krayina, an enclave in Croatia with a mainly Serb population that had been in existence since the seventeenth century. The result of this defeat was a newfound willingness of the Serbs to come to the conference table; a conference was held under US auspices in Dayton,

Ohio in November 1995, with Milošević representing the Bosnian Serbs, and an Accord was finally signed in Paris in December (Daalder, 2000; Holbrooke, 1999). In principle Bosnia-Herzegovina remained united, but in practice it was, and remains, effectively divided on ethic lines; a NATO-led International Protection Force, IFOR, exists to keep the peace, and a European 'High Representative' with his own office was established, effectively in a pro-consular role (Bose, 2002).

The operations in Bosnia-Herzegovina between 1993 and 1995, especially in 1995, constitute the first example of what Adam Roberts termed 'humanitarian war' (Roberts, 1993). This is a difficult term – it conveys the notion of war being fought for humanitarian ends, but with an undertone to the effect that the war should be fought as far as possible in a humanitarian way. Both notions are problematic. As to the latter, the 'casualty-aversion' of the leaders of those countries who engage in humanitarian war is obvious – no politician likes the idea of soldiers dying because of orders they have given, and most feel that their publics will be particularly unforgiving if the soldiers in question have not died for reasons of the national interest. In this they are probably correct – it is noteworthy that British public opinion was, on the whole, much more willing to countenance casualties suffered in retaking the Falkland Islands in 1982 than the much smaller loss of life entailed in keeping the peace in Bosnia. In any event, humanitarian war usually involves the use of air-power to avoid friendly casualties, even though reliance on killing at a distance may not actually be the best way to achieve the humanitarian goal of protecting civilian populations – indeed may actually involve risk to those populations.

The notion of engaging in war for humanitarian reasons is equally problematic. The classical conception of humanitarianism, as represented by the Red Cross, stresses impartiality and neutrality and is clearly not compatible with the idea that humanitarian reasons might be used to justify a war. Conversely, modern justifications for the use of force stress self-defence as the paradigmatic *casus belli*. 'Humanitarian war' involves a rethinking of both notions. Interestingly, in some respects, this could be seen as a return to medieval categories; as we saw in Chapter 3, for Aquinas a just *casus belli* involves righting a wrong and although self-defence fits this bill, it is not only self-defence that does so – force might also be seen as an appropriate response to grave violations of human rights. This resonates with new understandings of humanitarianism, which are also oriented towards human rights. A key feature of the 'new humanitarianism' is the desire to address the underlying causes of humanitarian crises; whereas the classical notion of humanitarianism would provide relief to the victims of the war in Bosnia whoever they may be, this newer, human-rights based humanitarianism asks who is responsible for the suffering that is taking place – and once the wrongdoer is identified it is a short step to justifying the use of force to rectify the injustice. Pull together this new meaning of humanitarianism and an expanded sense of the legitimate grounds for the use of force, and the possibility of a doctrine of 'humanitarian intervention' emerges, and in the light of this doctrine, humanitarian war is no longer the contradiction in terms it might seem to be (Barnett and Weiss, 2011).

But, even if we agree on the potential legitimacy of the notion of humanitarian war there are still many questions that are unanswered. Who is able to wage humanitarian war? Who is entitled to wage humanitarian war? And under what authority? In the case of the Bosnian war the latter two questions were easier to answer than would be the case with later interventions. NATO's military action was undertaken in Bosnia and Croatia in co-operation with the internationally recognised governments of those two countries and so this was not a case of an intervention that went against the grain of sovereignty, even though those people attempting to establish a Serbian republic in Bosnia might not have seen things that way. As noted above, Bosnia's friends did not always actually behave as though they took the country's sovereign status seriously, but nonetheless from a legal point of view this was action in support of the sovereignty of a friendly country, not in violation of the sovereignty of an enemy. Moreover, the UN Security Council had, in effect, legitimated warlike activities by establishing no-fly zones and safe areas.

From a political perspective, the most troubling aspect of this, and later, humanitarian wars concerned the first question above, which concerned the ability to wage humanitarian war. The answer to this question is actually clear, but unpalatable. Only powerful countries, those capable of projecting military force at a distance, are capable of conducting humanitarian interventions; moreover, such interventions presume a high degree of asymmetric power. Humanitarian war is fought by the powerful against the weak – even though the weak in question may well be locally powerful, as was the case in Bosnia where the Serb army-supported local Serbs outgunned the Bosniaks, but were in turn outgunned by NATO. The danger here is that the interveners will look like bullies – this may be an unfair perception, and if anyone deserved to be bullied it would be Mladić's Serbs after Srebrenica, but it is very damaging. To pick up an earlier theme, attitudes towards American power are of particular importance here. NATO's action was possible only because of the American contribution, and even in other military operations in the 1990s and since where the US was not directly involved, American logistic support was always crucial. For those who see US power as essentially imperial, the distinction between humanitarian wars and wars of aggression is immaterial – both are expressions of a will to dominate in international affairs.

The most controversial humanitarian war in the 1990s was the war in Kosovo in 1999, a war that directly followed from the political deals made at Dayton in 1995, which left Milošević in power in Serbia and provided no support for the people of Kosovo. However, this war, precisely because it was so controversial provided the impetus for the emergence of the idea of a 'responsibility to protect', and it will be examined in the next chapter along with the evolution of that doctrine. Here the focus of the rest of this chapter will be on two African tragedies, state-failure in Somalia, and genocide in Rwanda.

The new politics of state failure

State failure is not a new problem, but it is a new problem for the contemporary global order as opposed to being a problem for the state itself and its people. In the old society of states, its members were expected to be able to preserve themselves. Constitutional or political failure left states open to predators as indeed did any form of weakness, and unless they were able to protect themselves, directly or indirectly via a balance of power, they would disappear; the principle of legitimacy provided some protection after 1815, but over the centuries running up to 1914 a large number of states succumbed. After 1919 change in the norms and practice of twentieth-century international relations lessened the danger posed by predators; norms of non-aggression and self-determination made it more difficult for states to be absorbed by their neighbours. However, the problem of state failure has not gone away, indeed the decolonisation that took place after 1945 created more potential state failures. Many of the new states that emerged in this period were what Robert Jackson has called 'quasi-states', states with negative but not positive sovereignty – that is with the protected status of a sovereign state but without the capacity to maintain that status without assistance (Jackson, 1990). Instead of being the product of successful state-building, many new states were actually tasked with state- and nation-building. These states with weak administrations and insecure social foundations are vulnerable to internal disorder and collapse or external influence, but predation is no longer a legal solution to their failure. Territory can no longer be acquired legally by conquest. Weak or failed states become an international problem.

This is now widely recognised, and every year *Foreign Policy* magazine publishes a 'Failed States Index', ranking countries on a range of social indicators in order to arrive at a holistic judgement as to exactly the level of failure involved. It should be said at the outset that there are problems with this procedure; the implicit definition of a successful state is essentially a modern liberal capitalist democracy and it may well be the case that such a society is not actually appropriate for many of the states under consideration. Arguably, it is the state-form which is the failure in these cases, and those states deemed to be failing are failing an examination that they did not ask to sit. On the other hand, there is a reason why the state-form has become ubiquitous – effectively the alternative to the state after 1945 was the continuation of empire which was politically unacceptable to all concerned, including, in the end, the imperial powers.

The fate of Somalia – usually the 'winner' in the annual Failed States Index – illustrates all these points and more. Somalia was formed in 1960 by the fusion of Italian and British colonies; it has the advantage of being mono-ethnic and with but a single religion, Islam, but Somali society was, and is, clan based, with five or six major clans. In pre-colonial times conflict between the clans was endemic, but it was also limited, partly by the weaponry available, partly by compromises negotiated by clan elders. In modern times both of these limits disappeared. Compromises between the clans became more difficult to negotiate once a modern state was formed – the advantages that would accrue to whichever clan controlled the state apparatus were too great to be balanced by compromise; modernity created a 'winner takes all' system of rule (Lewis and Mayall, 1996). And, because of Somalia's strategically significant location on the Horn of Africa, its Superpower sponsor (the Soviet Union up to 1977, the United States thereafter) was prepared to pump in money, $100 million per annum in the 1980s, which could be used to buy modern weapons; AK47s and 'technicals', trucks mounted with recoilless rifles, replaced older, single shot firearms.

At the end of the 1980s, with the Cold War winding down, the US felt able to pay attention to the poor human rights record of Somalia's military dictator since 1969, General Mohammed Siyad Barre, and cut off all aid to his regime. The result was a multi-party civil war, the fall of Barre in January 1991, a general collapse of authority, rule by 'warlords', widespread banditry, an internal refugee problem, and large-scale hunger caused by crop confiscations and the control of whatever food production was taking place by the warlords. The UN provided food aid in association with NGOs but the warlords' control of airport and ports gave them the ability to divert aid to their own purposes. A small-scale UN protection force (UNISOM I) was ineffective, but a UN mediator, Mohamed Sahnoun, made some progress working with the clan elders until he was replaced in the summer of 1992 (Sahnoun, 1994 and in Moore, 1998). Pressure from NGOs and the UN Secretary-General for a more extensive military operation was initially resisted in the US; famously, General Colin Powell, US Chief of Staff and mastermind of the campaign in Kuwait, was said to have opined that 'we do deserts, we don't do cities' – the kind of subtle operation that would be needed in Mogadishu went against the current US doctrine of maximum force.

In December 1992, after losing his bid for re-election, President George H.W. Bush agreed to a US-led operation, Operation 'Restore Hope', an intervention by US, French, and Italian forces formally known as UNITAF (Unified Task Force). This heavily armed intervention, based on UN Security Council Resolution 794 was the first occasion in which a UN force was inserted without the approval of a host government and for humanitarian reasons – admittedly there was no 'host government' at the time but this was still an interesting precedent. UNITAF had at its core a strong force of US marines, with the capacity to change the situation least in Mogadishu, but the mandate of UNITAF was unclear – it was designed to assist aid deliveries and did so, but the famine was almost over; 'nation-building' was a different matter, given the absence of a government or effective state apparatus.

In the event, in spring 1993, US efforts were scaled down with only a 'Quick Reaction Force' of US Rangers remaining in the country and a new set of UN troops (UNISOM II), mostly from Muslim countries came in with a new mandate, this time including nation-building. Initially the Mogadishu warlord General Aidid was seen as a potential national leader but when it became clear that he was unacceptable to others, fighting broke out again. Attempts to disarm the participants were unsuccessful and in June 24 Pakistani UN peacekeepers were murdered by Aidid's forces – this was another precedent-making event; in the past the persons of UN peacekeepers had rarely been targeted, this was an indicator that the UN's status as an impartial actor was no longer to be taken for granted. In effect UN/US forces were at war with Aidid. In July at attempt to capture him led to the deaths of numerous elders of his clan, the Hawiye, and on 3 and 4 October 1993 the so-called 'Battle of Mogadishu' saw a fight in which 18 US Rangers were killed, and their bodies displayed in the street – the infamous 'Black Hawk Down' incident (Bowden, 1999). Soon after the US withdrew its forces and the anarchy continued; there is now a government in Somalia supported by the African Union, Ethiopia and the West, but pirates and radical Islamic groups remain disruptive, a reminder that failed states are not only a problem for their own people.

There are generic and specific lessons to be drawn from the experience of the international community in Somalia between 1991 and 1993. Poor intelligence and confused mission objectives always lead to problems, and certainly did in this case – the UN and US forces were singularly ill-prepared for the task they set themselves and repeatedly violated local customs through sheer ignorance. But, even if they had been better prepared, it is not clear that 'nation-building' would have been possible; nation-building in the circumstances of a failed state involves taking sides and picking potential leaders and it is not clear that outsiders, however well informed, are in a position to do this, let alone have the right to act in this way. A decade later these points resonate with the Western experience in Afghanistan and Iraq. In any event dealing with 'failed states' at a minimum requires a medium- to long-term commitment and that is difficult to achieve unless vital interests are at stake.

This is particularly true if casualties are involved; US casualty aversion has already been discussed and its affects can be seen after the 'Black Hawk Down' incident. In the wider scheme of things the loss of 18 soldiers, sad though it is for their families, ought not to have strategic significance for a nation of over 300 million, but on this occasion it did. Although the initial reaction in the US was a determination to stay the course, President Clinton, never convinced by the operation, took the decision to withdraw rather than risk further casualties; given Clinton's skills as a communicator it is possible that he could have sold the mission to the American people, but he did not make the effort. Instead, Presidential Directive 25 of 1994 restricted future US engagement in UN operations, stating that in future US soldiers would not be placed under UN command – the fact that the effective commanders of UNISOM II were actually American seems to have escaped the attention of the Administration. The end of US involvement in Somalia, and in particular the way it ended, was to have implications beyond the immediate, not least in terms of how the Clinton Administration handled the crisis in Rwanda in 1994. The wider point was that it drew attention to the extreme casualty aversion of the US; the message went out that it was only necessary to kill a small number of Americans to have a big impact on their policy, and this was a message heard in Bosnia-Herzegovina and by Islamic radicals.

The international community and genocide

Sadly, mass murder has been a feature of human history, but genocide is a relatively new phenomenon, identified and named by Raphael Lemkin in the middle of the Second World War in response to contemporary reports of the Holocaust, which he linked to the massacre of Armenians in the First World War (Lemkin, 1946, 1947). Lemkin's insight was that what linked these two atrocities was that they both involved the organised mass killing of a category of people – in other words this was not simply an aggregate of individual killings, and not just a question of the numbers involved. The deliberate extinction of at most 15,000 Tasmanian Aborigines in the nineteenth century constitutes a genocide, but the murder of between 200,000 and 300,000 in Nanjing in 1937 does not. An essential feature of a genocide seems to be that it is the product of modern nationalism and (illiberal) democracy; traditional autocracies wished to dominate and exploit, and murder some in order to terrorise the rest (such was the case with the Japanese massacres in Nanjing), but the aim of a genocide is to eliminate a whole category of people, thereby 'ethnically cleansing' territory to make it available for the perpetrators of the crime (as was the case in Tasmania) (Mann, 2005).

After 1945 Lemkin led a campaign to establish genocide as a specific crime under international law, and in 1948, the day after the Universal Declaration of Human Rights was passed in the UN General Assembly, The Genocide Convention was adopted. This defined genocide as follows:

Article II In the present Convention, genocide means any of the following acts committed with intent to destroy, in whole or in part, a national, ethnical, racial or religious group as such: (a) killing members of the group; (b) causing serious bodily or mental harm to members of the group; (c) deliberately inflicting on the group conditions of life calculated to bring about its physical destruction in whole or in part; (d) imposing measures intended to prevent births within the group; (e) forcibly transferring children of the group to another group.

At one level this is a very broad definition – causing mental harm to part of a group could constitute genocide – but at another level it is quite narrow – national, ethnical, racial and religious groups are included but not political or class-based groups, which means that on this definition the mass murder of approximately one-quarter of the population of Cambodia between 1975 and 1979 in the late 1970s did not constitute a genocide. The Convention committed states to 'prevent and punish' genocide, but without setting up any kind of mechanism to ensure that this would happen. Article VIV stated that the Convention would apply for ten years initially, then be extended for five years at a time; this has now been amended and the Convention is a permanent part of international law, but the inclusion of time limits indicates clearly that, in 1948 at least, it was past horrors that were in people's minds, rather than setting up a long-term mechanism to prevent genocide.

In recent years, the value of the Convention has been disputed; the argument in brief is that by putting so much emphasis on national, ethnic, religious or racial groups attention is drawn away from mass atrocity crimes in general. Alternatively, the notion of genocide is widened beyond the Convention to, in effect, cover most mass atrocity crimes (Shaw, 2007). Moreover, the category of genocide has taken on symbolic importance to the extent that a great deal of energy is focused on whether such-and-such a situation is 'really' a genocide without any real consequences following from the designation. For example, the Armenian desire to have the killings of 1915 termed a genocide, and the Turkish resistance to this designation, has distorted the political relationship between these two countries, with third parties drawn into the quarrel, and, arguably, with no real interests being at stake. Still, during the Cold War there was very little interest in the Convention, which was rarely referenced in public discourse – even in the case of Cambodia, although great horror was expressed at what was going on, the Convention was rarely invoked. As with the other crises examined in this chapter, it is the changes that came about at the end of the Cold War which created a context in which the notion of genocide comes to the fore, and in this case it did so in Rwanda in 1994.

Pre-colonial Rwanda was a complex, highly organised kingdom composed of two main groups, the 'Hutu', approximately 85 per cent of the population, stereotypically negroid and agriculturalist and the 'Tutsi' circa 15 per cent, stereotypically Nilotic and pastoralist (Prunier, 1998; Uvin, 2001). Post-colonial writers deny that there are actual differences between Hutu and Tutsi, and the leaders of both groups agree, portraying the conflict between them as based on class, and a struggle for control over the land, however it is worth noting that Hutu propaganda clearly identified Tutsis as 'other' and not simply as class-enemies, and in 1994 individuals were murdered on the basis of their physical appearance. What everyone agrees is that colonial race theories reinforced and rigidified whatever divisions were actually present; before colonialism the two categories had been only very loosely defined, but the introduction of identity cards marked Tutsi or Hutu eliminated such flexibility. The colonists, first German and then, after 1919, Belgium under a League of Nations Mandate and later a UN Trusteeship, initially privileged the Tutsi as 'natural leaders' (i.e. more European in appearance) then, in the 1950s, gradually shifted privileged status to the Hutu as the majority community. After independence in 1962, the 'Hutu Republic' was established – massacres of Tutsi led to around half a million Tutsi refugees in Burundi, Tanzania and Uganda. In 1973 Juvenal Habyarimana undertook a military coup, and established Rwanda as a one-party dictatorship. His rule was repressive but effective; as a small, relatively well-organised, French-speaking country Rwanda became an important part of Francophone Africa, receiving large amounts of aid from France, Switzerland and Canada, as well as Belgium. Tutsis suffered some repression, but were exploited rather than murdered, following the pattern of pre-democratic authoritarian rule.

Tutsi refugees and their descendants formed a major component of the personnel and leadership of Yoweri Museveni's National Resistance Army, the ultimate victor of the wars in Uganda in the 1980s and 1990, and in 1987 they formed the Rwanda Patriotic Front (RPF) with a view to returning to their original homeland by force of arms. In 1990 the RPF launched an invasion of Rwanda which was initially unsuccessful, but which initiated a military campaign that continued for the next four years. The Rwandan army was assisted in repelling the RPF by French forces; apart from its existing commitment to the Habyarimana regime, France saw the English-speaking Tutsis of the RPF as a threat to Rwanda's membership of Francophone Africa. The situation was complicated by the fact that after 1990 the Habyarimana regime came under pressure from its French and other foreign backers to democratise; most of the political parties that emerged as a result were Hutu-dominated and unwilling to countenance a deal with the overwhelmingly Tutsi RPF.

The international community brokered negotiations between the RPF and the government in Arusha, Tanzania, producing an agreement in September 1993 to form a government of national reconciliation in which the RPF were represented – perhaps over-represented, given their numbers – but which excluded the more extreme Hutu nationalists. The process of forming a new government and integrating the Rwanda Army and the RPF did not go smoothly and in April 1994 Habyarimana's aircraft was shot down while attempting to land at Kigali Airport. This was the signal for the murder of the government and the implementation by Hutu extremists of a policy of genocide, murdering all Tutsi who could be identified and those Hutu moderates who had supported peace. The genocide was carried out by Hutu militia (the *interahamwe* – 'those who act together') aided by the Rwanda Armed Forces. Between April and August 1994 around c. 800,000 Tutsi were killed; the genocide was only stopped by the victory of the RPF and the expulsion of the *'génocidaires'*, which created some 2 million new refugees, most of whom entered Zaire and have been at the root of the wars that followed in that country, wars which have claimed several million lives and which continue to this day (Gourevitch, 1999; Prunier, 2011).

The Rwanda genocide was a disaster of epic proportions and one that poses an obvious question – how could the world have allowed such a terrible occurrence to take place? Why was not action taken to end the killing? Here was an obvious case where a humanitarian intervention would have been justified and could, indeed, be declared mandatory given the commitment by states in the Genocide Convention to prevent that crime from taking place. No such intervention took place except towards the end of the genocide, and even then the French 'Operation Turquoise' had very little effect. In essence, the international community was a bystander to the genocide, and the reasons for this need to be probed.

The first thing to be said is that it is important not to begin the story in April 1994, or in September 1993, or even in 1990, because this gives the impression that the international community was uninvolved in Rwanda before those dates. This is often how such crises are narrated; the impression is given that a problem is generated locally and the international community only becomes involved when the pot boils over, as it were, and outsiders rush in to rescue, or not, as is more usually the case. This is wrong – the international community in the form of national and international aid agencies and missions, mostly but not entirely Francophone, had been present for decades in Rwanda and had done more or less nothing to relieve the tensions between Hutu and Tutsi that exploded in the 1990s. The government of Habyarimana had been very popular with the international community, which had focused on its effectiveness and ignored its repression of the Tutsi and other domestic opponents. It is unreasonable to suggest that the events of 1994 were, in detail, predictable, but the possibility of large-scale civil strife certainly was, and those in and knowledgeable of Rwandan society cannot claim to have been completely surprised by the way things turned out.

In any event, the UN did become involved in supporting the Arusha Agreement, and established UNAMIR (United Nations Assistance Mission to Rwanda) as a neutral military monitoring force, initially with around 2,500 troops drawn from *inter alia* Belgium (acceptable to the RPF in a way that the French were not), Bangladesh and Ghana, under the command of the Canadian General Roméo Dallaire. In January 1994 the latter, sensing what was to come, requested permission from the UN Peacekeeping Office, then run by Kofi Annan to act against the Hutu militia; permission was refused and he did not press home the point. Immediately after the murder of the President in April 1994, Dallaire provided a bodyguard of ten Belgian and five Ghanaian soldiers for the Prime Minister, Agathe Uwilingiyimana; she was attacked, her bodyguards attempted to protect her, she tried to slip away but was caught and murdered. The bodyguard then surrendered – the Ghanaians were allowed to leave but the Belgians were tortured and killed. Belgium then removed the rest of her troops (partly to prevent retaliation), the UN Security Council refused to reinforce UNAMIR, indeed cut its numbers to 270 men, and the force becomes a helpless observer of the genocide (Melvern, 2000, 2006).

Part of the problem was that Rwanda lay within the informal French sphere of interest in Africa, and France throughout interpreted events as a civil war, with atrocities being committed on both sides – this interpretation had wide implications because they had better sources of information than most other UN Security Council members, and their interpretation was backed up by the official Rwandan delegation at the UN, which, in an unfortunate coincidence, currently held one of the Africa seats on the Council. Clearly the French position was partly a reflection of the fear that an RPF victory would lead to Rwanda leaving Francophone Africa – which has indeed happened, as English has been adopted along with French as an official language, and Rwanda has joined the Commonwealth. It should also be said that French policy in this matter reflected the views and interests of a small number of 'Africa hands' working out of the President's Office, led by his son Jean Christophe Mitterrand (Wallis, 2006; Kroslak, 2007) – when ordinary French soldiers taking part in Operation Turquoise found that they were being greeted as allies by the *génocidaires* many were horrified.

It is worth stressing the role of the French in the Rwanda catastrophe, because so much of the Anglophone literature focuses on what the US did, or more to the point didn't do (Power, 2002). Certainly the US had good information on what was happening in Rwanda through their intelligence agencies, and the refusal of the State Department to acknowledge the genocide, referring instead to 'acts of genocide' on the grounds that intentions were unclear, did it little credit – still, Rwanda was never a high priority for the US in the way that it was for the French, and the matter never reached the highest level for decision. Anglophone newspapers, and for that matter groups such as Human Rights Watch did not identify what was going on as a genocide until quite late in the process and so very little pressure was exerted on the Clinton Administration to take a more active stance.

Could an intervention have been effective? Many of the victims, especially in Kigali, were killed very early on before an hypothetical intervention could have taken effect, but it should be remembered that the genocide was not a spontaneous popular reaction but something organised by a well-administered state, and disruption of communications might have had some effect (Kuperman, 2000a, 2000b; Des Forges, 2000). In the early days of the genocide around 1,000 French, Belgian and Italian troops landed in Kigali to evacuate 4,000 Europeans (leaving behind locally recruited embassy staff, but providing refuge to some Hutus implicated in planning the genocide). Had these troops joined with UNAMIR while it was at full strength giving an effective force of 3,500 soldiers they could have exerted considerable influence towards ending the genocide.

Most NGOs left Rwanda during the genocide, but in July and August 1994 the UN High Commissioner for Refugees, the Red Cross and several major NGO staffed refugee camps in the Democratic Republic of the Congo (then Zaire). They were responding to a major humanitarian crisis – disease and malnutrition were rife – but they were also providing assistance to the *génocidaires*, and the camps soon came to be dominated by Hutu extremists. The problem this posed to the humanitarian organisations concerned was simple – if they left, as some did, they were abandoning the needy, but if they stayed they were complicit in giving support to genocidal groups. A clearer example of the problems posed by both classical and the new humanitarianism is difficult to imagine. The truth is that the new global politics that emerged post-1989 simply does not have a solution to problems of this kind.

Genocide studies identify four roles: victims, perpetrators, rescuers, bystanders. French activity came close to complicity with genocide in this crisis, a view that the Rwandan Government certainly holds and was expressed in a speech by President Paul Kagame of Rwanda at the 10th anniversary memorial to the genocide; France retaliated by attempting to implicate Kagame and the RPF in the murder of Habyarimana, an attempt only abandoned as recently as January 2012. The international community 'stood by' in 1994 – the UN has acknowledged as much in the Carlsson Report of 1999. In March 1998, President Clinton visited Kigali Airport and gave a quasi-apology to Rwandans for the international community 'not doing enough'; it is not clear what Clinton thought the international community had done – certainly the US did nothing and actively obstructed some who would act, by, for example, refusing to transport the troops of other countries to Rwanda, citing Presidential Directive 25 and post-Somalia traumas, conveniently ignoring the fact that PD25 makes an exception for genocide.

Conclusion

This brief survey has covered only a sample of cases from the 1990s, but even on this limited evidence it ought to be clear that this was a decade in which all those concerned were struggling to find a new normative framework within which to situate the problems thrown up by the end of the Cold War. As writers such as Brendan Simms, Samantha Power and James Gow have argued, there were failures of will in the 1990s when it came to dealing with the horrors of war, ethnic cleansing and genocide; national leaders who had the power to act to at least mitigate these evils frequently failed to do so because they feared the consequences of action more than the consequences of inaction. But in their defence is should also be said that they were having to deal with situations that were in many respects unprecedented – moreover, they were expected to navigate these difficult waters without reliable charts. The old understandings of right and wrong conduct associated with the idea of an international society seemed no longer appropriate, but the new global politics that was emerging in the 1990s had not yet created a set of ideas that could replace them. At the end of the decade, the hope was that the mostly unfortunate experiences of the 1990s might at least prepare the way for new thinking in the next century. The next two chapters will relate how these hopes were partly realised by the notion of a 'responsibility to protect', but also undermined by another narrative, of the 'war on terror'.

Further Reading

A number of collections published in the early 2000s are, in effect, sets of reflections on the experience of the 1990s – see for example Mats Berdal and Spyros Economides (2007), Deen Chatterjee and Don Scheid (2003), J.L. Holzgrefe and Robert O. Keohane, (2003), Terry Nardin and Michael Williams (2006), all of which contain much that is of value. Jonathan Moore (1998) is rather different in so far as he has many practitioner contributors, including Mohamed Sahnoun. Individual reflections on the decade include Michael Ignatieff (2003), Nicholas Wheeler (2000), Simon Chesterman (2001), Anthony Lang (2003) and Alex Bellamy (2002). The thesis that the new interventionism amounts to a new American imperialism is associated with figures such as Noam Chomsky – of his many books (1999) is perhaps the best way into his writings in this area – John Pilger, ditto, see (2003) as illustrative and, altogether more scholarly, David Chandler (2005).

In-chapter references cover most of the points one would like to make about the Yugoslav Wars of the 1990s – to single out a few highlights, Brendan Simms (2001) is an unmissable indictment of British government policy, David Campbell (1998) relates Bosnia to the identity politics discussed in Chapter 6 of this book, and rejects comprehensively the 'ancient tribal hostilities' interpretation of the conflict, Noel Malcolm's two histories of Bosnia (1994) and Kosovo (2002) are very useful for gaining perspective. Alex Danchev and Thomas Halverson (1996) is a collection of essays that attempted to summarise the experience of the main participants, probably prematurely.

James Mayall and Ioan Lewis's contribution to Mayall (1996) is an account of Somalia which incorporates Lewis's anthropological studies of that country and is illuminated thereby. Scott Peterson (2000) also provides background, this time from a journalist who has spent much

(Continued)

(Continued)

time in the area. See in-text references for more on Somalia and failed states. The *Foreign Policy* Annual 'Failed States Index' is worth looking at, but should not be taken too seriously.

Jens Meierhenrich's *Genocide: A Reader* (2014) is a good starting point for the subject, Samantha Power (2002) is not – the basic assumption of her work is that it is America's unique responsibility to act in cases of genocide, a perspective that leads her badly astray on Rwanda where France was at the centre of the story in a way that America was not, see Andrew Wallis (2006) and Daniela Kroslak (2007). Malcolm Shaw's take on genocide (2007) is idiosyncratic but interesting. Michael Mann's (2005) exploration of the dark side of democracy shines a new and disturbing light on the phenomenon of ethnic cleansing and genocide. Specifically on Rwanda, Gérard Prunier and Linda Melvern are invaluable and complementary – all of their books (referenced in the text of the chapter) are outstanding, and on the background causes of the genocide, Peter Uvin (2001) packs a great deal into a short space. Philip Gourevitch (1999) conveys the horror very well, but is perhaps a little too favourably disposed to the RPF and Paul Kagame. Prunier (2011) tells the story of the aftermath of the genocide and traces the progress of 'Africa's World War'.

8

THE RESPONSIBILITY TO PROTECT

Kosovo prelude

In the last chapter the story of the wars of former Yugoslavia and their implications for international political theory was told up to the Dayton Peace Conference and the establishment of an uneasy peace in Bosnia-Herzegovina. As noted there, this peace left the issue of Kosovo, whose autonomy within Serbia had been removed in 1989, unresolved; prior to Dayton the Albanian majority community in Kosovo had engaged in a campaign of passive resistance aiming to undermine Serb rule and attract support from the international community. When Kosovar claims were ignored, this lead to a change of tactics, and the formation of the Kosovar Liberation Army (UCK); guerrilla attacks on the Serb police and army in Kosovo took place with predictable Serb reprisals and the creation of refugees. In effect, the Kosovars realised than in order to attract international support they needed to become victims, or perhaps better, to dramatise their victim status. This policy was successful; in March 1998, UN Security Council Resolution 1160 called for an end to violence, and in September 1998, Resolution 1999 recognised a Chapter VII 'threat to peace and security', although it did not explicitly authorise military action. NATO took up the cause of the Kosovars and threatened action, at which point the Yugoslav Government agreed to a ceasefire, and the presence of unarmed OSCE inspectors. However, violations of the ceasefire continued and January 1999 saw a massacre of civilians in the village of Racak by Serbs in retaliation for attacks on police. The unarmed OSCE inspectors withdrew on the principle that their presence was serving no useful purpose (Malcolm, 2002: Weller, 2009).

Talks between the parties were held at Rambouillet near Paris but failed, either because of Serb intransigence or because of the unreasonable demands made by NATO; the result was a NATO bombing campaign that lasted from 23 March 1999 to 3 June. Initially this was directed at Serb targets within Kosovo but then shifted to targets in Serbia proper including parts of the infrastructure of the state; the immediate result of the campaign was an even large refugee crisis with Kosovars forced from their homes into Macedonia, but after the eventual Yugoslav acceptance of an EU-Russian plan and withdrawal from Kosovo the flow of refugees was reversed. The ten week campaign resulted in the defeat of Serbia with zero NATO casualties, largely because only air-power was involved and then only aircraft flying above the operational ceiling of Serbia's air defences, a tactic which allegedly protected NATO personnel while increasing the likelihood of civilian casualties (Daalder and O'Hanlan, 2000; Freedman and Karsh, 2000). This raised all the problems with the conduct of asymmetric humanitarian wars discussed in the last chapter. The fact that NATO killed without being prepared to risk being killed was seen by some as undermining the legitimacy of the campaign; the argument was that if NATO members believed themselves to be fighting in a just cause they should have been willing to risk the lives of their soldiers. It is also noteworthy in this respect that the success of the campaign came about in part because serious preparations were being made for a ground campaign.

In any event, the result was the establishment of an international protectorate and the eventual establishment of an independent Kosovo, although as yet without recognition from Yugoslavia or the UN. Unlike the situation in Croatia and Bosnia-Herzegovina in 1995, Kosovo in 1999 was recognised by the UN and by all the parties to the conflict as under the sovereignty of Yugoslavia; NATO action was clearly in breach of Yugoslav sovereignty and this raises all the questions about the authority to act that were avoided in 1995. NATO argued that the various UN Security Council Resolutions in effect authorised action – but they did not explicitly authorise force (for example, by using such conventional phraseology as 'by whatever means necessary') and Russia and China made it clear that they would have vetoed them if they had. On the other hand, a draft resolution condemning NATO's action was defeated by 12 votes to 3 (Russia, China, Namibia) which was taken by some to confer a degree of legitimacy on the action; it should also be said that NATO and EU members were firm in their support for the action, albeit with the occasional wobble from Greece. A positive resolution in the Security Council would clearly have been vetoed by Russia and China – some Council members (in particular Argentina and Germany) argued that this would have been an illegitimate use of the veto – a position the three Western veto-powers firmly rejected, doubtless on the principle that they did not wish their own powers to be limited in this way.

During the war, one of its chief advocates in the West, Britain's then Prime Minister Tony Blair, set out in a speech in Chicago a *Doctrine of the International Community* designed to lay out the conditions under which a humanitarian intervention ought to be considered legitimate; these included such traditional

Just War notions as just cause, last resort and reasonable prospects of success, but also recognised the importance of having national interests involved, and was somewhat ambiguous on the issue of the role of the UN, arguing that it needed to be reformed but implying that in the meantime its authority was not needed (Blair, 1999). This was a serious contribution to the debate, and the speech is still worth reading for the way in which these points are integrated into a wider account of contemporary globalisation – but, inevitably, the speech failed to convince opponents of the action.

After the war an *Independent International Commission on Kosovo* was established with civil society luminaries as its members; the Commission declared the intervention to be 'illegal but legitimate'. The response to this judgment, and to the war itself, varied; many people in the West thought 'illegal but legitimate' to be a fair summary – in effect this was saying that there was a strong presumption against breaching the norm on non-intervention unless there was UN sanction for so doing, but that occasionally, all things considered, an intervention might nonetheless be the right thing to do. There is an analogy here with the law on euthanasia – euthanasia is illegal in most jurisdictions but it is clear that sometimes doctors 'ease the passing' of terminally ill patients, and as long as there is no benefit to the doctor involved, a legacy for example, most people are happy that this should be so, but the same people would resist a change in the law making euthanasia easier because of the perceived dangers associated with such a step. In short, euthanasia is 'illegal but (sometimes) legitimate'. Such a judgement rests on the idea that the doctor who prescribes the additional morphine that kills the patient is disinterested, has no axe to grind, and that is where the analogy breaks down as far as many observers of Kosovo were concerned. Russia, China, India and some other important states, along with much opinion on the left within the West itself, were not prepared to accept the idea that NATO, or the US in particular, was a disinterested actor (Chomsky, 1999). Instead the Kosovo War was interpreted as an imperial act, and the fact that it was supported by figures with solid left-wing credentials such as Clare Short in Britain and Joschka Fischer in Germany mattered not at all – indeed, Fischer, the leading Green in the Red-Green German coalition was attacked with red paint at a Green Party conference for defending the action.

Sovereignty as responsibility and the ICISS

These debates brought to a head controversies that had been present throughout the 1990s. During this decade, there had been a concerted push to change the meaning of 'sovereignty'. Whereas in 1945 the UN Charter established with Article 2 (7) the principle that the domestic jurisdiction of states should be unchallenged save in the interests of international peace and security – a principle compatible with the understanding of sovereignty that international society had developed over the previous three centuries – the move now was to establish new standards of international legitimacy. Some cosmopolitan writers and lawyers argued that, in effect, only liberal democratic states could be regarded as truly legitimate and thus entitled to the protection of Article 2(7). UN officials such as Dr Francis Deng, and future Secretary-General Kofi Annan were not prepared to take that step, but they did argue for a conception of 'sovereignty as responsibility', that is to say for a conception of sovereignty that required of states that they accept responsibility for the well-being of their people and for the protection of their human rights (Deng et al, 1996). Such a conception of sovereignty could be seen as having been behind the various interventions that took place in the 1990s, but these interventions were plagued by doubts about the criteria for action and double-standards being applied, and by an obvious lack of consensus on the Security Council, especially among the Permanent Five members.

Kosovo crystallised the problem; responding to the view that the intervention in Kosovo violated the principle of sovereignty. Kofi Annan summarised the difficulty as follows:

> if humanitarian intervention is, indeed, an unacceptable assault on sovereignty, how should we respond to a Rwanda, to a Srebrenica – to gross and systematic violations of human rights that affect every precept of our common humanity? (*ICISS* Report, viii)

This question formed the starting point for a Canadian Government-sponsored *International Commission on Intervention and State Sovereignty* (ICISS) established in 2000, and composed of a mixture of politicians, intellectuals and international civil servants drawn from around the world, and co-chaired by former Australian Foreign Minister Gareth Evans, and Algerian and UN diplomat Mohamed Sahnoun – other members included Canadian philosopher Michael Ignatieff, US Congressman Lee Hamilton, South African trade union leader Cyril Ramaphosa, Russian human rights activist Vladimir Lukin and Indian civil servant and academic Ramesh Thakur.

The Commission's approach involved a change in terminology that they believed signalled a different kind of politics. Instead of 'humanitarian intervention', with its implication of outsiders interfering in local politics, they focused on the 'responsibility to protect' (sometimes shortened in the language of texting to R2P or, RtoP), which was meant to indicate a much more general obligation towards local populations, to be understood as held in the first instance by the state itself. Following on from the work of Francis Deng and others, sovereignty is defined in terms of responsibility, specifically the responsibility to protect. This responsibility is located initially with the sovereign state, which is enjoined not to commit atrocities or to allow them to be committed, but when the state is unwilling or unable to act to end mass atrocities, the principle of non-intervention must yield to an international responsibility to protect. The responsibilities of the international community are threefold, ranging from *prevention* of mass atrocities in the first place, via *reaction* to them when they occur, to an obligation to assist *rebuilding* after the conflict is ended.

The second stage here – reaction – is the most controversial, taking the matter back towards humanitarian intervention, and must, the Commission argues, be seen in the context of these three dimensions. The Commission's position is that in extreme cases, which they define by conventional Just War criteria, that is, just cause, last resort, and proportionality, it may the duty of the international community to act militarily in response to a mass atrocity. The authority to act (the 'right authority' to use Just War terminology) is granted by the UN Security Council. The Commission is aware of the difficulties with relying on the Security Council to act in such cases, and proposes that it should establish guidelines to govern its responses to claims for military intervention, and the Permanent Five should agree in advance not to cast vetoes when these guideline criteria are clearly met. In the absence of such an agreement, if there is a clear cut case, the Commission argues tentatively that the UN General Assembly, and Regional Organisations may provide legitimacy for action; there is also an even more tentative reference to 'world public opinion' – but the Commission places most of its eggs in the basket of the UN Security Council which is also charged with meeting the other two dimensions of prevention and rebuilding.

The ICISS Report *The Responsibility to Protect* was published by the Canadian Government in December 2001; this was not propitious timing. The September 11th attacks in Manhattan and Washington had taken place a few months earlier, and the 'Global War on Terror' had been declared by the Administration of George W. Bush in response. Already when the Report was published the war in Afghanistan was underway, and over the next two years the focus would be on the intervention in Iraq in 2003. It would be 2004/5 before the Report would really start to influence official thinking in the run up to the UN's 60th anniversary World Summit in 2005. Before looking at that event and the incorporation of some of the ICISS's ideas in the World Summit Outcome Document, it may be worth looking in a little more detail at the ideas themselves. Does the notion of a responsibility to protect do what its authors hoped it would do, that is establish firm criteria for handling major humanitarian crises, and disassociate itself from the idea of 'humanitarian intervention'?

The ICISS Report and the underpinnings of the Responsibility to Protect

The ICISS authors acknowledge that what they were asking for is that 'the international community change its basic mind-set with respect to mass atrocity from a 'culture of reaction' to a 'culture of prevention' (3.42). What is not acknowledged, at least not explicitly, is that this requires not simply a change of mind-set on the part of the international community, but rather a substantial *political* shift to actually create the context in which this change could take place. Or, to put the same point differently, it is not acknowledged that the 'culture of reaction' that is criticised is only shared by part of the international community, the part that had in the 1990s supported humanitarian intervention, while another part of the international community, in so far as it had a collective position at all, could be seen as offering a 'culture of inaction' rather than a culture of 'reaction'. Those states and commentators who had opposed humanitarian intervention in the name of state sovereignty were obviously not part of the aforementioned 'culture of reaction' and a different kind of argument would be needed to change their mind-set in the desired direction.

Chapter 3 of the ICISS Report, on the *Responsibility to Prevent*, assumes that it would be a good thing if the current *ad hoc* and unstructured approach to early warning about deadly conflict which at the moment involves a wide range of players were to be centralised and concentrated around the UN Headquarters under the general oversight of the Security Council. In the event of prevention failing, the *Responsibility to React* (set out in Chapter 4) would also fall to the UN which would oversee the application of targeted sanctions against the offending state, and, *in extremis*, would authorise the resort to force, strictly in accordance to the criteria established by Just War theory. Chapter 5 gives the UN *Responsibility to Rebuild*, if necessary through international administration, with a view to eventually re-establishing local ownership.

The picture painted in these three chapters is of an embryonic central administration for the world, with the UN Security Council acting as a kind of global executive, spotting potential conflicts before they turn deadly, if possible managing them without direct intervention, but if necessary taking the parties by the scruff of the neck and making sure that they behave, then clearing up the mess that the latter part of the operation might have created, before benignly returning things to local control. From one perspective one might see this as an appropriately cosmopolitan picture of an emerging global polity, but this is not the only interpretation that could be put on such a vision. Some writers, Anne Orford in particular, have seen this as a description of an authoritarian international administration legitimated by a political theory that has its roots in a kind of Hobbesian reaction to a time of troubles, with the need for 'protection' overriding all the other functions that we might hope an enlightened, democratic, political authority could provide (Orford, 2011). The rhetorical justification of protecting populations has frequently been used to justify acts of aggression – from Czechoslovakia in 1938 to Crimea in 2014 – and the idea that the right to protect in this way could be transferred to a global executive is not an encouraging thought.

If the Security Council could, in fact, act in the way that Chapters 3–5 of the ICISS Report set out, Orford's fears would be justified – this would indeed be a case where a coalition of powerful states would be authorised to engage in 'pacification'; weak states would be pacified in the name of protecting their populations, and certainly some members of the international community would regard the denial of local agency that this process would involve as a very good thing. Needless to say, others would take a very different position on this exercise of international authority; the point is, however, that Orford's fears are made groundless by the fact that both of these positions are represented in the Security Council and among the Permanent Five veto-powers. Whereas sometimes the UK and France, and perhaps even the US, might actually be prepared to see the Council acting as this kind of Global Leviathan, bringing peace and order to the world, Russia and China, although not averse to imperialist enterprises on their own account, see the world rather differently, and in this are likely to be joined by at least some of the non-permanent members of the UN Security Council. As noted above, the Kosovo intervention of 1999 crystallised Russia and China opposition to international interventions and they are unlikely to agree to give legitimacy to any future attempts at pacification in the name of protection.

The ICISS was aware of the problem posed by the politics of the Security Council and the blocking potential of the Permanent Five powers, and proposed that

> there be agreed by the Permanent Five a 'code of conduct' for the use of the veto with respect to actions that are needed to stop or avert a significant humanitarian crisis. The idea essentially is that a permanent member, in matters where its vital interests were not claimed to be involved, would not use its veto to obstruct the passage of what would otherwise to a majority resolution. (6.21, p. 51)

The problem here is that, given that it is left to a Permanent Five country to determine whether or not its vital interests are involved then nothing would actually be changed by the adoption of such a code. It is interesting that although the Permanent Five countries have often criticised each other's use of the veto power, they have generally refrained from suggesting that any particular use of the veto is actually improper, as opposed to unwise or malicious. So, the idea that the P5 would pre-commit to a code of conduct that would determine how they would react in response to a humanitarian crisis has no legal weight behind it – but it is revealing of the way in which the Commission understood their own activities. Such a code of conduct would make sense if humanitarian crises could be understood as essentially non-political events likely to attract consensus about the appropriate response, in other words if the kind of disagreements about humanitarian action that were seen over Kosovo and had been present before in the 1990s did not exist. One could then treat the response to a situation where a gross violation of human rights was taking place in a technical manner, choosing the appropriate method to stop or avert a significant humanitarian crisis. For better or worse, this is not the way most states actually treat such crises.

The Commission were well aware that the Security Council might fail to discharge its duty in such matters and alternatives are discussed, such as moving the case to the UN General Assembly or to Regional Bodies. However, it is acknowledged that these bodies do not have the Security Council's power to authorise the use of force and the aim of these steps is to put pressure on the Security Council to do the job, to, as it were, shame it into action. The Commission also acknowledges that if all else fails and the situation is particularly dire, the possibility of an *ad hoc* group of states, or even an individual state acting alone arises – a possibility that is accompanied by serious warnings about doing the right thing for the wrong reason (6:39, p. 55). It is also pointed out that if unauthorised action takes place, and is successful and is widely seen to be so this may have 'enduringly serious consequences for the stature and credibility of the UN itself' (6:40). Again, the assumption seems to be that the Permanent Five will be sufficiently concerned by this possible outcome that they will prevent it from coming to pass by acting themselves. And, again, this underestimates the genuine political divisions that exist in the world. Since the superficially successful intervention in Kosovo by a group of states who did not have UN Security Council authorisation was one of the reasons for the establishment of the Commission in the first place one might have expected a little more depth on the subject, but at this point the chapter ends and the Report moves on to more congenial topics such as the operation of peacekeeping forces in the rebuilding stage.

To summarise these comments, the aim of the ICISS Report is to answer Kofi Annan's question – but the terms of the question are such that no satisfactory answer is likely to be forthcoming. In effect, the Commission attempted to produce a doctrine that legitimates intervention in some circumstances, but would not constitute an assault on sovereignty. But the notion it comes up with is actually most likely to be acceptable to those who are perfectly content to envisage an assault on sovereignty in some circumstances, while being largely unacceptable to those of an opposite view. The world tour undertaken by the ICISS Commissioners to promote their Report confirmed this judgement. The account of this tour presented by Gareth Evans in his very helpful and revealing book on the subject makes it clear that he and his fellow commissioners were generally unsuccessful in persuading their audiences that what they were offering was not a doctrine of humanitarian intervention (Evans, 2008b). Writing nearly ten years after he and or his fellow-commissioners visited Beijing, Pretoria, Moscow, Brasilia and other world capitals, he still finds 'five major misunderstandings', the first of which is that 'Responsibility to Protect' is just another name for humanitarian intervention' (p. 56). He is, of course, right that the aim of the ICISS Commissioners was to make the notion of a Responsibility to Protect different from humanitarian intervention, but they tried to do so by taking the politics out of the question of responding to gross violations of human rights, and their audiences insisted on putting the politics back in. For these audiences Responsibility to Protect looked like humanitarian intervention because they did not accept that protection issues could be depoliticised in the way that the Commissioners believed they could be. Effectively, their interlocutors applied the 'duck principle' – 'if it looks like a duck, swims like a duck, and quacks like a duck, then it probably is a duck' – and decided that, whatever Evans et al. might say, this looked like humanitarian intervention and would operate in the same way if push came to shove.

Responsibility to Protect: From the World Summit 2005 to UNSC1973

As noted above, the ICISS Report landed on the desks of international statespersons and bureaucrats at a time when minds were focused on the Global War on Terror, intervention in Afghanistan, and the well-advertised forthcoming war in Iraq. This was not a good time to ask the world to re-focus on the appropriate response to major humanitarian crises and to do so in a non-partisan manner, although this was a period in which, for once, the UN Security Council was acting as the kind of embryonic global executive looked for by the Commission, and feared by others. In the immediate aftermath of 9/11 the Security Council adopted a wide-ranging series of measures designed to counter terrorist activities, imposing sanctions on organisations and individuals and authorising state operations to the same end. For a short period at least, the Permanent Five on the Security Council were of one mind in respect to this issue at least – but in a context somewhat removed from that required for the adoption of the ICISS Report. In addition, the 2003 Iraq War did the Report no favours – even though this was not an operation that was officially justified in 'Responsibility to Protect' terms, the fact that it was seen as a kind of humanitarian intervention by some, including one of the Commission members, Michael Ignatieff, muddied the waters for the Report with those who, often vehemently, opposed the war.

Still, the work of the Commission remained available as an important contribution to debates over the appropriate response to humanitarian crises, and, moreover, a response that had a quasi-official status within the UN system. Although the ICISS was technically an initiative of the Canadian Government, from the beginning its work was closely linked to the UN – apart from the fact that it all began with a consideration of the question posed by UN Secretary General Kofi Annan, referred to above, the Co-Chair, Mohamed Sahnoun, was a Special Adviser to the UN Secretary General, another member, Ramesh Thakur, was Vice-Rector of the UN University in Tokyo, and, again as noted above, the Commission was informed by the thinking on 'sovereignty as responsibility' of

Francis Deng, a former Sudanese diplomat and a UN official in the 1990s (and later South Sudan's first UN Ambassador). So it was natural that, when the UN Secretary-General established a *High-Level Panel on Threats, Challenges and Change* in November 2003 in preparation for the UN's 60th Anniversary World Summit in September 2005, the ICISS Report would play a major part in their thinking – especially since Gareth Evans Co-Chair of the Commission was a member of the Panel – and so it transpired. The *World Summit Outcome Final Document* contained at paragraphs 138–140 much of the language of the ICISS Report.

The UN's Fact Sheet for the Summit describes the section of the Final Document on Responsibility to Protect in very strong terms, claiming:

> Clear and unambiguous acceptance by all governments of the collective international responsibility to protect populations from genocide, war crimes, ethnic cleansing and crimes against humanity. Willingness to take timely and decisive collective action for this purpose, through the Security Council, when peaceful means prove inadequate and national authorities are manifestly failing to do it.

The actual Final Document wording states that:

> 139. The international community, through the United Nations, also has the responsibility to use appropriate diplomatic, humanitarian and other peaceful means, in accordance with Chapters VI and VIII of the Charter, to help protect populations from genocide, war crimes, ethnic cleansing and crimes against humanity. In this context, we are prepared to take collective action, in a timely and decisive manner, through the Security Council, in accordance with the Charter, including Chapter VII, on a case-by-case basis and in cooperation with relevant regional organizations as appropriate, should peaceful means be inadequate and national authorities manifestly fail to protect their populations from genocide, war crimes, ethnic cleansing and crimes against humanity ...

What is missing from this, as was immediately noticed, is any reference to the Permanent Five members of the Council establishing a code of conduct that would involve a self-denying ordinance when it came to the casting of vetoes. In effect, although the Document employs the language of responsibility and protection, it actually creates no new legal obligation on the members of the Security Council – and it is clear from the statements of the main drafters of the Document that it was precisely for this reason that key members of the Permanent Five, including the US whose UN Ambassador at the time, John Bolton, was a ferocious critic of attempts to extend the scope of international law, were prepared to sign on the dotted line.

It has been suggested that the version of Responsibility to Protect adopted in 2005 amounts to 'R2P Lite' given the amount of detail from the Report that did not make it into the Final Document, but as far as the veto is concerned, this criticism is misplaced. As noted above, the original language of the Report on the veto was, to all intents and purposes, mere verbiage. In any event, once the notion of a Responsibility to Protect, lite or heavy, was adopted by the UN, predictably a certain amount of institutionalisation of the concept took place. Thus, a Special Adviser to the Secretary General on Responsibility to Protect was appointed in 2008, a position held by Dr Edward Luck until 2012, and to which Dr Jennifer Welsh has recently been appointed, and in 2009 the UN Secretary General presented a report entitled *Implementing the Responsibility to Protect*. This Report filled out a lot of the detail that had been missed in 2005, and established the notion of 'three-pillar strategy' for advancing the agenda mandated by the Heads of State and Government at the Summit. Thus, pillar one, the protection responsibilities of the State; pillar two, international assistance and capacity-building; pillar three, timely and decisive response. In effect, the Secretary-General ran with the ball passed to him in 2005, in the process elaborating what was decided there in rather more detail than many of the heads of government who signed up to the World Summit Outcome Document had intended.

The result of this activity is that nowadays when humanitarian issues arise, and the possibility of intervention is raised, the language of Responsibility to Protect is routinely employed by at least some of the actors involved – it has been, in effect, mainstreamed in UN discourse. A few examples illustrate the way in which the language has been used; the conflict in Darfur was the first major crisis to be addressed after the adoption of the Summit Outcome Document in 2005 (Prunier, 2005, 2011; De Waal, 2007). There was strong support in Western civil society for action to end the conflict – for reasons that are not altogether clear, the case attracted extensive celebrity concern, with predictably overblown rhetoric as a result ('... this is your legacy, your Rwanda, your Cambodia, your Auschwitz' said George Clooney addressing the UN Security Council in September 2006). But Russian opposition in principle to international action, Chinese oil-diplomacy and Arab support for the Sudanese Government made effective UN action difficult to organise. Still, UN Security Council Resolution 1706 in August 2006 explicitly references the World Summit Outcome Document and the commitment therein to protection – the first example of Responsibility to Protect language being used in an UN Resolution. The push to create an effective UN force in support of the existing, rather ineffective, African Union force was eventually successful in 2007 with the formation of the hybrid UN/AU force UNAMID which eventually involved around 20,000 soldiers, but the peace-building and mediation efforts of the UN have been rather more important in bringing about the marginally more stable situation that now exists.

In 2008, Cyclone Nargis created a large-scale humanitarian crisis in 2008 in Burma/Myanmar, and when the government of that country refused external aid it was proposed by the French government (whose foreign minister at that time was Bernard Kouchner, a long-standing advocate of humanitarian interventions) that the failure of the local government to respond adequately to the crisis produced a case for international intervention under the aegis of the responsibility to protect (Haacke, 2009). This argument was unsuccessful – an illegitimate use of the doctrine to some, simply impractical of implementation to others – but the fact that it was made at all is evidenced of the mainstreaming of the doctrine. Finally, the post-election crisis that took place in Kenya in 2007 was ended by a successful mediation by African leaders, which, after the event, was interpreted as a successful exercise in pillar one prevention. Whether in this case the doctrine actually had any effect is doubtful, but as in the case of Cyclone Nargis, the very fact that it was referenced, albeit in this case after the event, is indicative of the fact that the concept of Responsibility to Protect now dominates the discourse of humanitarian action (Crossley, 2013).

Reference was made above to Gareth Evans's 2008 book *The Responsibility to Protect: Ending Mass Atrocity Crimes Once and For All* and his five 'major misunderstandings' about the Responsibility to Protect. The second of these major misunderstandings was – 'that R2P always means the use of military force' – and, on the basis of the examples given above, and others such as those listed on the excellent website of the International Coalition for the Responsibility to Protect, we can agree that this is, indeed, a misunderstanding. Still, it remains the case that for many the real test of the doctrine is when force might be involved and in 2011 the crisis in Libya, and to a more limited degree, the crisis in Côte d'Ivoire provided that test. In the latter country, Presidential elections in November/December 2010 resulted in the opposition leader Ouattara defeating the incumbent President Gbagbo; the latter refused to accept the result, civil unrest and a major refugee crisis followed. UN Security Council Resolution 1962 extended the mandate of the existing UN Peacekeeping Force (UNOCI) to June 2011, and provided it with additional troops and support. On 4 April 2011 the UN Secretary-General instructed UNOCI to co-operate with French troops in the country and on 11 April Gbagbo was overthrown, largely by those French troops with UN support. This was not a full-scale R2P operation but showed a willingness of the international community to act – Libya made the point more unambiguously.

Libya and Syria – success and failure?

In the spring of 2011, upheavals took place in a number of Arab countries, beginning in Tunisia and spreading eastwards. In Tunisia and Egypt the 'Arab Spring' was relatively peaceful, but in Libya the regime of Colonel Gaddafi reacted violently to threats to its power, using the army and the police against the people. The regime established control in the capital, Tripoli, but the opposition soon controlled the east of the country, including Libya's second city, Benghazi; regime forces moved to retake the opposition-controlled areas, committing human rights abuses in the process. On 26 February 2011 the UN Security Council unanimously passed Resolution 1970 condemning human rights abuses, imposing an arms embargo, a travel ban and asset seizures on named regime officials along with other sanctions, also referring the situation to the International Criminal Court. Gaddafi was not deterred and as his troops approached Benghazi threats of extreme retaliation against its population were made, along with the use of extreme language ('cockroaches' and the like) to characterise the opposition. Perhaps these threats were simply rhetorical, but opposition forces in Benghazi had good reason to be concerned given the regime's record in dealing with dissent, and the possibility of a mass atrocity seemed high.

On 17 March 2011, Resolution 1973, proposed by Britain, France and the Lebanon and with the support of the Arab League and the African Union, passed in the Security Council by 10 votes to 0 with 5 abstentions (Russia, China, Brazil, South Africa and, somewhat strangely, Germany); 1973 reaffirmed the responsibility of the Libyan authorities to protect their civilian population and abide by international humanitarian law but, crucially, also called on member states to take 'all necessary measures' (including a no-fly zone, but explicitly excluding a foreign occupation force) to protect civilians and enforce sanctions. On 19 March air-strikes began, and on 31 March NATO took control of the operation – the initial airstrike to disarm regime air defences was carried out by the US, thereafter European NATO members took over, albeit with US assistance on targeting and resupply. Air-power prevented the fall of Benghazi, but NATO soon interpreted its mandate rather more widely than had been intended by some of those who voted for, or abstained, on UNSC Resolution 1973 and in effect acted as the air arm of the opposition, whose ground forces were armed and trained by NATO and some Gulf States, and, perhaps, assisted covertly by Arab Special Forces from Qatar, the UAE and Jordan. In any event, in late August Tripoli fell to the opposition, and on 20 October Gadaffi was captured and killed by opposition forces.

This small-scale tragi-comedy provides a wealth of material for contemplation on the concept of Responsibility to Protect (e.g. Hehir, 2013; Kuperman, 2013; *Ethics & International Affairs*, 2011). The initial reaction was that this was Responsibility to Protect as intended by the ICISS, with action authorised by the Security Council, as a last resort, and in response to a clear threat of a 'mass atrocity crime'. However, this sense of optimism soon dissipated. The use of air-power to establish a no-fly zone involved a bombing campaign to disarm Gaddafi's air force and ground-to-air defences, and inevitably the image of Western planes bombing Arab targets – however careful they were to avoid civilian casualties – went down very badly in the Global South. Brazil's introduction of the notion of 'Responsibility While Protecting' in a speech by Brazilian

President Dilma Rousseff at the opening of the 66th UN General Assembly in September 2011 reflected this sentiment, although since Resolution 1973 explicitly forbade the introduction of an occupation force of ground troops it is difficult to see how civilians could be protected without using air-power against the regime. More important in the long run were two other factors; the expansion of the mandate provided by Resolution 1973, and the selective nature of the campaign against Gaddafi, given that no such effort was launched to protect the peoples of Syria, Bahrain or the Yemen.

Resolution 1973 called for the protection of civilians, and NATO's official position was that it was prepared to use airpower to prevent both regime and rebel forces from attacking civilians. This was disingenuous – in effect NATO interpreted Resolution 1973 as giving support for regime change, on the principle that getting rid of Gaddafi was the best, perhaps only, way to protect the Libyan people. Russia and China – who had abstained on Resolution 1973 rather than cast their customary veto on intervention, largely because of pressure from Arab and African states – now expressed regret for their acquiescence in the action, and made it clear that in future they would not support such resolutions. South Africa likewise withdrew its support from the operation once the Libyan opposition refused the good offices of the African Union unless Gaddafi left the country (Alden and Schoeman, 2013; de Waal, 2013).

On the issue of selectivity, clearly Russia and China were not in favour of further interventions – and have vetoed Resolutions on Syria in 2011, again in 2012 on 4 February, in the latter case being the only two votes cast against a resolution calling on Assad to step down, and yet again in a minority of two on 19 July 2012 – but they, and other critics, have used the double-standards argument to critique the different approaches of the West to events in Libya and, say, Bahrain. The latter is the home to the US 5th Fleet and a crucial Western naval base, which has undoubtedly influenced Western action, or more accurately inaction, in regard to the repression of its majority Shia population. It is perhaps worth making the point that Gaddafi was also a de facto ally of the West prior to the spring of 2011, as a result of his surrender of chemical and biological weapons in 2004 – but his strategic significance was much less than that of the rulers of Bahrain, who had the backing of Saudi Arabia, another key Western ally in the region.

The case of Syria will be discussed below, but for the time being what is significant is the extent to which the events in Libya and in other parts of the Arab world bear out elements of the critique of the notion of Responsibility to Protect presented above. The point was made there that the ICISS Report attempted to treat 'protection' as something that could be considered in an apolitical manner and that this simply would not do. The fate of Resolution 1973 confirms this diagnosis. The Resolution seems to have been voted for by some members of the Security Council, South Africa in particular, precisely on the basis that it was in some way possible to protect the Libyan people without interfering in the politics of Libya; a moment's thought would reveal that this was obvious nonsense. Gaddafi wanted to re-establish control over Benghazi and NATO were preventing him from doing so; it is hard to see how that could be described as anything other than a political act and a direct intervention into the internal affairs of Libya – which, of course, is not to say that it was not justified, rather the point is that sometimes a spade has to be called a spade.

Once NATO's air-power had intervened and stabilised the front-line outside Benghazi it would, perhaps, have been possible to think about negotiating a settlement with the regime. That was the South African position, and the African Union delegation led by President Jacob Zuma did indeed gain Gaddafi's consent to a truce in April 2011 – but the opposition made it a condition that Gaddafi leave the country and the deal fell through. Clearly the opposition felt a distinct – and understandable – lack of trust in anything Gaddafi agreed to, and were aware that they had the support of the Western powers in adopting this stance. Apart from threatening the Libyan opposition, Gaddafi had threatened to 'go crazy' in the Mediterranean if the Europeans supported the rebels, and there was every reason to take this threat seriously given past atrocities attributed to the Libyan 'brother leader'. In effect, once the intervention took place, regime change was certain to be the order of the day – the politics of the situation demanded the end of Gaddafi's rule.

In fact, what we can see in Libya in 2011 is the playing out of a logic that had been demonstrated in Bosnia in the 1990s, this time speeded up over a few months rather than four or five years. Intervention in Bosnia began as a neutral operation to provide humanitarian aid protected by the UN (UNPROFOR, the UN Protection Force), but it gradually became apparent that neutrality wasn't actually an option. If side A is trying to starve side B, and is in a position to do so, then providing food to both sides is, in effect, an intervention which benefits B and disadvantages A; A will resist this kind of intervention. In the case of Bosnia, the failure of neutrality became too obvious to ignore after the fall of Srebrenica and NATO intervened on behalf of the Bosnian Government, who were usually the 'side B' in the above equation. In Libya in 2011 NATO did not wait to be taught this lesson – right from the beginning its leaders understood that this was an intervention that had to end with the departure of Gaddafi, one way or another, and if that meant surreptitiously arming the opposition, so be it.

Again, the belief that it is possible to approach the reaction to humanitarian crises in a politically neutral way, such that it is illegitimate to be 'selective' in determining where interventions take place is another manifestation of the antipolitical nature of the thinking behind Responsibility to Protect. States, like persons, have projects which they do not abandon simply because the kind of situation where the Responsibility to Protect is invoked is taking place. The United States has interests in the Middle East which it believes require it to preserve a secure naval base in the Gulf; regrettably all of the Gulf states with suitable port facilities are, to one degree or another, somewhat repressive and in

2011 oppression in Bahrain certainly went up a notch or two – hardly the site of a 'mass atrocity crime' but certainly the site of serious human rights violations. Very likely there was, behind the scenes, pressure from the US to end the oppression, but the 5th Fleet did not get up steam and sail away, and US Marines were not sent ashore to protect the population from their rulers. In any event the rulers of the Gulf states were providing essential assistance in Libya, making it even less likely that there would be effective action against them. Just as intervention is always a political act, so it always takes place in the context of a broader understanding of the general state of global politics. In the case of Libya there were no compelling political reasons not to intervene, given the nature of the Libyan regime, its lack of friends within the Arab world, or anywhere else, and the relative ease with which it was anticipated, rightly, that an intervention could be conducted.

In other areas the calculation pointed in a different direction. One can argue about whether the calculation was performed correctly in all such cases – perhaps more could have been done in Bahrain – but the idea that there should be no calculation at all doesn't make sense. Tony Blair got this right in his Chicago Speech setting out his *Doctrine of the International Community*; the fifth of his 'major considerations which have to be taken into account before intervening' was 'do we have national interests involved'. From the perspective of the doctrine of Responsibility to Protect, references to the national interest are unacceptable, but Blair's formulation stays in touch with the realities of global politics in a way that the ICISS Report does not. States do not simply clear their in-trays and abandon all other considerations when faced with gross violations of human rights – even when the atrocities in question are worse than they were in 2011 – and it is implausible to expect that they will do so. As Blair recognised in 1999, but the ICISS Report did not in 2001, altruism alone is a poor basis for expecting action in world politics.

Returning to the Libyan case, an assessment in terms of the 'three pillars' of the 2009 Report tells a sobering story. The first pillar concerns the protection responsibilities of the state, and it is very clear that Gaddafi's regime had been failing to meet these responsibilities for four decades, and that the international community had known this and largely stayed silent – indeed, after 2004 when Gaddafi gave up his WMD programme, he was actively courted by the international community, the grotesque features of his regime were dismissed as amusing eccentricities and the severe repression was ignored. To take one, very sad, example, his famous corps of female bodyguards were a source of amusement to visitors and observers; it now turns out that these unfortunate women were kidnapped, forced to join Gaddafi's harem and systematically raped by the 'brother leader' and his supporters (Cojean, 2013). The world did nothing to help opponents of the regime until 2011, and although then there was, perhaps, a timely response as called for by pillar three, the assistance and capacity building mandated by pillar two has been conspicuously absent. Partly because Resolution 1973 expressly prohibited any kind of occupation by external ground troops, the situation in Libya post-Gaddafi remains near anarchy. Libya in 2011 can only be seen as a success for Responsibility to Protect from a very limited perspective – at least a tyrant has been overthrown, and the Libyan people have a chance of putting together a better future.

The situation in Syria puts the Libyan case into another perspective. Here what began as repression of dissent has turned into a multi-faceted civil war, which has taken the lives of over 100,000 people and turned perhaps half the population of Syria into refugees. External powers have certainly intervened in the crisis – Russia and Iran in support of President Assad, Turkey, Qatar, Saudi Arabia, and more gingerly, the West in support of various factions amongst the rebels – but there has been no concerted intervention by the Security Council under the auspices of the Responsibility to Protect. As noted above, even resolutions not containing words which might sanction armed intervention have been vetoed by Russia and China (Bellamy, 2014). And, although in the summer of 2013 it seemed for a while that there would be an armed response to the use of chemical weapons by the Assad regime, even on that limited issue the will was not present for a non-UN sanctioned intervention, and the situation was resolved by a compromise that removed the chemical weapons while allowing the regime to continue fighting with conventional arms.

The most obvious reasons for this lack of action have already been discussed. Unlike Colonel Gaddafi, President Assad has powerful friends who will arm him and block moves against him; he also has a capable air force and good air defence systems – NATO could overcome these, but it would not be the one-sided affair that Libya was. In Libya the opposition forces had a geographical base in the east of the country which could be defended by air-power, whereas in Syria the opposition were to be found in pockets throughout the country, including in the suburbs of Damascus itself. Perhaps also the rhythm of the conflict made intervention less likely; in the early months it seemed very likely that Assad would fall without Western action, and by the time that it was clear that this was not going to be the case the opposition had fractured and radical Islamic groups had come to the fore. In short, there are many reasons why the international community has not acted in Syria – but none of them take away from the sense that there is something shameful about such a prolonged conflict persisting without effective action to bring it to a close.

The Responsibility to Protect and the International Criminal Court

Before moving to an overall assessment of the doctrine of Responsibility to Protect there is one further issue that is of some significance in terms of the overall theme of this book, the putative shift between a society of states and a global polity, and that is the relationship between R2P and the development of international criminal law. As was set out in Chapter 5, the development of international criminal law is one of the features of the emergent global polity, and the notion of individual criminal responsibility clearly has some connection to the idea of sovereignty as responsibility and the responsibility to protect. If under the putative new normative framework of international relations it is agreed that states have responsibilities towards their citizens then if the individuals whose duty it is to discharge this responsibility fail to act upon that duty, or blatantly act against it, it follows that they should be held criminally responsible for their misdeeds. Such is the position set out in the Rome Statute of the International Criminal Court – the interesting question is how this notion of criminal responsibility fits within the three pillars of the Responsibility to Protect? One answer to this question is, very uneasily. The argument here is that there is a potential clash between the requirements of peace and those of justice (Snyder and Vinjamuri, 2004).

Consider, for example, the decision of the ICC Chief Prosecutor to issue indictments against President Bashir of Sudan during the Darfur crisis, and against Colonel Gaddafi and his son Saif al-Islam Gaddafi in Libya in 2011. The argument goes that these indictments, rather than undermining these individuals actually stiffened their resolve by making it more difficult for them to compromise, or take their ill-gotten gains into exile. The spectacle of a tyrant enjoying a well-funded exile, living off the proceeds of exploitation, is not very attractive, but may be preferable to the costs of a continuing conflict. In fact, it is not at all clear that the ICC's indictments did have that effect – Bashir is, after all, still President of the Sudan, and Gaddafi's decision not to go into exile does not seem to have been based on fear of the ICC; indeed, his son Saif was, allegedly, trying to find a way to surrender to the Court when he was taken prisoner by the militias. But in other contexts, indictments issued by the Court may have made things more difficult, and the fact that once issued an indictment cannot be withdrawn adds to the complication.

The first Chief Prosecutor of the ICC, the Argentinian human rights lawyer Luis Moreno Ocampo took a hard line on such matters, arguing that justice was what was important and that the kind of crimes dealt with by the ICC were of such a serious nature that they transcended the political needs of conflict-resolution in any particular context. A crime against humanity was just that, against humanity and not against the country in which it was committed, and if prosecuting such a crime had adverse consequences then that was regrettable, but a price worth paying in the long run. His successor in the post since June 2012, Fatou Bensouda of the Gambia appears to take a less rigid approach to the issue. She has made it clear that in her view the ICC should develop a close relationship with the Security Council and that the pursuit of justice cannot be seen as entirely independent of the needs of peace. This seems sensible, even if the pristine purity of Ocampo's position did have the virtue of stressing the independence of the Court, and the aligning of the Court with the Security Council adds evidence in support of those who argue that the doctrine of Responsibility to Protect is providing a blueprint for an undemocratic, bureaucratic form of global governance.

Conclusion: The future of Responsibility to Protect

Where does the notion of Responsibility to Protect go from here? Two propositions seem clear – unfortunately they point in different directions, so answering this question is not going to be easy. On the one hand, it is clear that the notion of Responsibility to Protect has been mainstreamed into the UN system to such an extent that it has driven out other vocabularies for describing the appropriate ways of reacting to gross violations of human rights or mass atrocity crimes. Those supporting or calling for intervention in such circumstances will, in future, be obliged to employ this rhetoric; the language of humanitarian intervention is no longer employable by those wishing to save strangers. For better or worse, the notion of 'sovereignty as responsibility' is now orthodox within the UN system.

On the other hand, the political future of Responsibility to Protect looks less rosy. Although Russia and China accepted the wording of the World Summit Final Document in 2005, and abstained on UNSC 1973, their current position is best summarised as 'once bitten, twice shy'. Over the last two decades they have consistently taken the view that interventions in the internal affairs of UN members are illegitimate; in 2011 they were persuaded by allies in the Global South not to veto the key Libyan Resolution and more or less immediately came to regret this deviation from their usual practice. Their willingness to find themselves on the wrong end of a 13 to 2 vote on Syria in the Security Council in February 2012 (and an 11 to 2 vote in July 2012) suggests that even in the most propitious circumstances they are unlikely again to allow collective enforcement action to be legitimised. However, what is more damaging to the political feasibility of the concept of a Responsibility to Protect is the repeated failure of its advocates to convince the Global South, and in particular the emerging powers, India, Brazil and South Africa as well as China, that this doctrine is anything other than a rebranding of the idea of humanitarian intervention. It is striking that although these states, unlike Russia and China, have been willing to call for President Assad to leave Syria, they have made it very clear that they would not support a direct intervention to bring about his expulsion.

Here we return to the origins of the notion; the aim of the ICISS Report was to replace the idea of a 'right to intervene' with that of a 'responsibility to protect', to take the issue of dealing with mass atrocity crimes out of the realm of world politics and place it in a more elevated context where political considerations will no longer apply. In the twelve years since the Report the major Western powers have given lip-service to this ambition, while *sotto voce* reserving to themselves the right to decide when it will be applied. The Global South, on the other hand, has never accepted that this replacement has actually taken place. The third of Gareth Evans's five major misunderstandings, referred to above, is 'that R2P only applies to weak and friendless countries, never strong ones' (p. 56) – but, far from being a misunderstanding, this is a cold truth about world politics, and if the advocates of Responsibility to Protect do not understand this, countries in the Global South most certainly do.

So what can we expect in the future? The answer is probably some version of 'business as usual' for the twenty-first century. Atrocities will happen and, unlike, for example, the situation with regard to Rwanda in 1994, usually the new social media will combine with advances in news-gathering to ensure that the world knows about them in real-time. This will guarantee that the familiar cry of 'something must be done' will be heard, and those states that are actually in a position to do something will be forced to be engaged with the problem, whether they wish to be or not – again, the Syrian conflict illustrates the point. Still, they will, as always, calculate their response in terms not of an abstract principle but of the national interest and act accordingly; inaction will be justi-fied by the lack of a Security Council Resolution, but if the calculation leads to action then, miraculously, some way past this obstacle will be found. The value of a principle such as the Responsibility to Protect lies not in its capacity to determine action on its own by taking the matter out of the realm of political calculation but in the way that, as the doctrine becomes widely accepted, it may actually feed in to the calculation of the national interest. Or, to put the matter differently, the future of Responsibility to Protect depends on its ability to tran-scend its anti-political ambitions and become part of the framework of world and national politics, such that states may define their 'national interests' as encompassing a concern for the victims of crimes against humanity. In this way, somewhat paradoxically, the hopes and desires of the promoters of Responsibility to Protect may actually be met even though the de-politicised conception of protection they incorporated in the doctrine has failed to take hold.

Further Reading

For the Kosovo campaign Lawrence Freedman (2000) and Ivo Daalder and Michael O'Hanlon (2000) are key references – Daalder and O'Hanlon's title, *Winning Ugly* tells the story in two words. Booth (2000b) explores the human rights dimension of the conflict. The *Report of the Independent International Commission on Kosovo* did its best to provide a neutral account of the rights and wrongs of the war, coming down with the controversial verdict 'illegal but legitimate'. The Report is available here: http://reliefweb.int/sites/reliefweb.int/files/resources/F62789D9FCC56FB3C1256C1700303E3B-thekosovoreport.htm. Lawyers such as Simon Chesterman (2001) are predictably unhappy with such a verdict, as are the opponents of (alleged) Western imperialism, see e.g. Noam Chomsky (1999).

The *International Commission on Intervention and State Sovereignty* was a Canadian Government initiative, welcomed by the UN – see the Canadian Government website which has links to the Report and its appendices – the appendices are a mine of useful information on thinking about intervention in the 1990s www.cfr.org/humanitarian-intervention/international-commission-intervention-state-sovereignty-responsibility-protect-report/p24228. The Report's proposal, to recognise a 'Responsibility to Protect' has been mainstreamed into the UN system after the World Summit of 2005 – see www.un.org/en/preventgenocide/adviser/responsibility.shtml and has generated an International Coalition of Supporters whose website is a great source of useful information – see www.responsibilitytoprotect.org/. Very influential on the ICISS's work was the thinking of Francis Deng on 'sovereignty as responsibility', Francis Deng et al. (1996).

The initial reception of the ICISS Report was overshadowed by 9/11 and the Iraq War of 2003. The argument that the latter could be seen as a humanitarian intervention was made by some – see Christopher Hitchens (2003) (and Simon Cottee and Thomas Cushman's (2008) collection on Hitchens) and, more scholarly, but less fun, see Fernando Tesón (2005a) and (2005b) and the collection edited by Thomas Cushman (2005); opinion was overwhelmingly against this reading of the conflict – for a crisp riposte to Tesón, see Terry Nardin (2005).

The partial adoption of the principle of a Responsibility to Protect in the *World Summit Outcome Document* 2005 has generated a very large literature. Book-length studies that are required reading include Alex Bellamy (2009), Gareth Evans (2008b), Aidan Hehir (2012), Anne Orford (2011) and James Pattison (2010) – of these Bellamy and Pattison are the most balanced, Evans is the most favourable to R2P, Orford the least, and Hehir regrets the lack of ambition of R2P advocates. The *Journal of Intervention and Peacebuilding* generally prints articles critical of R2P – see e.g. the Special Issue Vol. 4, 1, 2010 – while *Global Responsibility to Protect*, is more favourable to the concept. Noteworthy articles on R2P include Louise Arbour (2008) – but see the sharp response by Stephanie Carvin (2010a) – David Chandler (2010), Thomas Weiss (2007) and numerous articles by Jennifer Welsh, the new Special Representative for R2P to the Secretary General of the UN – see Welsh (2002), (2007) and (2010a) and (2010b).

(Continued)

(Continued)

The action in Libya in 2011 has generated a great deal of literature, and more will have been published by the time this guide is read. Aidan Hehir and Robert Murray (2013) is an early monograph; the *Ethics & International Affairs* Roundtable Vol. 23 (3) in the Autumn of 2011 brought together Alex Bellamy, Simon Chesterman, James Pattison, Thomas Weiss and Jennifer Welsh – a dream team who make this the first port of call for thinking about Libya and R2P, although it was published before the consequences of the intervention could be assessed. Other post-Libya articles of interest include Alex Bellamy (2014), Chris Brown (2013b) and Aidan Hehir (2013), but this is an area where an avalanche of books and articles is on the horizon so there is no substitute for a search of the relevant journals.

9

THE ETHICS OF WAR AND VIOLENCE IN A POST-WESTPHALIAN AGE

War once was an institution of the society of states, a recognised method of conflict resolution between legal equals, and it was regulated (very imperfectly) by the Laws of War (International Humanitarian Law) which were in turn based in part on the principles of the Just War which were first established by Medieval Christian theologians. In the modern world many of the terms that appear in this sentence are no longer valid. War is no longer accepted as a legitimate conflict-resolving mechanism, and it is rarely engaged in by juridical equals; violence is still a feature of international politics but in the emerging global polity it only rarely takes the form of conventional inter-state war – instead we have the kind of 'humanitarian' wars discussed in the last two chapters, alongside asymmetric conflicts between states and national- or religious-based movements, conflicts which over the last decade and half have been summarised under the rubric of the 'global war on terror'. Wars are no longer the international equivalent of a duel, a formalised conflict between legal equals, and the kind of regulations summarised in International Humanitarian Law are much more difficult to sustain. On the other hand, although Just War thinking has developed over the last 300 years in the context of inter-state conflict, as we have seen, the standard categories for analysis – proper authority, right intention, just cause – date back to a pre-Westphalian age, and may still be appropriate (Johnson, 2001; Bellamy, 2006; Brown, 2013a). In much of what follows in this chapter, such categories will be applied to such iconic modern issues as drone warfare, targeted killing and 'enhanced interrogation techniques', but first it may be useful to rehearse the conditions under which restraints in inter-state war emerged and were sustained – this may help to show why such restraint is more difficult to achieve in the modern world.

The laws of war have never been wholly effective; but when they have worked to restrain the behaviour of combatants it is because they have been underpinned by the interaction of four general principles; the 'golden rule', immediate reciprocity, the 'shadow of the future' and military necessity. The 'golden rule' refers to the widespread existence of common ideas about fairness and right and wrong conduct; this may seem rather insubstantial in the context of the systematic application of violence but there is a great deal of evidence to the effect that soldiers in conventional wars do have clear ideas of right and wrong which influence their behaviour. Soldiers do not want to think of themselves as killers, and adherence to a moral code is one way in which that label can be set aside; such a code may be taught via international humanitarian law, but ultimately it rests on the soldier's sense of common morality. Immediate reciprocity is connected to the golden rule – the latter is sometimes summarised as 'do as you would be done by', and soldiers are very conscious of the application of this principle to their situation. Soldiers are much more likely to obey the laws of war if they believe that the opposition will do likewise, and the moral economy of the soldier is far more sensitive to this principle than it is to lectures on what ought to happen. The 'shadow of the future' refers to the behaviour of leaders rather than individual soldiers, and points to the assumption that wars end, and that peaceful relations with the current enemy will someday be desirable – hence the need not to do anything now, such as ill-treatment of prisoners, that would damage the possibility of future peaceful relations. Finally, military necessity provides a counterpoint to each of these principles; this is tricky notion, because if military necessity is regarded as capable of trumping all the other principles then there would be no laws of war – on the other hand, clearly, the resort to force takes place because something important is at stake, the achievement of which is unlikely to be compromised by too nice an attitude towards the rules.

The influence of these features is never unambiguous or uncomplicated, but in the humanitarian wars and asymmetric conflicts of the modern era it has become particularly problematic. The shadow of the future is very short indeed when the aim is to eliminate the enemy, not simply to defeat them; although in the past peace has actually often been made with so-called terrorists, this tends to be forgotten in the current war on terror – and with some reason since a peaceful future with non-state groups like Al Qaeda is difficult to imagine. Nationalists who engage in terror such as the Irish Revolutionary Army may be brought to the table and a compromise struck, as has happened in Northern Ireland, but it is difficult to imagine what kind of bargain could be struck with Islamic radicals whose territorial claims are hazy at best. Again, common morality and the golden rule may not actually apply when one or both of the combatants believe themselves to be inspired by God and believe the enemy to be the devil incarnate. In such circumstances, even if one side believes itself bound by the rules of war, it may find it difficult to act accordingly if it knows that the other side would not reciprocate. In a recent Court Martial in the UK where a British marine was convicted of shooting a prisoner, the marine was captured on tape acknowledging that he'd just broken the Geneva Convention, but also saying, correctly, that 'he'd have done the same to us' – the lack of reciprocity does not justify breaking the rules but it goes some way towards explaining why the rules are broken. In short, if wars are fought to bring about, or to prevent, ethnic cleansing, or against 'terrorists' or 'crusaders', neither of whom are seen as legitimate enemies, then many of the normal factors that produce some degree of restraint in war cannot be relied upon.

In addition, modern technologies of violence complicate things even further. In the first place, small groups of people can do very large amounts of damage, either by putting the technologies of peace to destructive ends, as was the case on 9/11 2001, or by weaponising such technologies, as is the case with chemical and biological weapons, or the use of malevolent computer software. Such threats are difficult to deal with and may produce counter-terrorism tactics that are as worrying as the threats that they are designed to combat. But, second, conventional militaries now increasingly employ technologies that undermine the possibility of restraint built on the notion of a 'warrior ethos'; the phenomenon of killing at a distance is obviously not new, but drone warfare takes it to a new level, making it possible to kill without any risk of being killed, a possibility which certainly undermines mutual respect between combatants.

All these factors make it difficult to produce a modern ethics of war and violence, which has even the limited effectiveness of older notions of international humanitarian law. In what follows in this chapter, the focus will be first on a number of specifically modern problems and then on some general considerations of contemporary Just War theory.

Non-combatant immunity: Unlawful combatants

One of the main aims of International Humanitarian Law, as set out in the *Geneva Convention* of 1949 and Protocols I & II to the Convention of 1977 is to protect persons taking no direct part in hostilities (including prisoners of war) – i.e. non-combatant immunity – and to define the rights of combatants. Initially this referred to combatants in international conflicts, but one of the points of the Protocols to the Convention of 1977 was to extend the same kind of protection to combatants in non-international armed conflicts – thus, what used to be the 'laws of war' is now properly referred to as the 'law of armed conflict', and such requirements for combatant status as, for example, the wearing of a distinctive uniform, have now been relaxed somewhat. The legal notion of non-combatant immunity is a crude way of translating the moral principle that innocence should not be violated into something with practical application, and it has sometimes been challenged because of this crudity, the argument being that some non-combatants are not in fact 'innocent' at all, but the general principle that it is important to discriminate between those who are, and those who are not legitimate targets in war has rarely been challenged. Unfortunately, this situation has now changed, and this principle is sometimes challenged, and its application has become increasingly difficult as the line between combatant and non-combatant has become more blurred even than in the past.

As to straightforward challenges to the principle of non-combatant immunity, a good starting point might be Al Qaeda's Second Fatwa of 23 February 1998, in effect declaring a holy war against America and its allies. After rehearsing the sins of the 'Crusader-Zionist Alliance', in particular the stationing of troops in the Arabian Peninsula, and declaring these sins a clear declaration of war on God, the statement continues:

> On that basis, and in compliance with God's order, we issue the following fatwa to all Muslims: The ruling to kill the Americans and their allies – civilians and military – is an individual duty for every Muslim who can do it in any country in which it is possible to do it, in order to liberate the al-Aqsa Mosque and the holy mosque [Mecca] from their grip, and in order for their armies to move out of all the lands of Islam, defeated and unable to threaten any Muslim. (www.pbs.org/newshour/updates/military-jan-june98-fatwa_1998/)

The thinking behind this is that the Americans and their allies are to be killed not on the basis of their status as combatants or potential combatants, but because they are American or allied to America; the distinction between civilian and military is explicitly ignored in the Fatwa – they are to be killed 'all together'. The most dramatic cashing out of this position came on 11th September 2001. Even if, by the exercise of a certain amount of mental gymnastics, the civilian and military workers who were attacked in the Pentagon could be regarded as combatants, that status clearly did not apply to the workers in the World Trade Center, or the passengers on American Airlines Flights 11 and 77, and United Airlines Flights 175 and 93. They were regarded as legitimate targets simply on the basis that they were American or working in America.

This was a clear breach of international law, a crime against humanity, and recognised as such by, for example, the UN Security Council and by nearly all governments, but most of the difficulties with non-combatant immunity are nowhere near as clear cut, and are created, not by a wilful refusal to recognise the status of non-combatant, but by the genuine difficulty there sometimes is in recognising practical applications of the principle. Consider, for example, the employment of civilians as so-called 'human shields' to protect military installations or to protect actual fighters. International humanitarian law is relatively clear on this matter; using civilians in this way is illegal, a war crime, and the responsibility for any harm that comes to them lies with those who placed them in this situation. But although the use of force in such circumstances may be legal, modern armies, acting under the scrutiny of global media and world public opinion, and unwilling to deliver death to the innocent may well refrain from acting. In short, the employment of human shields is actually a very effective military tactic against an army that attempts to draw a distinction between combatants and non-combatants. But from the point of view of this discussion what is interesting is whether this is actually a case of the misuse of the principle of non-combatant immunity or whether the 'civilians' who make up the human shield are, actually, combatants.

To bring home the point, consider an actual example, reported by Michael Gross (Gross, 2009, 2013). During Operation Cast Lead, the Israeli response to shellfire from Gaza at the end of 2008, at one point the Israeli army identified a particular block of flats as being used as a command post by Hamas fighters – since it was also occupied by civilians, the Israelis telephoned the inhabitants to warn them to leave because the block was about to be attacked. Instead, the inhabitants poured on to the roof believing, correctly, that this would deter the Israelis from attacking. This could be read in one of two ways, posing two different questions: first, if we assume that this was a spontaneous action by the inhabitants of the block of flats, have they made themselves combatants thereby? Second, should we think about things differently if they were actually herded onto the roof by Hamas militants? Had the Israelis attacked civilians would have been killed and this would have generated a lot of bad publicity, but it is by no means clear that the civilians were actually innocent victims as opposed to active participants in a conflict. The moral of the story is that identifying those entitled to the protection of the norm of non-combatant immunity is difficult even for those who take the norm seriously.

This story will be continued later in in this chapter in the context of putative civilians killed by drone attacks, but here another blurring of the distinction between combatant and non-combatant will briefly be considered. During the wars in Afghanistan and Iraq, the United States initially declared that some of the prisoners they had taken were 'unlawful combatants' and therefore not entitled to the protection of the Geneva Conventions. In fact, under pressure from their own military lawyers who were afraid of the precedent they might be creating the US soon went back on this position and gave these combatants their Geneva rights, but it was not wholly unreasonable to draw attention to the difficulty of categorising some of those taken prisoner. Consider, for example, the standing of a British citizen, a Muslim who has travelled to Afghanistan in order to engage in combat against NATO forces in that country, forces he regards as Crusaders attacking his Muslim brethren (disregarding the inconvenient fact that many Muslims in Afghanistan are actually fighting for the Afghan Government, alongside NATO and against the Taliban). This foreign fighter is clearly not a bandit or criminal in any normal sense of the term, but neither is he a member of a recognised national force – 'unlawful combatant' is an unfortunate description if it is meant to imply that he has no protection under the Geneva Convention, but then it is quite difficult to see how such a figure ought to be characterised. He is a prisoner of war, but even that anodyne description carries with it implications that may not apply in this case; normally, prisoners of war are released when the war is over, but what would count as the war being over in this case? The problem in all these cases is that the moral language we have doesn't quite fit the new circumstances of armed conflict in the twenty-first century, and although international humanitarian law can be made to apply in these anomalous cases the fit is very imperfect, and leads to a general sense of dissatisfaction.

Torture and rendition

One of the most disturbing features of the Global War on Terror has been the way that prohibitions on torture have been violated by participants on both sides of the 'war'. This is an area of international law that until the last decade or so was regarded as relatively clear-cut and settled. The *Convention against Torture and Other Cruel, Inhuman or Degrading Treatment or Punishment* which entered into force on 26 June 1987 in Article 1 defines torture as follows:

> For the purposes of this Convention, the term 'torture' means any act by which severe pain or suffering, whether physical or mental, is intentionally inflicted on a person for such purposes as obtaining from him or a third person information or a confession, punishing him for an act he or a third person has committed or is suspected of having committed, or intimidating or coercing him or a third person, or for any reason based on discrimination of any kind ...

Two points should be made here: first, many lawyers would argue that there was already a peremptory norm against torture and that the Convention merely codifies this norm, but, second, in spite of this norm and the Convention many states have used torture more or less routinely and continue to do so – the fact that there is a strong international norm barring torture doesn't of itself prevent the practice. Still, torture has certainly been regarded as a blot on the international standing of the states that employ it, and the latter are usually very unwilling to admit that they actually do so.

The War on Terror changed the situation here quite dramatically. In the first place, groups such as Al Qaeda and the Taliban routinely tortured prisoners, and made no secret of the fact that they were doing so – witness the proliferation of videos showing the decapitation of their opponents. More disturbing, because more unexpected, during the first Bush Administration, the US openly acknowledged that it was using what it called 'enhanced interrogation techniques';

these included 'waterboarding' (inducing the sensation of drowning by immersing the victim), a technique that when it was employed by the Gestapo in the Second World War was certainly regarded as torture (Bowden, 2003). Moreover, some persons suspected of terrorist offences were subject to rendition to 'black sites' beyond the jurisdiction of the US Constitution or the European Convention on Human Rights, or to third parties, allies of America who were less prone to engage in euphemisms when employing torture.

These practices were, of course, intensely controversial. The US Administration for a time held that these practices did not amount to torture because they did not cause lasting physical damage, a very poor argument given the definition cited above. More to the point, the Administration argued that these practices extracted information that could not be achieved in any other way and that lives would be saved thereby. This was a position that did attract some support. A stock question in applied ethics is based on the 'ticking bomb scenario'; suppose it were known with certainty that a bomb was planted in the city which would explode in a few hours and that the only way in which this bomb could be found would be by extracting the information from the person who placed it – would torture then be justified? Most writers either argue that the scenario is wholly artificial (how could one 'know with certainty' these things?), or that torture should not be employed even if the scenario is believable (Ginbar, 2008). However, some argue on consequentialist grounds that torture would be justified in such circumstances – famously, or perhaps infamously, the celebrity lawyer and Harvard Professor Alan Dershowitz argued that the practice should be regularised, and that judges should be able to issue 'torture warrants' which would prevent the unauthorised and excessive employment of torture, a proposal roundly condemned by most other commentators (2002).

In so far as it is possible at all to make a case for torture, it is the argument summarised by the term 'dirty hands' that best does the job. This position, which has a long history, has in recent times been articulated most clearly by Michael Walzer in an article by that name in *Philosophy and Public Affairs* in 1973. He argues that sometimes a person in a position of authority may find that the exercise of that authority requires them to get their hands dirty by doing something that they acknowledge breaks the moral code (Walzer, 1973). Paradoxically, doing something wrong might be the right thing to do, all things considered. A 'ticking bomb' scenario might be one such situation, and in *Just and Unjust Wars*, Walzer refers to a situation of 'supreme emergency' that might justify breaking the rules – the specific case he discusses is whether the deliberate bombing of German cities and civilians might have been justified had that been the only way to prevent the supreme disaster of a Nazi victory (which he acknowledges was not the case). Walzer is clear that a 'dirty hands' argument can only be made in extreme cases, but also that individuals who get their hands dirty in this way must be prepared to answer for what they have done in a court of law or if this is not feasible in the court of public opinion.

Is there actually any evidence that 'enhanced interrogation techniques' (EITs) have produced the goods, that is actually prevented terrorist attacks or led to the capture or killing of terrorists? The film *Zero Dark Thirty* sparked a debate along these lines by suggesting that the trail that led to Osama Bin Laden's hideout in Abbottabad in Pakistan began with acts of torture. Interestingly, some ex-CIA officials who had operated interrogation programmes denied that such a direct link could be found, though they acknowledged that indirectly torture had been significant in intelligence collection. The aim of EITs was to break the will to resist of prisoners, to get them to co-operate in general terms rather than to extract specific nuggets of information. Specific pieces of information might actually emerge in this way as a by-product of the process rather than as its direct aim – and it seems that this is actually relevant to the Bin Laden case; it was casual references by prisoners to a 'courier' that put the CIA on the track of the person who handled messages for Bin Laden.

The discussion between the ex-CIA interrogators yielded one other insight. The use of EITs lessened under the second Bush Administration, partly because other methods of intelligence gathering were more effective, and was ended altogether by President Obama as one of the first acts of his Presidency in 2009. The interrogators argued that one by-product of this decision was to increase dramatically the programme of targeted killing that has been a trademark of the Obama Administration's conduct of the War on Terror. In effect, once it was no longer possible to break the will of terrorists by the use of enhanced interrogation, the value of prisoners plummeted. The interrogators argued that the religious convictions of the terrorists meant that they were unlikely to co-operate unless they could tell themselves that they had been forced to do so and so taking them prisoner without that possibility was simply to store up a rod for one's back, especially since it was also an ambition of the Obama Administration, as yet unfulfilled, to close the camp at Guantanamo where the prisoners would be held. Better to eliminate them altogether.

Targeted killing and drone warfare

Drones (more properly, Unmanned Aerial Vehicles, UAVs) can be used for surveillance, and targeted assassinations can be carried out by manned warplanes or special forces, but still the association of this technology with that tactic does accurately summarise a distinctive feature of the Obama Administration's conduct of the War on Terror. By the summer of 2013 President Obama had authorised over 400 drone strikes since he came into office, targeting high profile Al Qaeda and Taliban leaders or technical specialists such as bomb-makers or propaganda experts in Pakistan, Yemen and Somalia, with an estimated 3,000 operatives killed, including 50 high-level leaders (Byman,

2013). So-called 'signature strikes' have also been conducted, in which groups of individuals who are suspected of being Taliban or Al Qaeda operatives are targeted; these strikes are not technically targeted assassinations because they are not aimed at specific named targets, on the other hand, since the individuals concerned are identified as enemy combatants on the basis of their behaviour patterns rather than by such indicators as wearing a uniform, they are also difficult to classify as regular military operations. Drone strikes put a great deal of psychological stress on their operators, but do not put the lives of US servicemen at risk. By removing capable leaders and specialists they undoubtedly damage the capability of the groups that are targeted, but they may also act as recruiters for these groups – and, in any event, sometimes removing experienced leaders is not a good idea if an eventual negotiated settlement is sought. The legality of drone strikes in countries with which the US is not at war has been challenged, as has been the extra-judicial killing of at least one American citizen.

All of these issues are important in the context of the politico-strategic efficacy of the drone campaign but there is also a normative issue at stake here – can a policy of targeted assassination be seen as consistent with the just conduct of the War on Terror? And, does the pursuit of this policy via drone strikes affect our judgement in this case? Picking up the latter point first, the reliance on drones represents the latest version of the US desire to fight zero-casualty wars. We have come across this desire in the context of the Kosovo campaign, where the preferred tactic was bombing from altitude to avoid the possibility of allied casualties; the point was made there that if the decision to intervene in a conflict of that nature was the right decision, then it ought not to have been conditioned on political considerations that valued NATO lives so much more than the lives of the people who were being intervened on behalf of. In Kosovo, the argument was that there should have been boots on the ground as well as planes in the air – on the other hand, over the last decade there have been plenty of boots on the ground in Iraq, in Afghanistan, and occasionally in Pakistan (for example in the raid on Abbottabad that killed Bin Laden), and drones are for the most part used in places where there are local political (or geographical) reasons for not committing actual soldiers. And on the positive side, the capacity that drone pilots have for maintaining extended periods of surveillance before actually striking should mean that civilian casualties are easier to avoid.

In fact, it is difficult to tell whether this potential for increased discrimination is actually being met. Part of the problem is that it is difficult to tell who is, or is not, a civilian in many of the contexts in which drones are used. In the frontier zones of Pakistan, for example, virtually all adult males routinely carry weapons and therefore when they become the casualties of drone strikes it is difficult to know whether they are actually associates of the known target, as the US authorities tend to assume, or simply bystanders. This is particularly a consideration in the case of strikes which are not directed at specific individuals, but at groups of people who are behaving in allegedly suspicious ways – what may be suspicious to a drone operator in the US may be routine behaviour in the area in question. However, there is another consideration here, which is that the training of at least the CIA drone pilots may not put as much stress on the laws of war as does that of regular air-force personnel – but still, for all these caveats, in principle, drones are weapons that make the discrimination that is central to Just War thinking easier to achieve.

In spite of these positives, it is still not too difficult to see why so many people worry about excessive reliance on drones. There is already something intuitively distasteful about the idea of killing without at least some risk of being killed, and this is somehow magnified when the 'killer' is sitting in a darkened room two continents away. It is important not to get too romantic about this – notions of chivalry and a warrior's honour have very little purchase where Al Qaeda or the Taliban are concerned – but the impersonality of drone warfare and also of long-distance cruise missile strikes, is an issue, and not just because the sense that such killings are 'unfair' acts as a driver for recruitment to terrorist groups. And this will become an even more pressing issue in the not too distant future when drones are replaced or supplemented by 'robots' – Autonomous Unmanned Aerial Vehicles – that is to say when the machines themselves are programmed to make the decision to kill. However subtle and sophisticated the programming, the use of robots will increase exponentially the sense of revulsion that the use of drones already clearly generates. Still, it is clear that the use of drones will continue, and it is also clear that it will become more widespread – while the US drone programme is still by far the most significant, other countries are forging ahead with their own attempts to match it, and we can expect that drone warfare will in future be a normal part of the repertoire of war. If any event, it is perhaps the use to which drones have been put – the policy of targeted assassinations – that in a way poses more problems than the use of drones as such.

Historically, International Humanitarian Law has operated on the principle that combatants are essentially anonymous, defined by the uniforms they wear – and, of course, the very name uniform suggests anonymity – or by other symbols which distinguish them from civilians. The principle of anonymity is also tied up with the idea of the moral equality of combatants, the idea that whatever the rights and wrongs of a war, the individuals who wear a uniform are to have equal moral standing, assuming, of course, that their behaviour is not such that they lose this status by e.g. committing war crimes – but that is not a judgement that is usually made on the battlefield. Anonymity also has played a part in the informal code with which combatants of (at least Western) armies have equipped themselves, hence the well-documented distaste in the First and Second World Wars for the infantry sniper, who identifies and kills in a way that is disturbingly personal, even though he acts within the laws of war. By the same token, the assassination of heads of state and individual army leaders in times of war is also regarded as morally ambiguous, perhaps justified in the case of a tyrant but generally undesirable; the basic principle that one should not carry out acts in time of war that make establishing peace at a later date more difficult is central. The key question is, how do these legal prohibitions and moral restraints play out in the war on terror?

In fact, they illustrate better than almost anything else the problems we have in coming to an intuitive moral understanding of how we should characterise the war on terror, at least in its present form. Obviously neither terrorists in general, nor their leaders in particular, wear distinctive uniforms or symbols that could convey anonymity; nor do they usually operate in the kind of context where direct contact between opposing forces is routine and where informal patterns of behaviour can thus emerge. On the other hand, they equally obviously carry out or order acts which are contrary to the laws of war, ignoring the requirement to discriminate amongst targets. In all three respects, they resemble members of a criminal gang rather than an army – although criminals often wear identifying marks such as gang colours and can operate within quite elaborate command structures – which is one of the reasons why critics of the War on Terror dislike the term and think it should be replaced by one that points towards the model of law enforcement rather than war fighting. But the law enforcement model only makes sense in those contexts where a judicial and police system exists which could identify and arrest members of a terrorist group, and this is a context which obviously doesn't exist in many parts of the world today, and, more specifically, certainly doesn't apply in parts of Yemen, Somalia and the frontier districts of Pakistan. These are regions where the writ of the central governments in question simply does not run, and, of course, there is the added complication that those governments in any event may not wish to exercise their legal powers when these groups are involved – had the US gone to the Pakistan authorities with the evidence they had on the probable presence of Bin Laden in Abbottabad, it is difficult to believe that this would have led to his capture. In short, the War on Terror is neither a 'war' in the conventional sense – which if it were, would tell against a systematic policy of targeted assassination – nor a police operation – where the targeting of criminals is a perfectly legitimate tactic, but where the aim is the arrest and conviction of the wrongdoers and their assassination would be a form of judicial murder. It is mostly fought not in a conventional war zone, nor in a zone of peace of the sort that might be found in relatively well-ordered societies adhering roughly to the rule of law, but rather in a kind of intermediate zone, neither of peace nor of war.

Perhaps what that suggests is that there is no big story to be told about targeted assassination; rather than trying to work out whether this is a morally acceptable policy in general terms we should instead focus on the specific. The moral demand should be that when killing takes place it should be on the basis of very good evidence as to the standing of the proposed victim, that civilian casualties should be avoided (difficult though that is when the status of non-combatant is so difficult to define) and that the wider political context should be taken into account, in other words the benefit from the operation should exceed potential political costs in terms of local support. Such a position would not satisfy those critics for whom any use of the tactic of targeted killing is illegitimate, but it would represent the best fit with the principle that the War on Terror should be fought justly. It would also rule out so-called 'signature strikes' where there is no direct evidence that the individuals concerned are members of a terrorist group. Modern campaigns against terrorist groups take place in a grey area where it is unacceptable to regard the local inhabitants as enemies unless they explicitly act as such – being in the wrong place at the wrong time may be suggestive, but it shouldn't be enough on its own to warrant a death sentence.

It is clear that President Obama has become conscious of the downside of his administration's use of drones. In a major speech in May 2013 at the National Defence Academy he defended the policy, arguing that:

> Under domestic law, and international law, the United States is at war with Al Qaeda, the Taliban, and their associated forces. We are at war with an organization that right now would kill as many Americans as they could if we did not stop them first. So this is a Just War — a war waged proportionally, in last resort, and in self-defense.

In his view the use of drones and targeted assassination has met those last requirements; however, he is clearly aware that this judgement is not as widely shared as he would like it to be. In the weeks before this speech a number of American and European commentators had begun to assess the scale of the use of these weapons and had come to the conclusion that Obama was, as they sometimes put it, every bit as bad as, or actually worse than Bush. In his National Defence Academy Speech, and in the State of the Union Address in January 2014, he acknowledged these criticisms, and promised to rein back the programme as far as was possible.

Surveillance, security and civil liberty

Does terrorism pose an existential threat to Western societies? At the most obvious, material, level the answer to this question is, no. Whereas, for example, during the Cold War the possibility of nuclear war certainly did pose an existential threat in the most literal sense of the term, terrorist attacks are on an entirely different scale, less deadly than any number of threats to life produced by the terms of modern living – dying in an automobile accident being the case that is often cited by those who argue we take the risk posed by terrorism too seriously. Of course, there is an important moral difference between an accident and a deliberate killing, but in terms simply of scale the former is indeed more of a threat to life than the latter, and neither constitutes an existential threat to our societies. On the other hand, existential threats are not necessarily to be defined quite so literally, as threats to one's physical existence; threats to a way of life as opposed to life itself are equally existential. Does terrorism pose this kind of threat? The operation of extremists within communities, the radicalisation of individuals, especially the young and impressionable, the 'capture' of mosques, the poisoning of inter-faith relations, these are all factors which impinge on everyone's lives in ways that actually constitute a more significant threat than the risk of dying in a terrorist attack. There is, however, a further point, well expressed by Philip Bobbitt who argues that the real existential threat posed by terrorism is that Western societies will find themselves obliged to change their nature in order to combat terrorism, that the very freedoms that define the West will be sacrificed as a result of the demands of an effective anti-terrorism policy, undermining the legitimacy of Western governments (Bobbitt, 2008). Followers of Carl Schmitt make a similar point arguing that the War on Terror forms the basis for a permanent 'state of exception' in which the normal processes of government are suspended, supposedly in the interests of national security, although, unlike Bobbitt, they do so from a position of general opposition to liberal, market states (Odysseos and Petito, 2007).

Responding to this danger, in his first Inaugural Address (2009) President Obama rejected as 'false the choice between our safety and our ideals' but for some critics the revelations about the level of surveillance conducted by the National Security Agency (NSA) and its foreign affiliates such as Britain's General Communications Headquarters (GCHQ) suggests that under his Administration our ideals have indeed been compromised putatively in the interests of our security, and Bobbitt's fears have come to pass. For these critics, Edward Snowden, the former analyst who has made it his mission to reveal the activities of the NSA, and his predecessor the serviceman Bradley (now Chelsea) Manning, who provided the vast quantities of diplomatic and military information disseminated by Wikileaks, are heroic 'whistle-blowers' acting in the public interest, rather than the criminals that the current Administration believes them to be. Interestingly, the critics on this occasion may be led by the usual suspects – Glenn Greenwald, the *Guardian* commentator who has never believed that terrorism constitutes any kind of threat independent of the behaviour of the US government, is Snowden's amanuensis – but they now include important figures on the libertarian right in the United States and realist IR scholars have also piled in to support Snowden (Walt, 2013). At the other end of the spectrum, Edward Jay Epstein has suggested in the *Wall Street Journal* that Snowden was a Russian agent (Epstein, 2014).

It is clear that the critique of US surveillance and data collection policy has struck a chord with public opinion in a way that earlier critiques of the conduct of the war on terror have not. How should this issue be assessed from the perspective of a concern with the normative foundations of the War on Terror? The first point that needs to be said is that very little evidence of actual illegal activity has been uncovered. The various programmes of data collection exist within a legal framework established by the Obama Administration and under the oversight of the Senate Intelligence Committee, now chaired by the liberal Senator from California, Diane Feinstein. Collecting intelligence on foreign nationals based abroad does not constitute a breach of US law. Some Europeans have been apparently outraged by US activities in Europe but, as Secretary of State Kerry remarked, all governments conduct espionage against their friends as well as their enemies, a fact highlighted by the revelation in *Le Monde* that the French Government has its own data collection programme, and without the cover of legality. However, the legality of US (and British) programmes may actually be formal rather than real – it seems that permission for specific operations is almost always given, and the suspicion is that the Senate Intelligence Committee has, in effect, been 'captured' by the NSA. Moreover, the suspicion remains that the close relationship between NSA and Britain's GCHQ allows the former to operate in the UK outside of British legal control and vice versa; in effect, the two organisations can work together to frustrate restrictions placed on each. This is denied by all concerned, but unfortunately there is no independent way of checking those denials.

Even if all the programmes run by the NSA are wholly within the law – and, to stress again, there is no evidence to the contrary – they still raise serious issues about the conduct of the War on Terror, and it is clear that the blanket assertion that such programmes are necessary to preserve our security will no longer pass unchallenged, and nor should it. Bobbitt's argument that it is in such programmes that the existential threat posed by terrorism lies deserves to be taken very seriously. As with the use of drones and the policy of extrajudicial killing, there are complex choices to be made here, which in this case come down to quite basic issues about personal freedom and security. The internet security that allows us to manage our bank account online relies on encryption algorithms that can also be used by other people to organise paedophile rings and terrorist plots. The capacity to prevent such activities (or at least make them less likely) may actually involve the security services possessing powers that impinge on the privacy of ordinary citizens – and it is difficult to see any way out of this dilemma, except to hope that the constitutional guarantees that countries such as the US and the UK have built up over the centuries will actually hold, and that the authorities will not betray the trust placed in them. This is an area where, as with the issue of drones and targeted killing, the desire to see a grey world in black and white terms is very strong, but ultimately unsustainable. It seems probable that, as a result of Snowden's revelations and shifts in public and congressional opinion, some elements of the surveillance and data-collection programmes run by NSA will be scaled back – but it is unlikely they will be eliminated altogether. A relatively small adjustment to the programmes would probably be enough to regain wide public support, although, of course, without satisfying the critics.

Just War thinking and modern warfare

The nature of war has changed almost beyond recognition over the last quarter century – of course, it is still the case that conventional inter-state wars are sometimes fought, but they have become the exception rather than the rule. Overall the incidence of war, however defined, has fallen, and most of those wars that do take place are either civil wars or asymmetric conflicts. As far as the latter are concerned, the French philosopher Jean Baudrillard wrote a book entitled *The Gulf War Did Not Take Place*, which attracted a certain amount of derision from literal-minded Anglo-Saxons, but the point he was making was actually valid; the 1991 Gulf War was so one-sided that to call it a war – with all the connotations of struggle that that term has – was misleading, and many modern wars have the same quality, Kosovo 1999 being a case in point (Baudrillard, 1995). In Iraq and Afghanistan things have looked rather different, and no one would suggest that these wars have not taken place, but still they bear very little relation to war as that term has been conventionally understood, at least in the Western world. Arguably, the kind of long-term frontier struggles between the civilised and the barbarian that characterised war for many centuries in Imperial China are rather more like the wars we see nowadays than the discrete conflicts that took place in Europe during the era of the society of states (Hanson, 1990).

Dramatic though these changes in the nature of war may have been, the Just War tradition set out in Chapter 3 of this book is well placed to cope with the shift in mind-set required to understand what is going on. Just War thinking crystallised in the middle ages at a time when the international order was not composed predominantly of clearly defined territorial states, when armies were rarely highly organised forces distinct from civil society and when many wars were low key and asymmetric (Johnson, 1985). The Scholastic philosophers who developed the notion of a Just War were concerned with the role of violence in preserving or regaining a just social order, and the categories they produced – just cause, last resort, proportionality and so on – were not tied to a system of nation states in the way that the international humanitarian law that developed in the nineteenth century was, or for that matter that the 'legalist paradigm' developed by Michael Walzer some forty years ago was (Walzer, 1977). Walzer, one of the most thoughtful of social critics, has recognised this point and has written on the ways in which his account of the legalist paradigm and the 'war convention' are difficult to apply when the zones of peace and war are not clearly defined, and so many activities, drone attacks for example, take place in an intermediate zone where neither the laws of war nor the laws of peace apply. Other scholars of the Just War who are more comfortable with the theological underpinnings of the original notion have had little difficulty applying Just War categories to modern conflicts. Jean Bethke Elshtain, a social theorist whose religious convictions have always been central to her work, has understood the War on Terror through Augustinian lenses, and James Turner Johnson, the historian of the tradition, has explored the ethics of the 2003 Gulf War through the standard categories set out by Thomas Aquinas (Elshtain, 2003; Johnson, 2005). Non-theologically minded writers, such as the present author, have looked at the War on Terror and the conflicts of the last decade through Aristotelian thought, moving behind the work of Aquinas to the Classical Greek origins of at least some of his categories (Brown, 2013a).

Critics of the Just War tradition have not been satisfied by these moves. There have always been those who have argued that Just War thinking actually encourages violence. The most serious of such enemies is perhaps Carl Schmitt, whose position, expressed most clearly in his book *The Nomos of the Earth*, is that to describe a war as 'just' encourages a self-righteous fury which will demonise the enemy and stand in the way of establishing limits in warfare (Schmitt, 2003). Every war becomes a total war, because every war is a war between good and evil, and with evil there can be no compromise. This is strikingly similar to the argument put forward, in different terms, by some modern students of 'critical security studies' who write of Just War theory as delegitimising 'the Other', encouraging a Manichean world view and so on. The difference between these superficially similar critiques, is that Schmitt was hostile to the notion of a Just War because of his nostalgia for an era when (allegedly) interstate war was regarded as a kind of duel between legitimate enemies, whereas modern critics are unclear on what alternative to the Just War they propose. Schmitt wanted to clear the space for war as an act of state within a European states-system and understood, correctly, that Just War thinking is incompatible with the idea that war is *simply* a political act of this kind. Schmitt clearly cannot accept the notion that war can only be waged for a just cause, and for that reason he is right to see his approach as incompatible with the tradition, but he is wrong to think that Just War thinking automatically leads to the demonising of enemies and the end of restraint. He may be right that it sometimes has this effect on people who think of themselves as just warriors – not difficult to find contemporary examples from all points on the political compass – but this self-satisfied approach is, or ought to be, contrary to a good understanding of what using Just War criteria as a basis for political judgement ought to involve.

Modern critics of Just War thinking from a left perspective, such as Ken Booth, are rather less clear about what they want than Schmitt (Booth, 2000a).

They make the same critique of Just War thinking as Schmitt, but crucially without the endorsement of war as an act of policy. The result is either a pacifist stance or an attempt to distinguish between 'progressive' and 'reactionary' uses of violence. Pacifism is, of course, a very well-established position with a long and distinguished pedigree, from Jesus to Tolstoy and Gandhi, but it is open to the obvious objection that an absolute rejection of violence, whatever the circumstances, puts power in the hands of those who are not similarly disposed and can lead to the perpetuation of injustice. Belief in a God who will provide an ultimate guarantee that justice will prevail may make this position tenable for some, but this is an argument that cuts no ice with non-believers, or, for that matter, with a majority of believers. In practice, most 'pacifist' thinkers are, actually, 'pacifistic', to adopt a term of Martin Ceadel, that is they are predisposed against violence but prepared to countenance it in some circumstances, which, of course, opens the door to Just War thinking, properly understood (Ceadel, 1987). The alternative position is to distinguish between the progressive and the reactionary use of violence, supporting the former, opposing the latter. At one level, this is simply an instrumental, Clausewitzian approach to violence in which matters of justice are irrelevant or, perhaps, predetermined – one side in a conflict is, by definition, just and therefore no further questions need to be asked about its conduct.

In summary, although clearly some of the rhetoric of the War on Terror has encouraged the kind of Manichean thinking criticised by Schmitt and Booth, Just War thinking, properly understood, should tell against such extremism. However, over the last two decades or so, what it means to 'properly understand' Just War thinking has gone through something of a transformation, as a number of very distinguished analytical political philosophers have addressed the subject, somewhat marginalising more traditional thinkers such as Johnson and Elshtain in the process. These thinkers have approached the classical categories of Just War thinking from a different angle, subjecting them to close analysis, and often finding them wanting. A few examples may be helpful here to illustrate the impact of this new kind of Just War thinking.

A fundamental principle of modern Just War thinking is the moral equality of actual combatants; thus, Walzer in *Just and Unjust Wars* argues that the 'War Convention' governing what is permissible in wartime, his equivalent of *ius in bello*, applies to all combatants. The justice or otherwise of a war is of great importance, but not something that should govern our attitude to the rights of soldiers fighting the war – the same rules apply to both sides and the rights or wrongs of the conflict are a matter for the political leadership. In David Rodin and Henry Shue's collection *Just and Unjust Warriors*, and in Jeff McMahan's *Killing in War*, this principle is challenged; the argument is that the same moral principles govern killing in war and in peace; killing in self-defence may be justified, but those who are engaged in an unjust war cannot claim such a defence (Rodin and Shue, 2008; McMahan, 2009). Thus, the rights of soldiers vary dramatically according to the justice of the war they are fighting – a soldier fighting for an unjust cause has no right to kill and cannot be regarded as the moral equal to a soldier fighting for a just cause.

McMahan's argument contradicts contemporary International Humanitarian Law but he could claim that his position on this matter is actually closer to Aquinas than is Walzer's notion of the moral equality of combatants, although Aquinas would be less sure than McMahan that anyone other than God could be sure which side in a conflict is actually just. More radical is the challenge to the principle of non-combatant immunity. Cecile Fabre has argued in *Cosmopolitan War* and elsewhere that the functional distinction between the military and civilians is irrelevant to their respective liability to be attacked; what matters is the extent to which particular individuals are responsible for wrongful deaths (Fabre, 2012a, 2012b). Matthew Bruenig takes the argument one step further; whereas in feudal and authoritarian regimes the sovereign who decides on war is not responsible to the people, in liberal democracies individuals have to be considered responsible for the decisions their governments make, and this means they cannot claim immunity from the consequences of those decisions (Bruenig, 2011). Perhaps slightly less controversial, many of the analytical political philosophers are very critical of the doctrine of 'double effect'; and therefore are much less willing than more conventional Just War theorists to accept that there is a clear moral distinction between so-called 'collateral damage' and the deliberate killing of civilians. This has considerable relevance for the moral assessment of terrorist attacks on civilians; conventional thinkers reject the idea that this is morally similar to the non-intentional deaths caused by, for example, drone attacks, but these thinkers are much less sure that such a distinction can be drawn.

There is no doubt that writers such as McMahan, Fabre, Rodin and Shue have revitalised Just War thinking by subjecting the traditional categories to a close analysis, but it may be that in the process they have changed the nature of the discourse in a way that is not particularly desirable. Part of the question here rests on what can be expected from Just War thinking. There is a distinction here that is best summarised by saying that whereas these writers look to Just War theory in the expectation that it will give them *answers*, more conventional Just War thinkers are more inclined to think of the tradition as a source of good *questions*. In the first case, the expectation is that Just War theory will tell us whether a particular war, or a particular action in a war, is just; in the second case, the hope is that Just War thinking will help us to make the wider judgement as to whether, in the particular circumstances of the case, a resort to force, or a particular forceful action, would be the right thing to do, all things considered. One of the features of contemporary analytical political philosophy is the belief that with the right amount of brainpower applied to any particular case, the right answer will emerge – the Scholastics who developed Just War theory also believed that the right answers could be found, but only by God's grace, while the Aristotelian roots of Just War thinking regard the discourse as an instance of *phronesis*, the opportunity to exercise political judgement and wisdom, without the kind of certainly that might be expected of the sciences.

An equally compelling critique is that the analytical Just War philosophers, in their search for a rigorous account of the Just War, have lost contact with the actual practices of war. This is what Michael Walzer had in mind in a recent interview when he remarked that for these writers 'the subject of just war theory is just war theory [whereas] I think the subject matter of Just War theory is war' (Interview with Nancy Rosenblum, see Further Reading in Chapter 3, p. 57), although it is worth pointing out that Walzer's emphasis on the *rights* of combatants was itself a step away from the tradition and in the direction of the writers he criticises. Refuting the notion of the moral equality of combatants, or challenging the principle of non-combatant immunity, may make sense in the seminar room, but neither position translates well to the battlefield – indeed, in practice, both positions could lead to disastrous consequences, as McMahan implicitly acknowledges by ending his book with a qualified endorsement of existing International Humanitarian Law, which contradicts the argument he has laid out in such detail. Of course, if one were to apply all the principles set out by McMahan et al. it would almost certainly be impossible to actually fight any war justly, and these philosophers would probably be happy with that result, concluding that therefore no war should be fought – but this is simply a back-door way of making Just War thinking the equivalent of pacifism, defeating the purpose of the exercise, which starts from the premise that violence is sometimes necessary.

Conclusion

There have already been more changes to the nature and practice of war and violence during the twenty-first century even than were seen in the twentieth century, and thinking about these changes has barely caught up. We are only just now beginning to work out how to think about the ethics of unmanned aerial vehicles, yet already the latter are on the verge of being replaced by true robots. The age of information warfare and the use of computer viruses has only just begun, and remains largely untheorised. The Just War tradition provides us with one set of tools for thinking through these new problems; the decades ahead will decide whether these tools are actually up to the job – for the moment we can only work with what we have.

Further Reading

Christopher Coker is an interesting guide to the changes in the nature of war in recent years – see Coker (2008) and (2013) among many other contributions. Michael Gross (2009) is an excellent introduction to the dilemmas generated by asymmetric warfare as is Anthony Lang and Amanda Beattie (2009). James Turner Johnson (2011) represents the traditional approach to Just War under modern conditions, as does Jean Bethke Elshtain (2003). Other useful overviews include Tim Dunne (2007), Wade Mansell (2004) and Stephanie Carvin and Michael John Williams (2014).

On specific issues, Stephanie Carvin (2010b) discusses judiciously issues such as the status of 'unlawful combatants'; specifically on Guantanamo see Karen Greenberg (2009). On torture, a good starting point would be the essay by Seamus Miller in the *Stanford Encyclopaedia of Philosophy* http://plato.stanford.edu/entries/torture/. Sanford Levinson's (2004) is a useful collection, as is Karen Greenberg (2006) and Greenberg and Joshua Dratel (2005). Alan Dershowitz's 'torture warrants' paper appears in Levinson and his book (2002) adds little to the argument. Yuval Ginbar (2008) takes the 'ticking bomb' scenario apart at great length. Neither Michael Ignatieff (2004) nor Michael Walzer (1973) actually defend torture, but they do manage to talk about the issues it raise in a more nuanced way than most others.

The issues surrounding UAVs (drones) are among the hottest topics in contemporary IPT; there are some book-length studies – Akbar Ahmed (2013), Christian Enemark (2014) and a good collection edited by Bradley Jay Strawser (2013) – but for the most part things move so quickly that even the journal literature is hardly up to date. Useful articles include Hillel Ofek (2010), Derek Gregory (2011), Stephanie Carvin (2012), Michael Boyle (2013), Daniel Byman (2013) and most usefully, McCrisken (2013). The Stanford/NYU Report 'Living Under Drones' is a valuable document, and the associated website has useful links www. livingunderdrones.org – still, the blogsphere remains the best source of material, to be used cautiously as always; Charli Carpenter's contributions to the *Duck of Minerva* are particularly worth looking out for.

The *Guardian* newspaper provides the 'official' version of the Wikileaks/Assange saga – David Leigh and Luke Harding (2010) – and of the Snowden Affair – Luke Harding (2014); Glen Greenwald (2014) is Snowden's amanuensis. The Kindle Special by Edward Lucas (2013) takes a more jaundiced view, arguing that Snowden has done great harm to Western interests. The jury is out on Mr Snowden – heroic whistle-blower, Russian spy or 'useful idiot'?

The key references for the new, individualist, Just War theory, works by Jeff McMahan, David Rodin, Cecile Fabre and Henry Shue, are given in the text of this chapter. Useful collections include Richard Sorabji and David Rodin (2006) and David Rodin and Henry Shue (2008). An *Ethics* Symposium on McMahan's *Killing in War* Vol. 122, No. 1 October 2011 has strong essays and a good response by McMahan. The *Oxford Institute for Ethics Law and Armed Conflict* is an important source for materials on Just War www.elac.ox.ac.uk/. Richard Norman (1995) is not an analytical philosopher, but was raising many of the issues that the new Just War theorists have focused on, and his contribution does not deserve to be forgotten.

10
GLOBAL JUSTICE

The last three chapters have focused on humanitarian intervention, a putative responsibility to protect on the part of the international community and the politics of war and violence in the twenty-first century. These are all important topics with considerable implications both for the way people live in the modern world and for the ways in which we think about global politics – but they are also topics which relate to unusual states of affairs, extreme acts of oppression, crimes against humanity, genocide and the like and the ways in which we respond, or do not respond to these events. In some ways a focus on such extreme events is rather misleading – there are many countries in the world where oppression is commonplace, but never reaches the level at which international action is even considered, never 'spikes' as the expression goes. Equally, there are many situations where violence at a relatively low level is also commonplace, but where esoteric technologies such as drones do not come into the equation. It is rarely suggested that the international community has a duty to intervene to protect women's rights in Saudi Arabia, or gay rights in Nigeria, or that the murder rate of 30.5 people per 100,000 pa in Southern Africa, thirty times higher than in Western Europe, constitutes an international problem – but these situations adversely affect far more people over longer time periods than the more exciting cases that reach the front pages of newspapers or that attract sustained academic attention.

Even more problematic is the issue of poverty and malnutrition. To take just one set of figures, *MsF* estimate that 20 million children globally suffer from severe malnutrition, of whom only 3 per cent receive the treatment they need and that malnutrition contributes to 3.5–5 million deaths in children under five annually (see www.msf.org.uk – the figures will have changed by the time you read this). Even if these figures exaggerate the problem – not impossible, given that charities such as *MsF* are engaged in a permanent struggle to raise funds which produces an incentive to over-dramatise – they are of a different order of magnitude to the estimated figure of 25,000 deaths in Libya in 2011, or the 120,00 who died in Syria between 2011 and 2014, tragic though these figures undoubtedly are. What this suggests is that even the 'normal' oppressions represented by low-level rights abuses pale into insignificance by comparison to the consequences of poverty, and, of course, the poverty in question takes place in the context of a world where many countries enjoy a very high standard of living, and are in a position to ensure that all their citizens can have their basic needs met – which, of course, is not to say that there are not pockets of poverty in the rich world, and, for that matter, pockets of great wealth in the poor but it is the overall situation that, for the moment, is the focus of attention.

In the world of the society of states as outlined in the first part of this book, poverty and inequality of this kind are not generally seen as an international problem. Within an imperial system such as the British Empire, in so far as intra-imperial inequality was considered at all, it was considered to be the responsibility of the imperial power, and, in any event, until the twentieth century it was probably the case that poverty and inequality were as much an issue within the imperial homeland as between the centre and the periphery of the empire. It has only been in the last century of so that the living standards of ordinary people within the core countries of the world economy have risen to the point that a clear delineation between rich and poor countries made much sense. But over the last fifty years with the widespread acceptance of the norm of self-determination and the accompanying collapse of the European empires, the politics of wealth and poverty has most definitely been internationalised – in this period poor countries have consistently pressed for this to be the case, for the global rich to recognise that they have responsibilities with respect to the global poor. The nature of these responsibilities, however, remains hotly contested and there is no consensus as to even the most basic questions such as whether the rich have a duty of assistance to the poor, and if so how far this duty extends and whether it involves recognising claims based on a global account of justice, let alone is there a consensus on whether global institutional reform is required, and if so in what form. Partly this lack of consensus reflects empirical disagreements as to the causes of poverty and the effects of the global institutional structure, but it also reflects deep normative disagreements about the obligations of both the global rich and the global poor. There are complex issues here, which will be explored in this chapter.

A duty of assistance? Two versions

The first attempts by political philosophers to explore these issues came in the early 1970s, at a time when a coalition based on the euphemistically described 'less developed countries' was forming at the United Nations devoted to establishing a

'New International Economic Order'. This coincidence in timing is not really surprising; by 1970 the major waves of post-war decolonisation had taken place between 25 and 15 years earlier, and it was already clear that the newly independent countries created thereby were not becoming richer at anything like the speed that some advocates of decolonisation had expected. Kwame Nkrumah, who led the British colony the Gold Coast into independence as Ghana in 1957 summarised this aspiration in an oft-quoted maxim 'Seek ye first the political kingdom and all else shall be added unto you...'. That Nkrumah, the most influential African independence leader of the 1950s, was overthrown by a military coup in 1966 symbolised the lack of progress experienced by the newly independent countries of Africa. If independence itself was no economic panacea, then perhaps these countries needed assistance and aid; economists debated what kind of aid would be appropriate, political philosophers considered the normative side of the problem – what actually are the moral obligations of rich countries or people towards poor countries or people, given the end of formal colonialism?

The journal *Philosophy and Public Affairs* was launched in 1972 precisely to provide a forum for debating this kind of question, and its very first issue contained a paper by the utilitarian philosopher Peter Singer which addressed the topic. 'Famine, affluence and morality' is an enormously influential work, anthologised repeatedly over the decades, the core argument of which reappears regularly in Singer's work, most recently in his book *The Life You Can Save: How to Play Your Part in Ending World Poverty* (2010). Singer is a radical utilitarian who presents a deceptively simple argument; unnecessary suffering and premature death are bad and if we can stop bad things happening without sacrificing anything of comparable moral significance (or, in weaker version, anything morally significant) morally we ought to do it. Distance is morally irrelevant to this principle and the 'we' in question includes individuals as well as governments. Radical implications follow from these simple ideas; to follow them, virtually all individuals within the advanced industrial world would be obliged to change the way they live by, for example, no longer purchasing goods that they do not need but instead transferring their wealth to those suffering from starvation or malnutrition. Two caveats are worth noting here; first, the assumption is that transfers from rich to poor will be effective; if not – and as we will see there is reason to question whether aid is effective – there is no obligation. Second, Singer, at least in the weaker version of his theory, is concerned with the meeting of basic needs rather than with equality and the actual level of transfer required by this duty of assistance may be low, although it will certainly be higher than current practice.

Singer's argument seems compelling, but he smuggles into his reasoning certain assumptions that we may not actually want to accept. As a utilitarian he follows Jeremy Bentham in assuming that all 'goods' and 'bad' are commensurable and that the 'greatest happiness' is the goal. Thus, at the outset of his paper he argues that the money spent on the Sydney Opera House, under construction in 1972, must be set against the sums spent on famine relief in Bangladesh; the fact that the opera house is attracting more money than famine relief is, for him, a sign that our priorities are wrong. But are these activities, famine relief and support for the arts, actually commensurable? Again, is 'distance' actually irrelevant as Singer asserts? It is certainly the case that modern news-gathering and transport technologies mean that we are now more familiar with distant suffering than we once were and have more ability to respond to it, but when we think of our obligations to others it is really social distance rather than geography that we have in mind. Most people believe that we have special duties towards those who are 'nearest' to us not in spatial terms but via kinship and friendship and Singer's argument seems to disregard this sense of the term distance – although in other work, for example his book *The Expanding Circle* (2011) he does acknowledge the point. Finally, in presenting his argument he offers as an illustration the obligations we would have towards a child drowning in a shallow pool; as adults, we should rescue the child even at the cost of ruining our clothes, because the moral significance of a child's life is obviously greater than the costs to us of so doing. All very well, but are the global poor to be understood as childlike, ultimately not responsible for their actions, and requiring the intervention of adults to save them?

These problems – if problems they are – stem from Singer's utilitarianism; as someone committed to a version of the principle that social arrangements and personal morality should conform to the 'greatest happiness' principle, he is not particularly concerned if this leads to downgrading the importance of family ties or the importance of self-determination. The fact that individuals value such ties, and would apparently be willing to sacrifice a degree of material well-being in order to be able to govern themselves may simply reflect a failure to think through the implications of the greatest happiness principle, or a sign that old-fashioned pre-utilitarian thinking still has a hold on many people. Others disagree, arguing that utilitarians do not take sufficiently seriously the right of individuals to shape their own projects, to manage their lives in the way that they wish to – obviously there are limits to this freedom, there are some projects that people ought not to be able to develop, but in general personal autonomy is a good, and one that the utilitarian approach to ethics does not take seriously enough. Moreover, utilitarian thinking runs into particular difficulties when dealing with international issues, because it is by no means clear how individuals personally can actually contribute to ending global poverty; giving to charitable NGOs such as Oxfam may achieve something, and arguing and voting for increased aid budgets may achieve more, but in neither case is it clear where the money will go and what actual effect it will have.

In so far as these are problems with utilitarian thought generally, the usual modern antidote to this way of thinking is provided by the moral theory of Kant, with its emphasis on deontology – the importance of moral rules being divorced from their consequences rather than being dependent on them, as consequentialists such as Singer maintain. Kant's *Perpetual Peace* and other explicitly international texts offer a cosmopolitan perspective that is not directly helpful to the issue at hand because he disregards the issue of global poverty (understandably, given the late eighteenth-century context) but some later Kantians and Kant-influenced scholars draw instead on his notion of the *categorical imperative* to derive principles that are relevant. Onora O'Neill is perhaps the most prominent such a Kantian: she writes on 'distant hunger' and helpfully distinguishes between duties and obligations of individuals and of those of institutions, and between perfect and imperfect duties (1986, 1991). One formulation of the categorical imperative is 'act only in accordance with that maxim through which you can at the same time will that it become a universal law' and from this it follows that we have a *perfect* duty not to establish international relations that are built on dishonesty or theft (because they would breach maxims that can be universalised) while we have an *imperfect* duty to support international aid programmes, (because we desire that such behaviour *should* be subject to such a maxim). Our duty to those suffering from distant hunger is to act charitably and to support programmes of poverty relief – but although this approach is helpful in distinguishing between personal and institutional responsibilities, it doesn't clarify the extent of the obligations of either.

Another writer who is critical of utilitarianism along not dissimilar lines is John Rawls, whose work on the 'Law of Peoples' we have already encountered in Chapter 4 as an example of modern thinking on how to reconcile the concept of human rights with the idea of a society of states (Rawls, 1999). Rawls is concerned with justice, which he sees as a property of institutions – get the basic institutions of a society right and individuals can be left free to pursue their own projects. In Rawls's 'realistic utopia' – his description of the Society of Peoples that he advocates – decent, well-ordered Peoples would have a duty of assistance towards those societies that do not qualify for membership of the Society of Peoples, and individual members of any particular People would discharge their personal responsibility in this way. This seems, in principle, to be a good way to approach the issue, but, as set out in Chapter 4, there are certain limitations to the duty of assistance that Rawls identifies, limitations that have been criticised by many scholars who take a more cosmopolitan stance on these issues. Essentially, Rawls argues in *The Law of Peoples* that liberal and decent peoples have a duty to assist what he calls burdened societies that do not have the human capital, the political culture or, perhaps, the material resources, to be well-ordered. Assistance for Rawls involves mainly the promotion of human rights and aid with the construction of just institutions. He holds out the possibility that material transfers might be necessary but he clearly regards this as a marginal concern by comparison with the issue of assistance to create the necessary institutions.

Given that the starting point of this chapter is that global poverty and extreme inequality are an issue for international political theory, Rawls's approach seems on the face of it to miss the point. Part of the problem here is that Rawls is actually not focusing on material inequality, and is not intending to create a theory of global justice. When he writes of 'burdened' societies, this should not be taken to equate to poor societies – extreme poverty may mean that societies are burdened in his sense of the term, but for the most part what he has in mind are societies with the wrong kind of institutions, institutions that prevent them from meeting the membership criteria of the Society of Peoples. A society with the right institutions could meet those criteria even if relatively poor, while comparative riches are no guarantee that a society will be well-ordered – a comparison here between India and Saudi Arabia is instructive; the former is much poorer than the latter, but also much closer to the ideal conditions for membership in the Society of Peoples. So, Rawls's duty of assistance is not actually primarily about combating poverty – but he does nonetheless offer the view that even in respect of combating poverty, it is internal factors and political culture that is crucial, and therefore aid should be directed towards developing the right kind of institutions rather than necessarily involving material transfers of any substantial kind.

This raises a crucially important issue which involves not just an evaluation of Rawls's work but also relates to all theories of global justice. Two quite closely related questions are posed by Rawls's argument. First, what is the relative importance of internal as opposed to external factors when it comes to an assessment of the causes of poverty? Rawls assumes in *The Law of Peoples* that internal factors are crucial and that given the right institutions and attitudes serious deprivation would become a thing of the past. Is this right? A second question, or perhaps a reformulation of the first question, is whether the existing global economic institutions – the International Monetary Fund, the World Bank and so on – are part of the problem of global poverty, or part of the solution? One response to Rawls's notion of 'burdened' societies is that these societies are not burdened by their own failings but are burdened by the effect of past and present global institutions and policies, from the institutions of formal imperialism through to those of contemporary neo-liberalism. Again, is this right? These are crucial questions, but they are not ultimately questions that political philosophers or international political theorists are in a good position to answer because they rely on empirical knowledge about how the world economy works, and how economic development takes place, knowledge which there is no reason to assume theorists of global justice actually possess. What is worse, those who do have some claim to possess this knowledge differ among themselves, and there is an obvious danger that the rest of us will choose to follow those who tell the story that best fits our view of how things should be.

Thus, for example, Rawls cites David Landes' *The Wealth and Poverty of Nations* (1998) in support of his view that domestic institutions are crucial, and had he lived he might have cited Paul Collier's *The Bottom Billion* (2007) or Darren Acemoglu and James A. Robinson's *Why Nations Fail* (2012), which both offer more nuanced arguments to the same effect. Backing up this position, works such as William Easterly's *The White Man's Burden: Why The West's Efforts To Aid The Rest Have Done So Much Ill And So Little Good* (2006) and Dambisa Moyo's *Dead Aid* (2010) provide provocative accounts of the ineffectiveness of aid programmes. On the other hand, writers such as Jeffrey Sachs in *The End of Poverty* (2005) argue strongly that, designed in the right way, development aid and investment from the West is needed to end poverty and can deliver the goods. Again there are many critics of the current global economic institutional order, but equally many supporters – and both critics and supporters can be found on the Left as well as the Liberal wing of contemporary politics. The critique of neo-liberalism by Left author Naomi Klein is not dissimilar from that by the liberal Joseph Stiglitz, and Marxist Meghnad Desai is as favourable to the contemporary order as his liberal fellow-countryman Jagdish Bhagwati, albeit for different reasons (Klein, 2001; Desai, 2002; Stiglitz, 2004; Bhagwati, 2004) .

Some things are reasonably clear, and not widely challenged. Under the current international order hundreds of millions of people have been pulled out of poverty in the last decade or two, which suggests that the claim that neo-liberalism necessarily works against the interests of the poor cannot be sustained. On the other hand, this reduction of poverty is largely down to the success of a relatively small number of states, especially China, and many others – Collier's *Bottom Billion* – have not benefited from this general development. The bottom billion, many of whom are to be found in sub-Saharan Africa, clearly lack sufficient capital, which suggests that transfers of wealth are needed, but they also clearly lack stable institutions and are often subject to internal war and major disruptions, which suggests that the Rawls–Landes position on institutions has much in its favour. As this brief summary suggests, this is a very complex situation with no easy answers. Still, it seems safe to assume that in some circumstances aid can be at least minimally effective, and that, whatever the importance of internal factors, to at least some extent international factors are important as well. These may seem very weak assumptions but they are all we need in order to make meaningful a discussion of the international dimension of global poverty and inequality. If poverty was simply produced by poor internal institutions, then Rawls would have the last word on the matter, but there is at least some reason to think that things could be improved by international action, and so it is worthwhile to ask questions about the moral responsibilities of the rich.

Global justice I

Rawls is prepared to consider a duty of assistance that well-ordered peoples owe to those societies that he describes as burdened, but, as set out in the first part of this book, he is working with a model of societies as self-contained and largely self-sufficient units which constitute *co-operatives schemes for mutual advantage* and this precludes the formation of principles of global social justice. According to Rawls, it is because societies are of this nature that principles of justice are required in order to determine the appropriate way to distribute the 'goods' that these co-operative schemes produce, and, by the same token, because the society of states, or, as he later calls it, the society of peoples, does not constitute a co-operative scheme for mutual advantage principles of global distributive justice are not required. There are no global goods to be distributed, therefore we have no need of principles to determine how they would be distributed if, in fact, they did exist. To put this another way, using language more consistent with *The Law of Peoples*, 'peoples' on his definition possess common institutions, common sympathies and a moral nature, and by this definition there is no global people.

This is a position that has never satisfied the majority of political philosophers – although theorists of international relations have, on the whole, been more sympathetic. The last forty years has seen a slew of theories of global justice by writers such as Chris Armstrong, Brian Barry, Charles Beitz, Gillian Brock, Simon Caney, Mathias Risse, Thomas Pogge and Kok-Chor Tan which vary quite considerably in the arguments they deploy, but which are united in their view that the way in which Rawls sets up the argument here is fundamentally misconceived. There are two distinct positions here; the first is that Rawls's basic approach is correct, but that he misunderstands the implications of his own theory; the second is that the perverse result of the international application of Rawls's principles indicates that there is something wrong with those principles. The most well-established versions of the first argument are those of Thomas Pogge and Charles Beitz, both of whom want to preserve Rawls's basic model; the fullest version of the second position is that of Brian Barry, who, while working under the shadow of Rawls – as do all modern contributors to the theory of justice – argues that the problem with Rawls's approach is more fundamental than Beitz or Pogge will allow.

Both Beitz and Pogge argue that Rawls is wrong to assume for the purpose of his theory that societies are bounded and self-contained; this might once have made a certain kind of sense, but no longer reflects the reality of complex interdependence (Beitz, 1979/2000; Pogge, 1989). Rawls is offering a morality of states but such an approach assumes a 'vanished Westphalian world' in the helpful phrase of Allen Buchanan (Buchanan, 2000). In Beitz's 1979 version of this argument, the reality of interdependence – nowadays one might say globalisation – mandates that there should be a global difference principle; global inequalities can be accepted as just only if they work to the advantage of the least advantaged. There is no justification for two different contracts, one within a society, and one between societies, because there is in reality only one global society. In this form, it has to be said that this is not a very good argument; global interdependence does not necessarily create a world which can plausibly be seen as a co-operative scheme for mutual advantage – one would have to hold a very benign view of the nature of the global political economy to see the world in that way. Rawls's later reasoning for rejecting the idea of a global people – the absence of common political institutions, common sympathies and a moral nature – is resistant to the idea that globalisation or interdependence has changed the situation from Westphalian days; we may have some common global institutions but most critics of Rawls would reject the idea that they act morally or reflect common sympathies. On the contrary, the usual criticism is that they exist for the benefit of the rich and powerful. Beitz in a later paper 'Cosmopolitan ideals and national sentiments' (1983) acknowledged that the idea of a global difference principle was non-viable, basing his cosmopolitanism instead on more straightforward Kantian lines. Pogge's cosmopolitan revision of Rawls was rather more coherent. In *Realizing Rawls* (1989) he argues that the contractarian logic of Rawls's position requires that there be a kind of meta-contract in which all persons decide upon the nature of the issues that they are prepared to allow to be decided at the state as opposed to the global level. The self-contained nature of schemes of co-operation is not something that ought to be assumed; instead this is a matter that should be subject to contractual agreement. A common critique of contractualist thinking is that it requires an arbitrary exercise in boundary drawing to determine who is and who is not a contractor – Pogge's version would get round this by including everyone in a meta-contract before the later versions of the contract come into play.

Both Pogge and Beitz provide cosmopolitan critiques of Rawls's position – they believe that Rawls's explicit rejection of cosmopolitanism is actually inconsistent with the premises of his theory. However, it should be said that both writers refer to themselves, at least in their earlier writings as 'moral' cosmopolitans rather than 'legal' or 'institutional' cosmopolitans. Pogge describes the difference as follows:

> *Legal* cosmopolitanism is committed to a concrete political ideal of a global order under which all persons have equivalent legal rights and duties – are fellow citizens of a universal republic. Moral cosmopolitanism holds that all persons stand in certain moral relations to one another; we are required to respect one another's status as ultimate units of *moral* concern … (Pogge, 1994, p. 90, emphasis in original)

Both writers recognise that a 'universal republic' is not on the cards, which is certainly true for the foreseeable future, but it must be questioned whether moral cosmopolitanism is actually enough to bring about the changes that Pogge at least believes to be necessary. Later in this chapter some proposals for institutional change will be considered, including proposals by Pogge, and it will be interesting to see if the moral/legal distinction can be sustained.

A global difference principle is certainly problematic, but there is another feature of Rawls's original model that is easier to challenge. In Rawls's second, international, contract it is asserted that the contractors under the veil of ignorance will accept the conventional international legal position that states own unconditionally the resources found of their territory. A good question, posed originally by Charles Beitz, is why states would agree to this when making their choices under an international veil of ignorance? One of the principles of Rawls's theory is that, as far as possible, no one should benefit from differences that are morally arbitrary. This raises interesting questions for his domestic theory – is, for example, musical talent to be considered arbitrary with the implication that a Mozart or a Schubert ought not to benefit from their natural gifts? – but it seems beyond question that the international distribution of natural resources is 'morally arbitrary'. No one could seriously argue, for example, that Saudi Arabia deserves the oil reserves it possesses. More plausibly, Beitz argues, contractors in the second, international contract, would plump for an egalitarian distribution of natural resources, to be achieved by some scheme of global taxation.

On purely normative grounds this is a solid argument, but it is one that could have perverse effects and operationalising the notion presents difficulty. The relationship between national economic success and natural resources is complex and changes over time; two hundred years ago Britain certainly benefited from the possession of coal and iron ore in close proximity to one another but in the twenty-first century might end up as a net beneficiary of an egalitarian distribution of natural resources. Part of the problem here lies in defining a 'natural resource'; one might argue that just as the land on which drilling can take place for oil is valuable, so is the land in the centre of London and both could be the subject of taxation – but this loses the link to the notion that natural resources are morally arbitrary; land in Central London is valuable because of the industry of the people who work there, which is hardly morally arbitrary.

For all these difficulties there are problems associated with the proposition that states own outright the natural resources of their territory and, in particular, with the convention that the government of the day can dispose of those resources as they wish. These well-established norms can actually provide support for oppressive governments and can distort development in those countries whose economies are dominated by the extractive industries. The phenomenon of the 'resource curse' is the subject of quite an extensive literature; the philosopher Lief Wenar is a central figure here (Wenar, 2008 and http://wenar.info/). This is certainly a serious argument, although it can be argued that the resource curse is actually a function of political institutions and culture rather than resources as such. Norway, for example, now has an economy that is substantially based on its share of North Sea oil revenues and yet it has avoided oppressive government, and its sovereign wealth fund is invested wisely. The difference between Norway and, say, Libya, where for 40 years Gaddafi ran a hydrocarbon dictatorship, is not a function of oil revenues but of political institutions and culture, which takes us back to Rawls's position.

Global justice II

The modified Rawlsian approach of Pogge and Beitz contrasts somewhat with the approach to global justice of those who reject the central apparatus with which Rawls approaches the problem, and who are unhappy with Rawls's notion of 'justice as fairness'. A central figure here is Brian Barry, who regards justice as fairness as giving far too much weight to mutual advantage, as witness Rawls's very definition of a society for the purposes of his theory as a 'co-operative scheme for mutual advantage'. The problem with mutual advantage as a basis for a social contract is that it assumes that all those who come to the table have something to offer which entitles them to be a contracting party, and this will exclude people who ought not to be excluded – it may be possible to give a virtual presence round the table to the severely disabled and to babes in arms, but future generations and foreigners are less easy to bring on board. Barry proposes an alternative formula, 'justice as impartiality' which he bases on principles established by Thomas Scanlon in his major study *What we Owe to Each Other* (Barry, 1995; Scanlon, 2000). Scanlon's contractualism is based on the proposition that

> [judgements] of right and wrong [are] judgements about what would be permitted by principles that could not reasonably be rejected, by people who were moved to find principles for the general regulation of behaviour that others, similarly motivated, could not reasonably reject.

This may seem a little convoluted but the intention is clear; this formula puts a lot of weight on motivation and reasonableness. Motivation to find agreement is important but often neglected. It probably is the case that most people want to think that their judgements on matters of right and wrong are defensible and so are motivated to seek agreement on them, but it would be foolish to expect that everyone will be so motivated. Some people who possess privileges may simply wish to defend them whether they are morally defensible or not, and it is foolish to think that they can be reasoned out of this position. Justice may sometimes involve coercion. Reasonableness plays a key role, and what is deemed reasonable is to be determined partly by engaging in thought-experiments such as Rawls's 'veil of ignorance' but also by invoking general principles. A great deal rests here on whether or not reasonableness is something that is cross-cultural – if it is not and what is reasonable in one culture is unreasonable in another then we have a real problem. One of the reasons why Barry is so critical of arguments that privilege culture is that he is sensitive to the high stakes that are involved here (Barry, 2000).

Having established a method, the aim is to find impartial principles: in this respect it is important to distinguish between 'first order' and 'second order' impartiality. The former means essentially equal treatment for all, the latter allows for differential treatment but only if the reasons for distinguishing between individuals apply to all. To give an obvious example of the latter, the argument that one is entitled to privilege the interests of family members and friends over strangers is consistent with second order impartiality, if and only if the same privilege is guaranteed to everyone else. The extent of this latter privilege is something that has to be subject to agreement, but there is nothing inherently wrong with the idea that we have greater obligations to those near to us than to strangers – whereas first order impartiality of the kind espoused by radical utilitarians would insist that everyone be treated alike, which is why, as we have seen, for Peter Singer, 'distance is irrelevant'.

The notion of second order impartiality is important in the context of this chapter because it seems a particularly appropriate notion in the international context. Rather than asking that we treat foreigners and our co-nationals equally in all respects, second order impartiality principles of global justice might involve some preferential treatment for co-nationals – the argument then becomes a matter of determining which areas might be characterised in this way. In other words, there is no longer an assumption of equal treatment; instead the assumption is that departures from equality are possible but need to be justified, and justified in such a way that all countries are able to go down the same route. No special privileges are available to my co-nationals simply because they are part of my tribe – rather, any privilege I claim for myself must be available for everyone else on the same basis. The criteria for determining which departures from equal treatment can be justified impartially are deter-mined according to Scanlon's principle as set out above. So, we can ask whether, for example, the principle of national ownership of national resources – which certainly meets the requirement of second order impartiality – is a principle 'that could not reasonably be rejected, by people who were moved to find prin-ciples for the general regulation of behaviour that others, similarly motivated, could not reasonably reject'? In answering this question we can have recourse to thought-experiments such as Rawls's second contract under a veil of igno-rance, but we can also ask whether such a principle is reasonable, given that it would result in radically unequal national endowments, which is a fact that would not be available to those working under a Rawlsian veil. We might con-clude that although this principle is consistent with second order impartiality it is not one that we ought to endorse.

Barry himself only examined the international dimension of justice in a small number of papers, of which his account of 'International society from a cosmopolitan perspective' is the most important (Barry, 1998a). In that paper he suggests three principles can be established as reasonable at the international as well as the domestic level; first, is 'the presumption of equality'; second, the notion of 'personal responsibility and compensation' which covers departures from equality which are the result of decisions freely taken by individuals; and third, and in this context most importantly 'the priority of vital interests', which he elaborates as the principle that 'in the absence of some compelling consideration to the contrary, the vital interests of each person should be protected in preference to the non-vital interests of anyone' (p. 148). It is clear that such a principle has very radical implications when applied to international relations, but although, as the title of the paper suggests, this is a cosmopolitan principle, it is interesting that it does not necessarily lead to global equality, *pace* the first of the three principles. The second principle, individual responsibility, offers scope for quite wide variation once the vital interests of all are met; if a particular society chooses a lower savings rate than the average then, over time and other things being equal, it will become poorer and this result would be 'reasonable' in the terms of the principles set out above.

What is interesting here is that Barry, Rawls and Singer end up more or less in the same place, though they have arrived there by very different routes. Rawls's *The Law of Peoples* sets out a duty of assistance on the part of the well-ordered to help the burdened to attain membership of the Society of Peoples; the weaker version of Singer's utilitarianism requires transfers to meet the basic needs of those who are subject to malnutrition or starvation, but makes no demand beyond that point, and Barry's reasonable principle requires that the vital interests of all be prioritised over everyone's non-vital interests. There is a surprisingly high degree of convergence here, reflecting perhaps the operation of a general commitment to beneficence working itself through different philosophical lenses. What it may also suggest is that a general theory of global justice can take us only so far down the road towards solving the problem of global poverty and inequality, and that what is needed is more attention to particular problems and the operation of particular institutions, and this is indeed the way in which the discourse on global inequality has actually developed. Whereas the work examined so far in this chapter has its origins in debates of the 1970s and 1980s, in the last decade or so the discourse has taken a somewhat different slant.

Global institutional reform

Most of the writers we have looked at so far in this chapter are 'moral cosmopolitans' in Thomas Pogge's terms, including in such works as *Realizing Rawls*, Pogge himself, but in the last decade or so the emphasis of global justice theorists has shifted towards institutional reform – not towards world government as such, but towards reform at a more modest but still significant level. One of the writers who has been most creative in this respect has been Pogge himself, and his *World Poverty and Human Rights* (2008) stands with Simon Caney's *Justice Beyond Borders* (2005) as one of the two most significant works in the field of the present century. To recapitulate, Pogge is a Post-Rawlsian justice theorist – he holds that Rawls's *Theory of Justice* is on the right lines, but is wrong to simply assume the existence of separate societies; such a Westphalian assumption would be legitimate only if validated by a single global original position in which all people are represented as individuals. Such a global original position would, he assumes, support global responsibilities even if separate societies were chosen as the mechanism by which they were met; this position underlies *World Poverty and Human Rights*.

Linking the issue of world poverty to human rights is, of course, not original to Pogge; what is distinctive in his approach to this issue is, first, his understanding that coping with world poverty should be seen as an issue of negative duties rather than positive duties, and, second, his proposal of institutional reform to remedy the situation. As to the first, his definition of negative and positive duties are more or less conventional; a negative duty is a duty 'to ensure that others are not unduly harmed [or wronged] through one's conduct', a positive duty is a 'duty to benefit persons or to shield them from other harms'. Pogge argues that we have negative as well as positive duties to the poor; these negative duties stem from the fact that we actively contribute to global poverty via the injustices embedded in the global economic system.

Here we return with a vengeance to an issue aired in an earlier section of this chapter – are the current global international economic institutions part of the problem or part of the solution? Pogge has no doubt that the former is the case – we in the West benefit from global institutions which have been imposed on the global South as a result of a common and violent history. The West called the shots in the past via formal imperialism, nowadays it uses more subtle techniques. The standard rules and norms of the world economy are instrumental in allowing illegitimate regimes to oppress their populations. First, such oppressive governments are allowed to borrow money from global institutions and to mortgage the natural resources that their country possesses – these 'borrowing' and 'resource' privileges enable oppressive regimes to stay in business, and since the debts so produced are regarded as incurred by the country in question they will burden and handicap successor democratic regimes. Moreover, as another instance of the way in which institutions that are supposed to work for the benefit of all actually help the rich, the World Trade Organisation forces open the markets of poor countries but allows rich country markets to stay protected, thereby denying the benefits of free trade to the poor. Thus, for example, the European Union's Common Agricultural Policy protects sugar beet producers in Europe at the expense of cane sugar producers elsewhere, and rice growers in Japan and the US are similarly protected from competition from poor countries.

Before looking at Pogge's remedies for this situation, it is worth noting that although there is clearly some substance to the charges being made, defenders of the current regime also have quite a strong case since, as noted earlier, very large numbers of people have been lifted out of poverty by the operation of the global economy over the last two decades. Still, it is difficult to avoid the impression that the important point for Pogge is actually about the effect of the argument rather than the detail that supports it. He clearly believes that arguments to the general public based on negative duties have persuasive power that arguments based on positive duties do not – the thought is that we will find it much more difficult to dodge the moral implications of global poverty if we can be persuaded that we have actually created the misery that is placed before us, than if we are simply told that we have a positive duty to relieve suffering regardless of its causes. This may actually be the case, but there are arguments that go in the other direction. Part of the problem is that Pogge is clearly so absolutely convinced of the general truth of his assessment of the current global economic system that he finds it difficult to believe that there are serious arguments in its favour – but if such arguments do actually exist then the argument from negative duties falls down, while the argument from positive duty remains unharmed. It is this latter thought that explains why writers such Simon Caney focus on positive duties, because that way the case for global action is dependent only on the existence of extreme need, and its causes can be set aside as morally irrelevant.

Returning to the proposals for reform made by Pogge, these form into three sets, concerned with democracy, sovereignty and redistribution. As to democracy, the basic idea is that democratising states should be protected from authoritarian predators by setting up institutional arrangements that prevent such predators from enjoying the aforementioned borrowing and resource privileges. The key institutional reform proposed is that a Democracy Panel should be created to judge when a democracy has been undermined by such predators. Contracts signed by regimes judged not to be democratic should have no legal binding force on subsequent regimes; this would make international lenders and multinationals reluctant to enter into agreements with non-democratic regimes, which in turn would reduce dramatically the resources available to such regimes. There would be an incentive to establish democracies, and a disincentive to overthrow them. This would, of course, only work if all states and corporations accepted the legitimacy of the Democracy Panel. Pogge proposed that it should be composed of respected international jurists, presumably along the same lines as the existing International Court of Justice and International Criminal Court in the Hague but with a much more politically charged mandate even than the ICC. Given that the rulings of the ICC and the ICJ are not universally accepted today it is difficult to be optimistic that the rulings of a Democracy Panel would be taken seriously in the absence of other changes in the global institutional order, and such changes are, in fact, envis-aged by Pogge.

These changes involve a new approach to sovereignty, compatible with, but rather more extensive than, the redefinition of sovereignty as responsibility that we encountered in Chapter 8. Pogge does not propose the establishment of a 'world government' but rather that national sovereignty should be undermined by a form of global federalism, with power dispersed at many levels, and the powers of national governments severely curtailed thereby. There is a certain vagueness about this approach to sovereignty, and it is informed by the view that 'Westphalian' sovereignty of the kind that existed in the old society of states is incompatible with federal systems – allegedly, federal systems have no ultimate centre of authority and such a centre is, again allegedly, required for Westphalian sovereignty to be valid. These claims can be challenged; while it is certainly true that federal systems do not have the kind of straightforward sov-ereigns that Thomas Hobbes regarded as important and necessary, they do have ultimate loci of power – in the US, for example, it could be said that the sover-eign power resides with the majorities of Congress and the separate states that are needed to propose and ratify constitutional amendments. In any event, Hobbesian sovereignty was never regarded as the norm within the Society of States, witness the survival as an effective political actor of the Holy Roman Empire for a century and a half after Westphalia (Simms, 2013). Still, the notion that the sovereign powers of national states should be limited is crucial to Pogge's world-view.

The final element of his reform programme concerns national resources and redistribution. Nations should continue to control their natural resources, sub-ject to the findings of the Democracy Panel, but, when they use or sell these resources, governments should pay a small percentage of their value into a fund which would be used to pay a Global Resource Dividend (GRD) to the global poor, who ought to be regarded as having an inalienable stake in these resources, a stake that at the moment brings them no benefits. This is an interesting idea, which actually has positive environmental consequences; unlike those notions that involve taxing the notional value of natural resources, the GRD provides a positive incentive to conserve such resources, since it is paid only when they are actually exploited. It also avoids the counter-intuitive consequences of a tax on the value of resources, because although some resource-rich poor countries would pay more into the GRD than resource-poor rich countries, they would get much more back. Ultimately the costs of the GRD would be borne by consumers.

Pogge's GRD falls into the same general category as the Tobin Tax – a tax on foreign exchange transactions designed to create a development fund and simul-taneously discourage exchange-rate speculation – or indeed a simple proposal to create additional Special Drawing Rights (SDRs) for poorer countries at the IMF, similar to the 'quantitative easing' or stimulus packages' which rich countries have used in recent years to prevent their economies from crashing in the aftermath of the 2008 financial crisis. All of these schemes have their merits and a case can be made that the implementation of any one of them would make for a better, fairer world – however, they all face the same problem of ensuring that the proceeds of the GRD or Tobin Tax or SDRs actually get to the right people. Pogge's Democracy Panel, if it could be made to operate effectively, would prevent oppressive governments sequestering the proceeds of such taxes, but even without this misappropriation it is difficult to reach the actual poor in poor societies, as so many studies of development aid over the years have shown.

World government and globalisation

Thomas Pogge's programme for institutional reform is ambitious but falls short of actual world government, and in any event in recent years he has shifted his attention to global health problems and 'health rights' – on which see his excellent website http://pantheon.yale.edu/~tp4/index.html – while Simon Caney has also shifted his attention away from the big picture towards, in his case, the moral implications of climate change (Caney, 2012a, 2012b). Interestingly, this shift has taken place simultaneously with a revived interest in world government on the part of IR theorists. Generally in the post-1945 discipline of International Relations world government has been regarded as an utopian project – and the arguments against such projects are standard in the IR literature: on the one hand, world government is impossible to achieve without the (implausible) consent of states, while, on the other hand, if it could be achieved it could only be in the form of an undesirable, undemocratic 'leviathan'. As was noted in Chapter 8 above, this latter fear has been expressed even in respect of the limited degree of UN Security Council consensus anticipated by the proponents of a Responsibility to Protect, which, in any event, has not been achieved. These arguments remain in place and, some would say remain valid, but still world government is back on the intellectual agenda of IR theorists, if not in the world of actual international politics.

This revival of the notion of world government is not actually a response to global poverty, but to the fear of nuclear war. Campbell Craig and William Scheuerman have revived the arguments of John Herz and Hans J. Morgenthau to the effect that nuclear weapons have brought about the 'demise of the territorial state' (Herz, 1959; Craig, 2004; Scheuerman, 2011). Morgenthau himself, rather contrary to his image as a hidebound realist, believed that world government had become a necessity with the emergence of nuclear power, the first real revolution in international relations for hundreds of years (Morgenthau, 1970). Daniel Deudney's 'republican security theory' set out in his masterwork *Bounding Power*, again concludes with the idea that what he calls 'nuclear one-worldism' based on 'violence interdependence' is mandated by the destructive power of modern weapons (Deudney, 2006). And, on similar lines, the constructivist theorist Alexander Wendt in a famous paper in the *European Journal of International Relations* sets out why the logic of anarchy explains 'Why a world state is inevitable' albeit only within the next one or two hundred years (Wendt, 2003).

Interestingly, these writers are working from within a state-centric account of international relations – their world government is a world state – and rather more relevant to the theme of the second half of this book, the putative emergence of a global polity, is the work on globalisation and global governance of writers such as David Held, Daniele Archibugi, Luis Cabrera and Mathias Koenig-Archibugi, and the scholars who are developing a model of global constitutionalism. Of the former group Held is a central figure; he began his career as a Critical theorist in the Frankfurt tradition and would maintain that he has stayed true to this perspective on the world, adopting a social democratic politics to the age of globalisation. His contention is that democracy is meaningful only if it applies to the places where power is exercised; the nation-state is no longer such a place, and democracy must therefore be globalised in a cosmopolitan politics which looks to the establishment of accountability and the rule of law at the global level (Held, 1987). He has elaborated these thoughts in numerous books, alone or in collaboration with Archibugi (Archibugi and Held, 1995; Held, 2004). His work has involved preparing proposals for institutional reform, for example, envisaging popular institutions running parallel to interstate bodies such as the UN, and enhancing the legitimacy of 'global civil society' bodies. The journal *Global Policy* and the LSE 'Global Civil Society' Project which produces the *Yearbook of Global Civil Society*, now in its tenth year, are cognate projects. These initiatives dovetail with arguments made by Mathias Koenig-Archibugi on the possibility of global democracy, and the work of Luis Cabrera on 'global citizenship' (Cabrera, 2010; Koenig-Archibugi, 2011). Cabrera's argument is interesting in so far as it moves beyond the moral case for global citizenship to analysing the work of immigration activists in the US and in Europe as examples of those who think and act globally, who are, already, global citizens.

These theorists are simultaneously analysing the emerging global polity, and attempting through their actions to make it a reality. This at times presents difficulties; the roles of advocate and analyst do not always sit comfortably together in the same individual. The analyst needs a degree of distance from the object of analysis, while for the advocate a close engagement is essential; one obvious critique of work of this kind is that the advocacy at times distorts the analysis – Held and his colleagues are so sure of the value of the position that they are advocating that they sometimes disregard the objections to that position that can legitimately be posed. The most important of these objections is that the vision of the world that they advocate is very much the view from a privileged, largely Western European standpoint, and that the values that are regarded as unproblematic by these writers actually are contested in much of the rest of the world. The assumption is that the peoples of the world really share a common vision of how they would like the future to play out and that democratising the world's institutions would produce a kind of global liberal democracy devoted to human rights and universal well-being. Perhaps so, but the difficulties experienced by the international human rights regime over the last two or three decades suggest that this assumption may well be optimistic.

The (West) European vision of world politics is even more precisely represented in the notions of 'global constitutionalism' which have become institutionalised in a number of British and German universities in recent years – see, for example, the Centre for Global Constitutionalism at the University of St Andrews and the new international journal *Global Constitutionalism*. Antje Wiener's 'Global Constitutionalism: Mapping an Emergent Field' is a useful overview of this movement, the product of a conference held at the Social Science Research Center in Berlin on *Constitutionalism in a New Key* in January 2011 (available online at http://cosmopolis.wzb.eu/program). The goal of this project is to Europeanise world politics – post-1945 Europe has managed to transform itself from the cockpit of global conflict into a security community in which violent methods of conflict resolution have been replaced by arguments within a constitutional structure. It would indeed be a great achievement if this shift could be generalised, but it is clear that, for the time being, the conditions that made it possible in Europe are not present globally – the aim of the global constitutionalism movement is to explore the ways in which this gap between Europe and the rest of the world can be closed.

Conclusion

As we have seen over the last five chapters, the normative shift from a Society of States to a cosmopolitan Global Polity has not proceeded smoothly; the ending of one obstacle to a human rights culture, the Cold War, provided a space within which other critiques of human rights could flourish; attempts to operationalise a new humanitarian sensibility in the 1990s threw up problems which the notion of a Responsibility to Protect in the new century only partially addressed; in the last decade or more the Global War on Terror declared in response to the rise of radical Islam has led to the deployment of new techniques of warfare which have challenged the conventional moral categories we use to consider the use of force without producing new ones. In this rather depressing context, notions such as global governance and global constitutionalism, melding with theories of global social justice, present an account of what a global polity might look like that is refreshingly optimistic. Writers such as Pogge, Caney, Held and Cabrera are presenting a programme of cosmopolitanism in action for the twenty-first century, symbolically represented by a new movement 'Academics Stand Against Poverty' (ASAP) which was announced in a Special Issue of *Ethics & International Affairs* edited by Pogge and Cabrera in the summer of 2012. The key question, though, is whether this cosmopolitan programme can actually leave the seminar room and take root in the real world.

Further Reading

The major works of Brian Barry, Charles Beitz, Thomas Pogge, Peter Singer and John Rawls are noted in the text of this chapter. The secondary literature on Rawls has already been noted in Chapter 4; Barry's collected papers (1989) contain a number of works on global justice produced before he fully formulated his ideas on impartiality, of particular note is 'Humanity and justice in global perspective' a friendly critique of Singer. A Symposium on Brian Barry's 'Justice as impartiality' in *Political Studies* 44, 2 (1996) is very useful and Paul Kelly (1998) is an excellent collection of papers on all aspects of Barry's work. The classic status of Charles Beitz (1979) was recognised by a Special Section of the *Review of International Studies* 31, No. 2 (2005). Thomas Pogge has one of the academic world's most informative websites, with a comprehensive guide to his publications http://pantheon.yale.edu/~tp4/index.html. Alison Jagger (2010) is a good collection of papers on Pogge's work.

Simon Caney's major book (2005) should not be missed; his later work on the ethics of climate change has been very influential – Caney (2012a) gives an overview, (2012b) is more substantial. Kok-Cho Tan (2000) is an important study; Chris Armstrong (2012) is a very useful textbook on global justice, covering the same ground as this chapter, but in more detail (and from a more cosmopolitan viewpoint), a competitor for Gillian Brock's text (2009). Mathias Risse's book *On Global Justice* (2012) stands alongside Caney (2005) and Pogge (2008) as a major contribution. Risse's book also produced a rather jaundiced review by Conor Gearty in the *Times Higher Education Supplement* which ended by asking 'Even if ... he is right, what difference can (yet another) set of self-contained right answers about justice by a bright university guy make?' – a question that might be posed to most of the works discussed here – although the 'bright university guys' would probably ask how else moral progress can be made www.timeshighereducation.co.uk/books/on-global-justice/421936.article. Leif Wenar's position on the 'resource curse' can be followed via Wenar (2008) and (2013) but as with Thomas Pogge, his website is where the action really is http://wenar.info/.

(Continued)

(Continued)

David Held's project for cosmopolitan democracy has been referenced in the text of this chapter – one of the most recent, and best, products is a collection edited by Daniele Archibugi, Mathias Koenig-Archibugi and Raffaele Marchetti (2012), while Archibugi and Held (1995) is one of the Ur-texts, along with Held (1987). Luis Cabrera's (2010) has been referenced in the text of this chapter – also noteworthy is his 'cosmopolitan case for a world state' (2004). Held, Cabrera et al. approach cosmopolitan democracy from a normative perspective – works by Daniel Deudney (2006), William Schuerman (2011) and Alexander Wendt (2003) look to the emergence of a world state but from an analytical viewpoint. The *Global Civil Society Yearbooks* produced at the London School of Economics offer a range of theoretical articles and case studies – see www.lse.ac.uk/internationalDevelopment/research/CSHS/civilSociety/yearBook/contentsPages/2012.aspx for the 2012 Yearbook, and links to earlier numbers.

CONCLUSION

THE RETURN OF REALISM IN THEORY AND PRACTICE

The second half of this book has been devoted to examining the putative evolution of the international order from a society of states to a global polity. This has involved an examination of the new international human rights regime that emerged after the end of the Cold War, humanitarian intervention and the rights-based humanitarianism of the 1990s, the concept of 'Responsibility to Protect' as it has evolved in the years since the ICISS Report of 2001, changes in the nature of Just War theory pointing it in the direction of individual rights and, in the last chapter, theories of global justice and global governance. All of these themes have converged on the notion of a cosmopolitan transformation of the normative basis of international relations. An examination of the new politics of war and violence and the Global War on Terror disrupted somewhat this narrative by placing conflict centre-stage, but even here it was clear that things had drifted away from an inter-state account of how the world works – groups such as Al Qaeda are as much part of the global polity as the cosmopolitans who have been behind the evolution of human rights norms and proposals for global social justice. It seems that even those who most want to disrupt our world can be fitted into a narrative of progress, albeit on the dark side of the story.

The purpose of this final chapter is to identify some challenges to the cosmopolitan story that the second half of this book has been telling, not with a view to disrupting the narrative altogether but rather with a view to identifying how the broad story of a move towards a global polity fits into the actual practice of international politics in the twenty-first century. The best way to summarise much of what follows is to say that it is concerned to trace how an essentially liberal conception of politics chimes, or does not chime, with a world that, in many respects, is the reverse of liberal. There are different dimensions to this story; it involves contrasting the liberal cosmopolitanism we have encountered so far with a different kind of cosmopolitanism, one more attuned to the importance of difference; it involves examining how an essentially European vision of how politics ought to work plays out in a world order where non-European states are coming to assume greater importance; and it involves looking at trends in the study of international political theory that are reviving and revitalising the realist tradition of political theory, a tradition that liberal cosmopolitanism had consigned to the past, but which is proving remarkably resilient.

Liberal cosmopolitanism and its critics

At the end of Chapter 6, as a way of signalling that there was more to be said about the story of human rights in a multicultural world, Tsvetan Todorov's account of the *Conquest of America* was briefly told, in order to highlight the proposition that liberal thinking – and perhaps European thinking more generally – finds it difficult to cope with the notion of 'different but equal'. Difference is either denied in the interests of equality, or understood as a sign of inferiority; to its credit, the former strategy is characteristic of liberalism, which rejects racism and intolerance as irrational and unreasonable – but on the basis of an account of rationality and reasonableness that is taken to be unproblematic. This is a position that pervades liberal thought, although it is most visible in the work of theorists of justice, whether cosmopolitan or not. Thus, John Rawls's 'realist utopia' is designed not to contradict what we know about human nature; in the 'original position' under the 'veil of ignorance' he assumes that contractors know that there are certain 'primary goods' that all rational persons want whatever else they want, and these primary goods include what people need in their status as free and equal citizens as well as what they need for their general welfare and survival. Again, Brian Barry's 'justice as impartiality' rests on a notion of 'reasonableness', which is assumed to be cross-cultural; his *Culture and Equality* is explicit on this – the assumption is that there is only one standard of reasonableness. Jürgen Habermas's thought, not examined elsewhere in this book, but important for many writers on global governance, assumes that the 'force of the better argument' would prevail in an 'ideal speech situation', that is to say a situation where the distortions of power and interest are removed; truth is built into the nature of speech and will come through if such distortions can be eliminated (Habermas, 1990). What all of these positions have in common is that they build the answer into the question; working out what constitutes the better argument, or which social institutions can be justified as reasonable, or will be chosen under the veil of ignorance becomes an exercise in reasoning from unquestioned premises and failure to get the right answer indicates either an ill will, or an inability to think straight.

But what constitutes a reasonable argument? Daniel Bell in a review of Barry's *Justice as Impartiality* in *Political Theory*, helpfully and amusingly lists arguments deemed not to be reasonable by Barry:

> [religious] 'dogma' is not allowed (pp. 29, 30, 122–3, 162–3); cultural communities that claim special advantages – what 'post-modernists' call the 'politics of identity' – are not being reasonable (pp. 8, 115); those who reject the authority of expert opinions, arguments, and evidence are not guided by a norm of reasonableness (pp. 104–6); those who hold false beliefs should be excluded (p. 208); those who lack knowledge that other societies do things differently and that their own could feasibly be different in various ways don't count either. (Bell, 1998: 107)

The point is not that, for example, 'religious dogmas' are held to be wrong, but rather that they are ruled out of order. Our own, putatively liberal, society is privileged over all others, past and present – we have 'higher cognitive adequacy' to quote a revealing formulation of Habermas. Progress has given us the opportunity to condescend to the past; we in the modern West are in a privileged position vis-à-vis the past and those societies that are mired in the past, that still hold to pre-modern positions.

This is, of course, a caricature – very few liberals would hold quite such strong views, although the late Norman Geras in his blog told a good story here about Brian Barry, on the occasion of the latter's death in 2009:

> I was at a discussion meeting in London some time between 1988 and 1992 in which Brian was a participant. Though I don't remember the precise terms of the question, at one point during the evening it was put to him (approximately) to say whether, in view of the great range of cultural forms, social practices and moral beliefs there had been historically, he was wanting to claim that liberal values were the best values for everyone. I do remember the precise terms of Brian's answer. 'Yes,' he said.

Barry was actually a little unusual in that he was prepared to say such things explicitly, but most liberal cosmopolitans believe something similar, and they have distinguished predecessors in so doing. Kimberly Hutchings traces this position to Immanuel Kant, and in particular to Kant's belief that thought requires orientation and that this orientation has to be based on the perspective of the present. As she puts it,

> Kant's orientation for political thinking organizes the world, spatially, temporarily and morally in a particular way … [to] the extent that others do not orient their

thought along Kantian lines they are in some kind of error [wilful or inadvertent]. This means that spatio-temporally distant people and peoples, from the perspective of the rational belief of the philosopher, precisely because they are moral equals are a priori identified as in need of either punishment or education to set them right. (Hutchings, 2011: 193)

As an example of the continuation of this orientation she cites Habermas's cosmopolitanism which is built on Kant, but looks to the growth of institutions in Europe in particular as the current bearers of the Kantian project. These societies face other cultures 'not as alien societies … [but] as previous phrases of our own social development'. From this we can deduce that our societies have responsibilities as bearers of the cosmopolitan ideal in the absence of a fully constitutionalised international order.

Charles Taylor summarises the issue very well when he makes the point in *The Politics of Recognition* that 'liberalism is not a possible meeting ground for all cultures, but is the political expression of one range of cultures, and quite incompatible with other ranges' (Taylor et al., 1994: 62). To treat liberalism as the end point of a process of development which means that contemporary liberals are in position to critique all alternatives is to make a serious mistake, and one that has real-world political consequences – resistance to cosmopolitan liberal political positions partly stems from a rejection of this privileged standpoint, although, as we will see later in this chapter, other motivations also come into play. Still, rejecting the liberal version of cosmopolitanism does not mean that cosmopolitanism as such has to be rejected – one critic of liberal cosmopolitanism, William Connolly, offers an alternative version that has at least some traction.

Connolly is a figure from the 'New Left' of the 1960s and 70s who has become a leading post-structuralist writer, someone whose work crosses domestic/international boundaries. A fundamental proposition about politics for Connolly is that there is no identity without difference – the key issue is how this fact is negotiated. Originally a student of C.B. Macpherson, Connolly now characterises the latter's problematic as based on:

> *Alienation/repression/collective realisation.* People are alienated from a harmonious identity; this alienation is fostered by institutions that both repress the self and disable the collectivity from forming a higher unifying consensus; and the highest institutional arrangements would enable individuals to flourish within a harmonious whole. (1995, p. 88)

In Macpherson's hands this is a socialist perspective but it shares qualities with liberalism. Now though, Connolly is committed to a different problematic:

> *Normalisation/depoliticization/pluralisation.* Pressures to normalization are deeply inscribed in the contemporary order; these pressures depoliticize consensual

conventions that harm many; a pluralizing political society would foster cultural diversities while relieving many of these injuries. (1995, p. 88).

The old emancipatory project, socialist and liberal, has proved to be a new disciplinary force, pinning down meanings, normalising identities, depoliticising issues by the use of a sovereign reason, imposing consensus in the name of anti-relativism. The aim instead must be a pluralising political society – characterised by 'agonistic' politics.

Does this point to communitarianism? Globalising factors based on wider/deeper interactions ('speed') mean that the traditional sovereign space is no longer adequate, but neither is a cosmopolitanism based on a morality grounded in one society (the Kantian position). Instead there are a plurality of cosmopolitanisms:

> Today, when speed compresses distance and intercultural action transcends state boundaries, cosmopolitanism becomes both unavoidable and diverse. There are military, corporate, Christian, Islamic, ecological, aboriginal, and feminist modes of cosmopolitanism for starters, with each type containing considerable variety in itself and involved in a series of alliances and struggles with the others. (Connolly, 2000, p. 603)

Agonistic pluralism at the global level is needed; Connolly's point is that a faith in secular rationalism can be as 'fundamentalist' as religious faith, and that the liberal propensity to moralise and legalise questions that are essentially political is unhealthy. This position has affinities with the work of the new political realism which we are about to encounter, but before moving on it may be worth adding a cautionary note. Benjamin Barber makes a compelling point in a review of Connolly's *Pluralism*:

> [Connolly] is consistently more distrustful of the hidden coercions of rationality and liberal tolerance than he is of the explicit brutalities of unreason and fundamentalist bigotry. (Barber, 2007)

This tendency is more pronounced in his recent work on 'neo-liberalism' which pulls together all the normalising features of the modern world into one, not altogether coherent package – and at times the impression is left that anything that disrupts this package is to be welcomed, whatever its particular orientation. There are echoes here of Michel Foucault welcoming the Iranian Revolution of 1979 on the basis that it offered a new way of doing politics in contrast to the liberal West; indeed it did, and many Iranians have paid and are still paying the price. Still, Connolly's 'agonism' does have one major incontestable benefit – it points us back to the importance of the political and the dangers of making politics subject to morality.

The problem with global justice and the new political realism

Connolly presents a critique of liberal cosmopolitanism from the perspective of an alternative understanding of cosmopolitanism, but cosmopolitanism is also contestable from within liberalism by those who stress the importance of membership in a political community and of patriotism – while acknowledging a duty of global benevolence writers such as David Miller and Michael Walzer – and for that matter John Rawls – reject the idea that this is a matter of justice. Such positions take us back to the 'Society of States' approach discussed in the first part of this book. Into this debate comes an interesting contribution from Thomas Nagel; in 'The problem of global justice' (2005) he offers a critique of liberal cosmopolitan theories of global justice from an unexpected direction. Nagel is a liberal, analytical, political philosopher who might be expected to sympathise with the discourse of global justice – instead he provides a compelling critique, and does so in the house journal of his opponents.

Much of his argument replicates Rawls's critique of cosmopolitanism; he renames Rawls's position on global justice as the 'political' conception and defends it as 'anti-monist'. There is no reason to think that there is simply one account of justice (this is what he means by 'monism'); justice should be governed by the Rawlsian principle that the correct regulative principle for a thing depends on the nature of that thing. This argument is not particularly original – it has close, albeit unacknowledged, affinities with the argument presented by Michael Walzer in *Spheres of Justice* (1983) – and more interesting is Nagel's defence of the Hobbesian proposition that there is a link between justice and sovereignty: he argues that:

> What creates the link between justice and sovereignty is something common to a wide range of conceptions of justice: they all depend on the co-ordinated conduct of large numbers of people, which cannot be achieved without law, backed up by a monopoly of force. (p.115)

This is important because it suggests that the distinction between 'moral cosmopolitanism' and 'institutional cosmopolitanism' does not do the work that figures such as Beitz and Pogge want it to and, if valid, it also undermines the idea that some form of 'global governance' can substitute for the sovereign state, or that a loose confederation, or set of networks can do the job. These are all different ways of getting round the absence of a global institution that possesses the monopoly of force and thus has the capacity to co-ordinate conduct.

What Nagel is presenting here is effectively a critique of the notion of 'ideal theory'; ideal theory assumes that every actor (whether individuals or institutions) is willing and able to comply with whatever principles of social justice are regarded as appropriate – what Nagel is suggesting is that the level of coordination required to bring about just social conditions goes beyond what can be achieved by such voluntary compliance. A legal system backed by a government in possession of the monopoly of force is required – presumably he would acknowledge that such a monopoly is never absolute, but that is beside the point, which is that theories of global justice which are expected to work in the absence of law and government are doomed to disappoint. Predictably this position has proved unpopular with those Nagel is criticising, but, perhaps unintentionally, it has some features in common with another move in contemporary political philosophy, sometimes called the new political realism.

The key texts of the new political realism are Raymond Geuss *Philosophy and Real Politics* (2008) and Bernard Williams *In The Beginning Was the Deed: Realism and Moralism in Political Argument* (2005) – in some respects the latter of the two books is the more interesting from the perspective of International Political Theory. Bernard Williams (1929–2003) was one of the leading British philosophers of the second half of the twentieth century. He wrote extensively on many subjects including ethics; he was a critic of 'meta-ethical' positions such as utilitarianism and Kantianism, instead focusing on the key question of Classical ethics, 'how should we live?'. He was a leading figure in the revival of so-called 'Virtue Ethics', which we have encountered in this book in the early work at least of Martha Nussbaum. Williams was a consistent critic of 'morality' as an abstract exercise, someone who instead focused on a secular, humanist account of how we should live in the here and now (Williams, 2006).

In the Beginning was the Deed is a posthumous collection of essays which explores the relationship between politics and morality and is vigorously critical of any account of political theory or political philosophy in which politics is seen as applied morality. In particular he criticises two models of political theory both of which have played a big part in the development of the theory of a global polity and global justice. First, he criticises what he calls *The Enactment Model* under which principles, concepts, ideals and values are formulated in theory and the role of politics is to enact these formulations via persuasion, the use of power and so on. Utilitarianism and other consequentialist theories are examples of this model; see, for example, Peter Singer's approach to famine relief which is to establish the relevant principle (we should stop bad things happening if we can) and values (suffering is bad) on the basis that political action should follow from this – we should enact his model in our political life. Thomas Pogge's account of the relationship of human rights and poverty takes a somewhat similar form, as do attempts to set out criteria for Humanitarian Intervention (for example, Tony Blair's Chicago 'Doctrine of the International Community') and some versions of Just War theory. *The Structural Model* on the other hand works rather differently: 'theory lays down moral conditions of coexistence under power, conditions in which power can be justly exercised' – morality doesn't directly tell us what politics must do but sets constraints on what politics can rightly do. The classic illustration is here is Rawls's

Theory of Justice where politics must meet the conditions laid down by the Original Position but where within this constraint limited variation is possible. In the *Law of Peoples* greater variation is offered – now 'well-ordered' societies are to be regarded as legitimate – but the basic idea holds. The idea of a 'Responsibility to Protect' could be seen as based on a structural model, constraining the legitimate use of power, to replace enactment models of humanitarian intervention. Structural models are also widely used in US political philosophy, where legal constraints based on the Constitution and interpreted or enforced by the Supreme Court cover many issues regarded elsewhere as more purely political.

Williams's point is that in both enactment and structural models, the moral is prior to the political – Williams terms this *'political moralism'* and contrasts it with *'political realism'*. Political moralism is unsatisfactory because it disregards the reality of politics and in particular fails to understand that the 'first political question' is always that of securing order; he adds to this that the 'basic legitimation demand' for any political order is that it be secured in such a way that it is acceptable to all. This position is compatible with a kind of liberalism, but it is the 'liberalism of fear' of Judith Shklar rather than the liberalism of ideal theorists such as Rawls and other theorists of justice (Shklar, 1996; Shklar and Yack, 1996). The basic units of political life are the weak and the powerful – the assumption is that the powerful will abuse their power unless constrained from doing so; building such constraints is, or should be, the task of political theory.

Raymond Geuss's *Philosophy and Real Politics* is a short essay making similar points especially against Rawls. The basic argument is similar to that of Williams – politics is not a branch of applied ethics, political theory should focus on real political actors. On the face of it, the 'new political realism' seems to be quite close to the 'classical realism' of IR theory – although Morgenthau and other classical realists are not referenced by these writers. This is strange, and may simply reflect the fact that Williams and Geuss are not as familiar with this discourse as perhaps they ought to be. For example, when discussing specifically 'international' issues such as human rights and relativism, Williams makes reference to a Weberian 'ethic of responsibility'; this is also a starting point for classical realism, and it is strange and a little disconcerting that Williams does not appear to recognise that others have been there before him. One of the essays in *In the Beginning was the Deed* addresses 'Humanitarianism and the right to intervene'; this short essay, written at the end of the 1990s, packs a lot into a short space, and touches on virtually all the standard issues – but Michael Walzer's 'Politics of rescue' (1995) article is the only International Relations source referenced. The article ends by expressing the sort of caution about humanitarian intervention to be expected from a classical realist or an English School pluralist.

Realism in practice

The new political realism and the old classical realism are movements within the realm of theory – what of the realm of practice? Much of the second half of this book has been devoted to looking at the emerging global polity and it is time now in this final chapter to look a little more closely at those forces that have opposed and are still opposing that emergence. The first thing that should be said here is that national governments are rarely supportive of shifts in the world that reduce their own significance, and none of the major world powers have behaved in such a way as to disprove this proposition. The shift away from a society of states towards a global polity is often associated with the West and more specifically with Europe but this can be rather misleading. The United States is clearly part of the West but has never accepted the full implications of a shift away from the society of states, although some American leaders such as Presidents Clinton and Obama have been willing to pay at least lip service to a new way of doing international relations. It is often and correctly said that the move towards understanding sovereignty as responsibility has been driven by European states, and certainly all European states west of Russia are members of the International Criminal Court and generally supportive of the new international politics, but that does not stop Britain and France in particular from acting according to their own vision of the national interest when it suits them to do so.

For all that, the major opposition to a new way of understanding notions such as sovereignty and human rights comes from the so-called 'emergent' powers, in particular from China and India, and, to a lesser extent, from South Africa and Brazil. Rather than discuss this in the abstract, it may be helpful to return to a specific case which has already been discussed in Chapter 8, namely the politics surrounding, and following from, the passing of UN Security Council Resolution 1973 in 2011 and the unfolding crisis in Libya during that year. It will be recalled that China, Russia, India and Brazil abstained on that resolution and, as the crisis developed, at least the first two countries so named expressed regrets that they did not cast a negative vote, which would have caused the resolution to fail. The voting record of these countries on this matter should not be over-interpreted, but does plausibly suggest the emergent powers collectively and individually have a rather different approach to issues of sovereignty from the European powers who have been behind the drive to establish sovereignty as responsibility over the last few decades – and different even from the attitude of the US which, as noted above, has, itself, been very ambiguous in its approach to this shift. Subsequent, repeated, Russian and Chinese vetoes of UNSC Resolutions proposing sanctions on the Syrian Government in late 2011 and 2012 confirm this difference and similar indications can be found in other aspects of the policy of the emergent powers – consider, for example, the position of China in Africa, where it has explicitly rejected any link between Chinese assistance and human rights (Alden and Hughes, 2009). The attitude of the emergent powers to sovereignty issues would benefit from further investigation.

Why have China, India and the other emergent powers adopted the attitude they have to the new thinking on sovereignty? More to the point, to what extent is the broadly hostile attitude they currently display towards this thinking likely to continue in the future, when their increasing general importance in international politics could enable them to reverse the normative shifts that have taken place over the last few decades? Is it possible that future generations will look back on the history of the international human rights regime since 1945 and the emergence of ideas of 'sovereignty as responsibility' not as laying the foundations for a radically different, less state-centric world order, but as the last gasp of the 'Vasco da Gama Epoch', that is a Europe-dominated world (Pannikar, 1961)? It is possible to offer a simple, uncomplicated answer to the first of these questions. It is certainly the case that that the emergent powers are deeply suspicious of the power of the United States and its allies, and are inclined to interpret an active human rights policy and the redefinitions of sovereignty adopted by the latter as moves in a power-political game rather than as normatively driven actions. Add to this generic suspicion the fact that China and Russia are deeply vulnerable to criticism on human rights grounds, and the fact that these two countries along with India have national minorities who would very much like to claim the protection of the international community if given the chance to do so, and resistance to the new thinking is easy to understand. In practice, of course, there is no possibility that the international community (which these states regard as a synonym for America and its friends) is going to actively intervene on behalf of Tibetans, Chechnyans or Kashmiris, but it easy to see why events such as the campaign in 1999 on behalf of the Kosovo Albanians send shivers down spines in Beijing, Moscow and New Delhi. Moreover, this general attitude of resistance to the new thinking is likely to continue even as China and India become more central to world politics, given that the capacity of the US to project its military power is likely to remain unchallengeable, even as its relative economic strength declines.

Still, emergent power resistance to new thinking on sovereignty and human rights cannot simply be understood in terms of the contingencies of power politics, important though such considerations may be when in comes to specific cases. There are principles involved here and not simply interests. When the representatives of China or India have opposed operations in Kosovo in 1999 or Libya in 2011 they have done so from principle and the thinking behind their opposition deserves to be considered in its own terms. In order to understand those terms it is necessary to begin with grasping the ways in which China and India have experienced the Westphalia System over the last few centuries. As was noted in the first half of this book, in the seventeenth through nineteenth centuries the European states-system had a rather more complicated and ambiguous approach to the notion of sovereignty than is usually conveyed by the term 'Westphalian', but rather more to the point in this context is that the intra-European 'rules of the game' of the society of states – however defined – were very different from the rules which applied outside Europe. Edward Keene has given one account of the rules 'beyond the anarchical society' of Europe, and Carl Schmitt, from a very different perspective, has given another – but what they both agree on is that the kind of normative framework which governed relations within Europe, Schmitt's *Ius Publicum Europaeum*, was absent from Europe's relations with the rest of the world, and indeed in the relations of European states with each other 'beyond the line' (Keene, 2002; Schmitt, 2003). Unlike the situation within Europe where European rulers recognised each other as legitimate, albeit sometimes legitimate enemies, European states did not recognise the rulers they came across in the rest of the world as possessing legitimate *dominium*, and their relations with them were, accordingly, governed simply by relative power.

In what became the Americas, such relations were wholly one-sided in favour of the European powers, while in the Indian sub-continent and the East until the late eighteenth or early nineteenth century they largely favoured the indigenous rulers – but in both cases it was power that counted, rather than the kind of minimal normative framework that existed in Europe. In acting in this way, it should be said, the Europeans who encountered Indian rulers or the Chinese Emperors were, in fact, conforming to the local rules of the game. Whereas in Europe the notion of the legal, if not political, equality of rulers had taken hold, China's relations with other peoples was based on a tributary system in which other rulers, however politically powerful, were in no sense to be understood as the equal of the Chinese Emperor, while in India the Mogul Emperor in Delhi had a similar – albeit rather more contestable – view of the world. The European intruders were not making themselves felt within a system of states in the European sense of the term, and their behaviour needs to be understood partly in this light. Nor was it the case that before the Imperial systems of China and India were established there had been in those lands a normatively grounded states-system. Certainly, in both cases, there had been multiple centres of power, sovereignties even, but without the European sense that this states of affairs was normatively desirable, and not simply the result of the contingencies of power. Thus, the period of the Warring States in China (approximately 475–221 BCE) produced a great deal of interesting international thought which is now beginning to be related to contemporary conditions – see, for example, the work of Yan Xuetong and the commentaries thereon translated as *Ancient Chinese Thought, Modern Chinese Power* – but it seems that this period did not produce the equivalent of the notion of an 'international society' (Yan Xuetong, 2011; see also Callahan and Barabantseva, 2012 and Zhang and Buzan, 2012). The normative goal of all the thinkers of this period seems to have been empire.

The notion of a normatively grounded international society was introduced to China and India via European imperialism once the forces of capitalist industrialisation (temporarily) delivered the East into the hands of Europe. Chinese and Indian civilisation initially experienced the idea of an international society of states from a subordinate position, which the new elites that imperialism created in place of the Chinese and Indian imperial governing class were understandably determined to overcome. However, and here a very long story is being cut short, these new elites – the nationalist movements of China and India, and the Chinese Communist Party – did not aspire to recreate the old empires, but rather to enter international society as independent and powerful members in their own right. The UN Charter of 1945, by divorcing the normative framework of the states-system from its European origins and providing an alternative grounding for a potentially universal international order, made this easier than it would have been previously. The new states that were created post-1945 no longer had to look to the old European powers for recognition, their international legitimacy was guaranteed by UN membership.

This entry into international society was by no means unproblematic. China was a founding member of the UN and a permanent member of the Security Council but the People's Republic of China's occupancy of China's seat at the UN did not take place until 1971. The PRC under Mao saw itself as a leader of world revolution rather than as a state in any conventional sense, and it was only in the 1970s under his successor that Chinese membership of international society became regularised. India was a founder member of the UN (albeit under ultimate British control between 1945 and 1947) but in the 1950s attempted to develop an alternative code for the conduct of international relations, the *Panchsheel* or Five Principles of Co-Existence, first formally established in a treaty with the PRC in 1954. These Principles were intended by India's Prime Minister, Jawaharlal Nehru to constitute a major break with the past and a signpost to a future world order not dominated by European norms, and they did have some influence in the thinking of the Non-Aligned Movement (NAM) which was established in Belgrade in 1961, but pre-figured at the Bandung Conference in 1955. However, a less enthusiastic reading of the principles would suggest they were actually an unnecessarily long-winded restatement of the traditional notions of sovereignty and non-intervention – and in any case the Sino-Indian Border War of 1962 revealed the hollowness of the pact with the PRC. This event led India into a de facto alliance with the USSR driven by balance of power thinking, and thereafter India's foreign policy has, somewhat reluctantly, followed conventional lines.

Thus by the mid-1970s both India and China had become fully functioning members of the post-war international order, members who, in the main, respected the central principles of that order – the procedural rules of international society, non-intervention, non-aggression, respect for treaties and so on. And these two countries remain more or less committed to this conventional account of what being a sovereign state involves, but – perhaps largely because of the long and difficult road they have had to take in order to have that status recognised by the major powers, their new peers – they are very resistant to the idea of revising that account, which was what the leading European members of that society were beginning to attempt to do at exactly the point when India and China finally achieved full membership under the old rules. Having only recently escaped from the experience of being dominated by European imperialism, these countries were now experiencing new attempts to circumscribe their freedom of action in the name of human rights and sovereignty as responsibility. In order to defend their hard-won freedom, they both became, and have remained, firmly committed to an account of sovereignty as untrammelled autonomy, an account that is in keeping with the formal rules of the 'Westphalian' order but which is not entirely consonant with the actual practice of Westphalian international society as outlined in the first half of this book. Moreover, this account of sovereignty seems out of kilter with the other developments in international society also noted in the first half of this book; still, out of kilter with the times or not, the substantial and increasing economic power of China and India probably means that their vision of what it means to be sovereign will be of increasing importance as time goes by – assuming, that is, that this vision does not itself evolve as their power grows.

Will this vision evolve? Will economic growth, rising wealth and an increasing stake in the success of the world economic system, within which this growth takes place, and upon which it is dependent, change attitudes in the emergent powers? This has become a subject for intense debate in academic and policy circles in the US and elsewhere, a debate which is generally cast in contemporary terms but which actually is grounded in classic notions of modernity and society. G. John Ikenberry and Daniel Deudney have summarised the arguments of the classics in modern terms in an article in *Foreign Affairs* (2009); capitalism leads to political democracy because rising wealth and education levels creates a demand for political participation, capitalist property systems need the rule of law and economic growth leads to a diversity of socio-economic interests and the need for political pluralism; autocratic regimes are disadvantaged by corruption, which can only be controlled by institutional checks and balances, by political struggles against the autocracy generated by the inevitable inequalities that accompany economic development and by weak accountability and information flows which hamper policy development. This article responded to an earlier article by Azar Gat (2007) who argued on the basis of past history that in practice authoritarian powers are by no means handicapped in the race for economic growth and that there is no reason to assume that as China and Russia become wealthier and more powerful internationally, they will become more democratic or that their attitudes on matters such as sovereignty and human rights will shift. The argument was continued in a debate later in 2009 rather portentously titled 'Which way is history marching' (Gat et al., 2009). This is an interesting discussion – but an argument that focuses on the long-term viability of authoritarian politics isn't quite to the point; India, after all, is a liberal democracy governed by the rule of law with a constitution that guarantees human rights at home, but it remains very sceptical about any attempt to promote human rights internationally. Even if those who believe that economic growth will eventually democratise China are right, it does not follow that China's views on the relationship between sovereignty and human rights will change.

More to the point is the possibility that the old liberal international economic order based on US hegemony will be replaced by a post-hegemonic international order which remains basically liberal capitalist in inspiration, but with an expanding core membership, increasingly interdependent security and economic regimes, and a further expansion of policy domains with new realms of network-based co-operation (Slaughter, 2004; Ikenberry 2011b). China, India and perhaps Russia and Brazil will arguably be obliged to take leading roles in preserving the global economy, accepting that they now have a stake in the system; the question posed here is whether they will be able to take over this role without to some extent buying into the kind of changes in the normative framework of international relations described in the second part of this book? If the emergent countries do become enmeshed in new forms of network-based co-operation in order to cope with an increasing number of international problems that can only be dealt with by generating higher levels of interdependence (such as global ecological degeneration, financial instability and threats to global health) will it be possible to keep human rights issues off the agenda? Increased co-operation will increasingly depend on social networks and the rapid exchange of information and, *pace* the 'Great Firewall' of China, it is difficult to see how even the authoritarian emergent powers will be able to control this process in such a way that unwanted topics are kept off the agenda – even behind the Chinese firewall, a very active blogsphere has developed, and Chinese 'netizens' seem unwilling to accept the restrictions on their freedoms that the Chinese government would like to impose. On the other hand, there is very little evidence that the burgeoning Chinese property-owning class is committed to political change.

The last few decades have seen two strong trends; the increasing importance of human rights-based policies and ideas of sovereignty as responsibility – summarised here as the emergence of a global polity – and the increasing importance globally of powers who reject these ideas. These two trends are now converging, and one or the other (or perhaps both) will be changed as a result. Is it possible to envisage that China, India and the other emergent powers could be integrated ever more tightly into a new global architecture which recognised their increasing importance in most spheres of human activity, while at the same time allowing them to opt out of being influenced and affected by the new meanings of sovereignty and human rights that have developed over the last two or three decades? The simply answer is, yes, it is possible to envisage such a future; the new understandings of sovereignty that have emerged did so initially in Europe, gradually spreading out to Latin America and Africa and beginning to establish toeholds in the East – it is not too difficult to imagine this process of expansion coming to an end and indeed being reversed. For much of the last 400 years there has been one rule for Europe and another rule for the rest of the world, and it is not impossible that in the future this will once again be the case – only this time it will be the rest of the world which is operating to Westphalian rules, while Europe (including in this category much of Latin America and the Anglosphere) moves to a different drum. When Stephen Hopgood refers to the 'endtimes of human rights' it is partially this possibility that he has in mind (Hopgood, 2013).

But there are some reasons to think that this rather depressing picture of a superficially unified but actually deeply divided world may not come to pass. Apart from the aforementioned changes that might come about in China and the other emergent powers as a result of increased prosperity, it is also the case that the self-confidence that will come from their universally recognised importance as mainstays of the new world order may translate into a more relaxed view of the need to maintain a rigid understanding of sovereignty. The passage of time will also help in this respect: as the era of colonialism, overt imperialism and Western dominance fades into the distant past, so it might be hoped that the rulers of these countries will be less influenced by the desire to avoid any interference with their hard-won independence.

In summary, it may be that the future will see a revived contest between the idea of sovereignty and the idea of human rights, and the fusion of the two notions incorporated in the idea of 'sovereignty as responsibility' will go into abeyance – but other futures are possible. Which of these paths is taken will depend, ultimately, on the peoples of the emergent powers themselves – but, final point, current advocates of the fusion of sovereignty and rights also have a part to play. They must show that respect for human rights is not simply something demanded of others but applies equally to their own societies; they must show that when, as in Libya, R2P demands the use of force, this is followed by generous aid in reconstruction; they must ensure that they did not arm the *génocidaires* they condemn. In short, they must demonstrate that the principles they promote are truly worthy of support, and in no way reflect Europe's past history of dealing with the rest of the world.

Further Reading

David Campbell and Morton Schoolman's collection on William Connolly (2008) is a good route into the latter's work. Connolly (1995) and (2002) are characteristic statements; Connolly (2013a) is a critique of neoliberalism

(Continued)

(Continued)

from the materialist perspective – a short version is Connolly (2013b). Wenman (2013) situates Connolly within the wider field of agnostic democracy. Kimberley Hutchings is a lucid critic of Kantian and neo-Kantian thought – Hutchings (2005) engages directly with Habermas, Hutchings (2008) explores ways of thinking time and world politics.

Michael Blake (2012) is a useful accompaniment to Thomas Nagel (2005). The *European Journal of Political Theory* published a Special Issue on 'Realism and Political Theory' (2010), which places Bernard Williams and Raymond Geuss in a wider context, alongside 'agonists' such as Connolly. Duncan Bell's (2009) collection also mixes different kinds of realist to good effect. A Special Issue of *Social Theory and Practice* (2008) explores the pros and cons of ideal and non-ideal theory.

On the role of 'emergent powers' Charles Kupchan (2012) has it right – 'no one's world'; see also the *Transatlantic Academy*'s co-authored ebook Trine Flockhart et al. (2014). Niall Ferguson (2011) offers an account of the West's 'killer apps' that are now more widely available. Robert Kagan (2012) worries about America reducing its role in world affairs, perhaps unnecessarily, US decline has been predicted frequently in the past – Paul Kennedy's thesis (1989) is currently on its third or fourth iteration. In any event, it is safe to say that China will be a key player in the new world order – assessing China's approach to world politics is a difficult but necessary task; William Callahan (2013) is more revealing than most of the instant commentary that is available, as is his (2009) volume.

BIBLIOGRAPHY

Acemoglu, Darren and Robinson, James A. (2012) *Why Nations Fail*. London: Profile Books.

Ahmed, Akbar S. (2013) *The Thistle and the Drone: How America's War on Terror Became a Global War on Tribal Islam*. Washington, DC: Brookings Institution Press.

Alden, Chris and Hughes, Christopher R. (2009) 'Harmony and discord in China's Africa strategy: some implications for foreign policy', *The China Quarterly*, 199: 563–84.

Alden, Chris and Schoeman, Maxie (2013) 'South Africa in the company of giants: the search for leadership in a transforming global order', *International Affairs*, 89 (1): 111–29.

Allen, Tim and Styan, David (2000) 'A right to interfere? Bernard Kouchner and The New Humanitarianism', *Journal of International Development*, 12 (6): 825–42.

Allott, Philip (1999) 'The concept of international law', *European Journal of International Law*, 10 (1): 31–50.

Allott, Philip (2001) *Eunomia: New Order for a New World*. Oxford: Oxford University Press.

Allott, Philip (2002) *The Health of Nations*. Cambridge: Cambridge University Press.

Alston, Philip and Goodman, Ryan (eds) (2012) *International Human Rights*. Oxford: Oxford University Press.

The American Journal of International Law (1999) Developments in International Criminal Law – Special Issue, 93 (1): 1–123.

Anscombe, G.E.M. (1981) *Ethics, Religion and Politics*. Minneapolis, MN: University of Minnesota Press.

Appiah, Kwame Anthony (2005) *The Ethics of Identity*. Princeton, NJ: Princeton University Press.

Appiah, Kwame Anthony (2007) *Cosmopolitanism: Ethics in a World of Strangers*. New York: W.W. Norton.

Arbour, Louise (2008) 'The responsibility to protect as a duty of care in international law and practice', *Review of International Studies*, 34 (3): 445–58.

Archibugi, Daniele and Held, David (eds) (1995) *Cosmopolitan Democracy: An Agenda for a New World Order*. Cambridge: Polity Press.

Archibugi, Daniele, Koenig-Archibugi, Mathias and Marchetti, Raffaele (eds) (2012) *Global Democracy: Normative and Empirical Perspectives*. Cambridge: Cambridge University Press.

Armstrong, Chris (2009) 'Basic needs, equality and global justice', *Journal of Global Ethics*, 5 (3): 245–51.

Armstrong, Chris (2012) *Global Distributive Justice: An Introduction*. Cambridge: Cambridge University Press.

Armstrong, David (2007) *International Law and International Relations*. Cambridge: Cambridge University Press.

Atack, Iain (2005) *The Ethics of Peace and War*. Basingstoke: Macmillan.

Barber, Benjamin (2007) 'William Connolly, *Pluralism*' Book Review, *Ethics*, 117 (4): 747–54.

Barkin, J. Samuel and Cronin, Bruce (1994) 'The State and the Nation: Changing norms and the rules of sovereignty in international relations', *International Organization*, 48 (1): 107–30.

Barnett, Michael N. (2011) *Empire of Humanity: A History of Humanitarianism*. Ithaca, NY: Cornell University Press.

Barnett, Michael N. and Weiss, Thomas G. (eds) (2008) *Humanitarianism in Question: Politics, Power, Ethics*. Ithaca, NY: Cornell University Press.

Barnett, Michael N. and Weiss, Thomas G. (2011) *Humanitarianism Contested: Where Angels Fear to Tread*. London: Routledge.

Barry, Brian (1989) *Democracy, Power and Justice*. Oxford: Clarendon.

Barry, Brian (1995) *Justice as Impartiality*. Oxford: Clarendon Press.

Barry, Brian (1998a) 'International society from a cosmopolitan perspective', in David Mapel and Terry Nardin T (eds), *International Society*. Princeton, NJ: Princeton University Press.

Barry, Brian (1998b) 'Statism and Nationalism: A cosmopolitan critique', in Leah Brilmayer and Ian Shapiro (eds), *Global Justice*. New York: New York University Press.

Barry, Brian (2000) *Culture and Equality: An Egalitarian Critique of Multiculturalism*. Cambridge: Polity Press.

Bartleson, Jens (1995) *A Genealogy of Sovereignty*. Cambridge: Cambridge University Press.

Bartelson, Jens (2014) *Sovereignty as Symbolic Form*. London: Routledge.

Bass, Gary J. (2000) *Stay the Hand of Vengeance: The Politics of War Crimes Tribunals*. Princeton, NJ: Princeton University Press.

Bass, Gary J. (2008) *Freedom's Battle: The Origins of Humanitarian Intervention*. New York: Alfred A. Knopf.

Baudrillard, Jean (1995) *The Gulf War Did Not Take Place*. Bloomington, IN: Indiana University Press.

Bauer, Harry and Brighi, Elisabetta (eds) (2008) *Pragmatism and International Relations*. London: Routledge.

Bauer, Joanne R. and Bell, Daniel A. (eds) (1999) *The East Asian Challenge for Human Rights*. Cambridge: Cambridge University Press.

Beitz, Charles R. (1979) *Political Theory and International Relations*. Princeton, NJ: Princeton University Press.

Beitz, Charles R. (1983) 'Cosmopolitan ideals and national sentiment', *The Journal of Philosophy*, 80 (10): 591.

Beitz, Charles R. (ed.) (1985) *International Ethics*. Princeton, NJ: Princeton University Press.

Beitz, Charles R. (1994) 'Cosmopolitan Liberalism and the States System', in Chris Brown (ed.), *Political Restructuring in Europe: Ethical Perspectives*. London: Routledge.

Beitz, Charles R. (2000) 'Rawls's Law of Peoples', *Ethics*, 110 (4): 669–96.

Bell, Duncan (ed.) (2009) *Political Thought and International Relations: Variations on a Realist Theme*. Oxford; New York: Oxford University Press.

Bell, Duncan (ed.) (2010) *Ethics and World Politics*. New York: Oxford University Press.

Bell, Daniel A. (1998) 'The Limits of Liberal Justice', *Political Theory* 26 (4): 557–82.

Bell, Daniel A. (2000) *East Meets West: Human Rights and Democracy in East Asia* Princeton, NJ: Princeton University Press.

Bell, Daniel A. (2007) *Confucian Political Ethics*. Princeton, NJ: Princeton University Press.

Bell, Lynda S., Nathan, Andrew J. and Peleg, Ilan (eds) (2001) *Negotiating Culture and Human Rights*. New York: Columbia University Press.

Bellamy, Alex J. (2002) 'Pragmatic solidarism and the dilemmas of humanitarian intervention', *Millennium – Journal of International Studies*, 31 (3): 473–97.

Bellamy, Alex J. (2003) 'Humanitarian responsibilities and interventionist claims in international society', *Review of International Studies*, 29 (3): 321–40.

Bellamy, Alex J. (ed.) (2005) *International Society and its Critics*. Oxford: Oxford University Press.

Bellamy, Alex J. (2006) *Just Wars: from Cicero to Iraq*. Cambridge: Polity Press.

Bellamy, Alex J. (2009) *Responsibility to Protect: The Global Effort to End Mass Atrocities*. Cambridge: Polity.

Bellamy, Alex J. (2011) 'Libya and the Responsibility to Protect: The exception and the norm', *Ethics & International Affairs*, 25 (3): 263–9.

Bellamy, Alex J. (2014) 'From Tripoli to Damascus? Lesson learning and the implementation of the Responsibility to Protect', *International Politics*, 51 (1): 23–44.

Bentham, Jeremy (1982) *An Introduction to the Principles of Morals and Legislation*. London: Methuen.

Bentham, Jeremy (2000) *On Utilitarianism and Government*. Ware: Wordsworth Editions.

Berdal, Mats and Economides, Spyros (eds) (2007) *United Nations Interventionism, 1991–2004*. Cambridge: Cambridge University Press.

Bhagwati, J.N. (2004) *In Defense of Globalization*. New York: Oxford University Press.

Biggar, Nigel (2013) *In Defence of War*. Oxford: Oxford University Press.

Blair, Tony (1999) *Doctrine of the International Community* (Speech given to the Economic Club of Chicago, 24 April 1999) (http://webarchive.nationalarchives.gov.uk/+/www.number10.gov.uk/Page1297)

Blake, Michael (2012) 'Global distributive justice: Why political philosophy needs political science', *Annual Review of Political Science*, 15: 121–36.

Blom, J.C.H. et al. (2002) *Srebrenica. Reconstruction, Background, Consequences and Analyses of the Fall of a Safe Area*. NIOD Report (Dutch Government Investigation). Amsterdam: NIOD Foundation.

Bobbitt, Philip (2008) *Terror and Consent: The Wars for the Twenty-first Century*. London: Allen Lane.

Booth, Ken (2000a) 'Ten flaws of Just Wars', *Journal of International Human Rights*, 4 (3/4): 314–324.

Booth, Ken (ed.) (2000b) *The Kosovo Tragedy: The Human Rights Dimensions*. London: Routledge.

Booth, Ken (ed.) (2011) *Realism and World Politics*. London: Routledge.

Booth, Ken and Dunne, Tim (eds) (2002) *Worlds in Collision: Terror and the Future of Global Order*. London: Palgrave Macmillan.

Booth, Ken and Smith, Steve (eds) (1995) *International Relations Theory Today*. Cambridge: Polity Press.

Bose, Sumantra (2002) *Bosnia after Dayton: Nationalist Partition and International Intervention*. London: C. Hurst.

Boucher, David (1998) *Political Theories of International Relations*. Oxford: Oxford University Press.

Boucher, David (2011a) *The Limits of Ethics in International Relations: Natural Law, Natural Rights, and Human Rights in Transition*. Reprint edition. Oxford: Oxford University Press.

Boucher, David (2011b) 'The recognition theory of rights, customary international law and human rights', *Political Studies*, 59 (3): 753–71.

Boucher, David (2012) 'The just war tradition and its modern legacy: *Jus ad bellum* and *jus in bello*', *European Journal of Political Theory*, 11 (2): 92–111.

Bowden, Mark (1999) *Black Hawk Down*. London: Bantam.

Bowden, Mark (2003) 'The dark art of interrogation', *The Atlantic,* October. (www.theatlantic.com/magazine/archive/2003/10/the-dark-art-of-interrogation/302791/)

Boyle, Joseph (2013) 'The necessity of "right intent" for justifiably waging war', in Anthony F. Lang, Cian O'Driscoll and John Williams (eds), *Just War: Authority, Tradition and Practice*. Washington, DC: Georgetown University Press.

Boyle, Michael J. (2013) 'The costs and consequences of drone warfare', *International Affairs*, 89 (1): 1–29.

Brock, Gillian (2009) *Global Justice: A Cosmopolitan Account*. Oxford: Oxford University Press.

Brown, Chris (1992) *International Relations Theory: New Normative Approaches*. New York: Columbia University Press.

Brown, Chris (1994) *Political Restructuring in Europe: Ethical Perspectives*. London: Routledge.

Brown, Chris (1997) 'Human rights', in John Bayliss and Steve Smith (eds), *The Globalization of World Politics: An Introduction to International Relations*. Oxford: Oxford University Press.

Brown, Chris (2001) 'Ethics, interest and foreign policy', in Margot Light and Karen E. Smith (eds), *Ethics and Foreign Policy*. Cambridge: Cambridge University Press.

Brown, Chris (2002a) *Sovereignty, Rights and Justice*. Cambridge: Polity Press.

Brown, Chris (2002b) 'The construction of a realistic utopia', *Review of International Studies*, 28 (1): 5–21.

Brown, Chris (2004) 'Selective humanitarianism: In defence of inconsistency', in Deen K. Chatterjee and Don E. Scheid (eds), *Ethics and Foreign Intervention*. Cambridge: Cambridge University Press.

Brown, Chris (2006a) 'From international to global justice', in John Dryzek, Bonnie Honig and Anne Phillips (eds), *The Oxford Handbook of Political Theory*. Oxford: Oxford University Press.

Brown, Chris (2006b) 'International relations as political theory', in Tim Dunne Milja Kurki and Steve Smith (eds), *Theories of International Relations: Discipline and Diversity*. Oxford: Oxford University Press.

Brown, Chris (2008) '"Delinquent" states, guilty consciences and humanitarian politics in the 1990s', *Journal of International Political Theory*, 4 (1): 55–71.

Brown, Chris (2009) *Understanding International Relations*. 4th edition. London: Palgrave Macmillan.

Brown, Chris (2011) 'On Gareth Evans, the Responsibility to Protect: Ending mass atrocity crimes once and for all', *Global Responsibility to Protect*, 2 (3): 310–14.

Brown, Chris (2013a) 'Just War and political judgement', in Anthony Lang, Cian O'Driscoll and John Williams (eds), *Just War: Authority, Tradition and Practice*. Washington, DC: Georgetown University Press.

Brown, Chris (2013b) 'The antipolitical theory of Responsibility to Protect', *Global Responsibility to Protect*, 5 (4): 423–42.

Brown, Chris, Nardin, Terry and Rengger, N.J. (eds) (2002) *International Relations in Political Thought: Texts from the Ancient Greeks to the First World War*. Cambridge: Cambridge University Press.

Bruenig, Matthew (2011) 'Rethinking noncombatant immunity', *Theoretical and Applied Ethics*, 1 (1): 26–33.

Buchanan, Allen (2000) 'Rawls's Law of Peoples: Rules for a vanished Westphalian world', *Ethics*, 110 (4): 697–721.

Bull, Hedley (1977) *The Anarchical Society: A Study of Order in World Politics*. London: Macmillan.

Bull, Hedley (ed.) (1984a) *Intervention in World Politics*. Oxford: Clarendon Press.

Bull, Hedley (1984b) *Justice in International Relations*. Hagey Lectures, University of Waterloo, Ontario.

Bull, Hedley (2012) *The Anarchical Society: A Study of Order in World Politics*. 4th edition. Basingstoke: Palgrave Macmillan (1st edition, 1977).

Bull, Hedley and Watson, Adam (eds) (1984) *The Expansion of International Society*. Oxford: Clarendon Press.

Burke, Edmund (2009) *Reflections on the Revolution in France*. Oxford: Oxford University Press.

Butterfield, Herbert and Wight, Martin (eds) (1966) *Diplomatic Investigations: Essays in the Theory of International Politics*. London: George Allen and Unwin.

Buzan, Barry (2004) *From International to World Society: English School Theory and the Structure of Globalisation*. Cambridge: Cambridge University Press.

Buzan, Barry (2014) *An Introduction to the English School of International Relations*. Cambridge: Polity Press.

Byman, Daniel (2013) 'Why drones work: The case for Washington's weapon of choice', *Foreign Affairs*, 92 (4): 32–43.

Cabrera, Luis (2004) *Political Theory of Global Justice: A Cosmopolitan Case for the World State*. London: Routledge.

Cabrera, Luis (2010) *The Practice of Global Citizenship*. Cambridge: Cambridge University Press.

Calderisi, R. (2006) *The Trouble with Africa: Why Foreign Aid Isn't Working*. New Haven, CT: Yale University Press.

Callahan, William (2009) *China: The Pessoptimist Nation*. Oxford: Oxford University Press.

Callahan, William (2013) *China Dreams: 20 Visions of the Future*. New York: Oxford University Press.

Callahan, William and Barabantseva, Elena (2012) *China Orders the World: Normative Soft Power and Foreign Policy*. Washington, DC: Johns Hopkins University Press.

Campbell, David (1998) *National Deconstruction: Violence, Identity, and Justice in Bosnia*. Minneapolis, MN: University of Minneapolis Press.

Campbell, David and Schoolman, Morton (eds) (2008) *The New Pluralism: William Connolly and the Contemporary Global Condition*. Durham, NC: Duke University Press.

Caney, Simon (2005) *Justice Beyond Borders: A Global Political Theory*. Oxford: Oxford University Press.

Caney, Simon (2012a) 'Addressing poverty and climate change', *Ethics and International Affairs*, 26 (2): 191–216.

Caney, Simon (2012b) 'Just emissions', *Philosophy & Public Affairs*, 40 (4): 255–300.

Caney, Simon and Jones, Peter (eds) (2001) *Human Rights and Global Diversity*. London: Frank Cass Publishers.

Caney, Simon, George, David and Jones, Peter (eds) (1996) *National Rights, International Obligations*. Boulder, CO: Westview Press.

Carvin, Stephanie (2010a) 'A Responsibility to Reality: A reply to Louise Arbour', *Review of International Studies*, 36, Special Issue: 47–54.

Carvin, Stephanie (2010b) *Prisoners of America's War: From the Early Republic to Guantanamo.* London: Hurst.

Carvin, Stephanie (2012) 'The trouble with targeted killing', *Security Studies,* 21 (3): 529–55.

Carvin, Stephanie and Williams, Michael J. (2014) *Law, Science, Liberalism and the American Way of Warfare: The Quest for Humanity in Conflict.* Cambridge: Cambridge University Press.

Cassese, Antonio (1999a) 'The statute of the International Criminal Court: Some preliminary reflections', *European Journal of International Law,* 10 (1): 144–71.

Cassese, Antonio (1999b) 'Ex iniuria ius oritur: are we moving towards international legitimation of forcible humanitarian countermeasures in the world community', *European Journal of International Law,* 10: 23–30.

Cassese, Antonio (2001) *International Law.* Oxford: Oxford University Press.

Cassese, Antonio (2008) *International Criminal Law* 2nd ed. Oxford: Oxford University Press.

Ceadel, Martin (1987) *Thinking About Peace and War.* Oxford: Oxford University Press.

Chandler, David (2005) *From Kosovo to Kabul and Beyond.* New edition. London: Pluto Press.

Chandler, David (2010) 'R2P or Not R2P? More statebuilding, less responsibility', *Global Responsibility to Protect,* 2 (1): 161–6.

Charvet, John (2008) *The Liberal Project and Human Rights: The Theory and Practice of a New World Order.* Cambridge: Cambridge University Press.

Chatterjee, Deen K. (ed.) (2013) *The Ethics of Preventive War.* Cambridge: Cambridge University Press.

Chatterjee, Deen and Scheid, Don (eds) (2003) *Ethics and Foreign Interventions.* Cambridge: Cambridge University Press.

Checkel, Jeff (1998) 'The constructivist turn in international relations theory', *World Politics,* 50 (2): 324–48.

Chesterman, Simon (2001) *Just War or Just Peace? Humanitarian Intervention and International Law.* Oxford: Oxford University Press.

Chesterman, Simon (2011) '"Leading from Behind": The Responsibility to Protect, the Obama Doctrine, and humanitarian intervention after Libya', *Ethics & International Affairs,* 25 (03): 279–85.

Chomsky, Noam (1999) *The New Military Humanism: Lessons from Kosovo.* London: Pluto.

Clark, Ian (2011) *Hegemony in International Society.* Oxford: Oxford University Press.

Coates, A.J. (2012) *The Ethics of War.* Manchester: Manchester University Press.

Cochran, Molly (1995) 'Postmodernism, ethics and international political theory', *Review of International Studies,* 21 (3): 237–50.

Cochran, Molly (1999) *Normative Theory in International Relations: A Pragmatic Approach.* Cambridge: Cambridge University Press.

Cochran, Molly (2009) 'Charting the Ethics of the English School: What "Good" is There in a Middle-Ground Ethics?', *International Studies Quarterly,* 53 (1): 203–25.

Cochran, Molly (ed.) (2010) *The Cambridge Companion to Dewey.* Cambridge: Cambridge University Press.

Cohen, Daniel (1998) *The Wealth of the World and the Poverty of Nations.* Cambridge, MA: MIT Press.

Cojean, Annick (2013) *Gaddafi's Harem: The Story of a Young Woman and the Abuses of Power in Libya.* New York: Atlantic Monthly Press.

Coker, Christopher (2008) *Ethics and War in the Twenty-First Century.* London: Routledge.

Coker, Christopher (2013) *Warrior Geeks: How the 21st Century Technology is Changing the Way We Fight and Think About War.* London: C. Hurst.

Collier, Paul (2007) *The Bottom Billion: Why the Poorest Countries are Failing and What Can Be Done About It.* New York: Oxford University Press.

Connolly, William E. (1992) *Identity-Difference: Democratic Negotiations of Political Paradox.* Ithaca, NY: Cornell University Press.

Connolly, William E. (1995) *The Ethos of Pluralization.* Borderlines. Minneapolis, MN: University of Minnesota Press.

Connolly, William E. (2000) 'Speed, concentric circles and cosmopolitanism', *Political Theory,* 28 (2): 596–618.

Connolly, William E. (2002) *Neuropolitics: Thinking, Culture, Speed.* Minneapolis, MN: University of Minnesota Press.

Connolly, William E. (2013a) *The Fragility of Things: Self-Organizing Processes, Neoliberal Fantasies and Democratic Activism*. Durham, NC: Duke University Press.

Connolly, William E. (2013b) 'The "New Materialism" and the fragility of things', *Millennium: Journal of International Studies*, 14 (3): 399–412.

Cook, Rebecca J. (ed.) (1994) *Human Rights of Women: National and International Perspectives*. Philadelphia, PA: University of Pennsylvania Press.

Coomaraswamy, Radhika (1994) 'To bellow like a cow: Women, ethnicity and the discourse of rights', in Rebecca Cook (ed.), *Human Rights of Women: National and International Perspectives*. Philadelphia, PA: University of Pennsylvania Press.

Cooper, Robert (2003) *The Breaking of Nations*. New York: Atlantic Books.

Cornell International Law Review (2005) Special Issue on Criminal Justice, 38(3).

Cottee, Simon and Cushman, Thomas (eds) (2008) *Christopher Hitchens and His Critics: Terror, Iraq and the Left*. New York: New York University Press.

Cox, Michael, Ikenberry, G John and Inoguchi, Takashi (2000) *American Democracy Promotion*. Oxford: Oxford University Press.

Craig, Campbell (2004) *Glimmer of a New Leviathan: Total War in the Realism of Niebuhr, Morgenthau, and Waltz*. New York: Columbia University Press.

Crawford, James (ed.) (1988) *The Rights of Peoples*. Oxford: Clarendon Press.

Crawford, James and Koskenniemi, Martti (eds) (2012) *The Cambridge Companion to International Law*. Cambridge: Cambridge University Press.

Crossley, Noele (2013) 'A model case of R2P prevention? Mediation in the aftermath of Kenya's 2007 Presidential Elections', *Global Responsibility to Protect*, 5 (2): 192–214.

Cushman, Thomas (ed.) (2005) *A Matter of Principle: Humanitarian Arguments for War in Iraq*. Berkeley, CA: University of California Press.

Daalder, Ivo H. (2000) *Getting to Dayton: The Making of America's Bosnia Policy*. Washington, DC: Brookings Institution Press.

Daalder, Ivo H. and O'Hanlon, Michael E. (2000) *Winning Ugly: NATO's War to Save Kosovo*. Washington, DC: Brookings Institution Press.

Danchev, Alex and Halverson, Thomas (eds) (1996) *International Perspectives on the Yugoslav Conflict*. Basingstoke: Macmillan.

De Waal, Alex (ed.) (2007) *War in Darfur and the Search for Peace*. Cambridge, MA: Global Equity Initiative, Harvard University.

De Waal, Alex (2013) 'African roles in the Libyan conflict of 2011', *International Affairs*, 89 (2): 365–79.

Deng, Francis M., Kimaro, Sadekiel, Lyons, Terence, Rothschild, Donal S. and Zartman, I. William (1996) *Sovereignty as Responsibility: Conflict Management in Africa*. Washington, DC: Brookings Institution.

Dershowitz, Alan M. (2002) *Why Terrorism Works: Understanding the Threat, Responding to the Challenge*. New Haven, CT: Yale University Press.

Des Forges, Alison L. (1999) *'Leave None to tell the Story': Genocide in Rwanda*. New York: Human Rights Watch.

Des Forges, Alison L. (2000) 'Shame: rationalising Western Apathy on Rwanda', *Foreign Affairs*, 79 (3).

Desai, Meghnad (2002) *Marx's Revenge: The Resurgence of Capitalism and the Death of Statist Socialism*. London: Verso.

Deudney, Daniel (2006) *Bounding Power: Republican Theory From the Polis to the Village*. Princeton, NJ: Princeton University Press.

Deudney, Daniel and Ikenberry, G. John (2009) 'The myth of the autocratic revival – Why liberal democracy will prevail', *Foreign Affairs*, 88 (1).

Donnelly, Jack (1989) *Universal Human Rights in Theory and Practice*. Ithaca, NY: Cornell University Press.

Donnelly, Jack (1998) 'Human rights: A new standard of civilization?', *International Affairs*, 74 (1): 1–23.

Donnelly, Jack (2006) 'Human rights', in John Dryzek, Bonnie Honig and Anne Phillips (eds), *The Oxford Handbook of Political Theory*. Oxford: Oxford University Press.

Donnelly, Jack (2007) 'The relative universality of human rights', *Human Rights Quarterly*, 29 (2): 281–306.

Dorfman, Ariel and Levinson, Sanford (2006) *Torture: A Collection*. Oxford: Oxford University Press.

Doyle, Michael W. (1983) '"Kant, Liberal Legacies and Foreign Affairs", Parts I and II', *Philosophy and Public Affairs*, 12, (1) and (2): 205–35, 323–53.

Doyle, Michael W. (2006) 'One world, many peoples: International justice in John Rawls's The Law of Peoples', *Perspectives on Politics*, 4 (1): 109–20.

Dryzek, John S, Honig, Bonnie and Phillips, Anne (eds) (2006) *The Oxford Handbook of Political Theory*. Oxford: Oxford University Press.

Dunant, Henri J. (1986) *A Memory of Solferino*. Geneva: International Committee of the Red Cross.

Dunne, Tim (1998) *Inventing International Society: A History of the English School*. New York: St. Martin's Press.

Dunne, Tim (2007) '"The rules of the game are changing": Fundamental human rights in crisis after 9/11', *International Politics*, 44 (2): 269–86.

Dunne, Tim and Wheeler, Nicholas J. (eds) (1999) *Human Rights in Global Politics*. Cambridge: Cambridge University Press.

Easterly, William R. (2006) *The White Man's Burden: Why the West's Efforts to Aid the Rest Have Done So Much Ill And So Little Good*. Oxford: Oxford University Press.

Elshtain, Jean Bethke (1982) *Public Man, Private Woman: Women in Social and Political Thought*. Oxford: Robertson.

Elshtain, Jean Bethke (ed.) (1992) *Just War Theory*. New York: New York University Press.

Elshtain, Jean Bethke (2003) *Just War Against Terror: The Burden of American Power in a Violent World*. New York: Basic Books.

Enemark, Christain (2014) *Armed Drones and the Ethics of War: Military Virtue in a Post-Heroic Age*. London: Routledge.

Epstein, Edward Jay (2014) 'Was Snowden's heist a foreign espionage operation?', *Wall Street Journal*, 9 May 2014.

Erskine, Toni (2009) 'Normative IR theory', in Tim Dunne, Milja Kurki and Steve Smith (eds), *International Relations Theory*. 2nd edition. Oxford: Oxford University Press.

Ethics (2000) Symposium on Martha Nussbaum's Political Philosophy, 111 (1).

Ethics (2011) Symposium on Jeff MacMahan's Killing in War, 122 (1).

Ethics & International Affairs (2011) 'Roundtable: Libya, Responsibility to Protect and humanitarian intervention', 25 (3).

European Journal of Political Theory (2010) Special Issue on 'Realism and Political Theory', 9 (4).

Evans, Gareth (2008a) 'The Responsibility to Protect: An idea whose time has come ... and gone?', *International Relations*, 22 (3): 283–98.

Evans, Gareth (2008b) *The Responsibility to Protect: Ending Mass Atrocity Crimes Once and For All*. Washington, DC: Brookings Institution.

Evans, Gareth (2010) 'Response to reviews by Michael Barnett, Chris Brown and Robert Jackson', *Global Responsibility to Protect*, (2): 320–7.

Evans, Tony (1998) *Human Rights Fifty Years On: A Reappraisal*. Manchester: Manchester University Press.

Fabre, Cecile (2012a) *Cosmopolitan War*. Oxford: Oxford University Press.

Fabre, Cecile (2012b) 'Internecine war killings', *Utilitas*, 24 (2): 214–36.

Favez, J-C (1999) *The Red Cross and the Holocaust*. Cambridge: Cambridge University Press.

Ferguson, Niall (2011) *Civilization: The West and the Rest*. Harmondsworth: Penguin.

Festenstein, Matthew and Thompson, Simon (eds) (2001) *Richard Rorty: Critical Dialogues*. Cambridge: Polity Press.

Finnemore, Martha (1996) 'Constructing norms of humanitarian intervention', in Peter Katzenstein (ed.), *The Culture of National Security: Norms and Identity in World Politics*. New York: Columbia University Press.

Finnemore, Martha (2003) *The Purpose of Intervention: Changing Beliefs About the Use of Force*. Ithaca, NY: Cornell University Press.

Finnemore, Martha and Sikkink, Katherine (1998) 'International norm dynamics and political change', *International Organization*, 54 (4): 887–917.

Finnis, John (1996) 'The ethics of war and peace in the Catholic Natural Law tradition', in Terry Nardin (ed.), *The Ethics of War and Peace*. Princeton, NJ: Princeton University Press.

Finnis, John (1998) *Aquinas: Moral, Political, and Legal Theory*. New York: Oxford University Press.

Finnis, John (2011a) *Human Rights and Common Good*. Oxford: Oxford University Press.

Finnis, John (2011b) *Natural Law and Natural Right*. New edition. Oxford: Oxford University Press.

Finnis, John, Boyle, Joseph and Grisez, Germain (1987) *Nuclear Deterrence, Morality and Realism*. Oxford: Clarendon Press.

Flint, Julie (2008) *Darfur: A New History of a Long War*. Revised and updated edition. London: Zed Books.

Flint, Julie and De Waal, Alex (2005) *Darfur: A Short History of a Long War*. London: Zed Books.

Flockhart, Trine, Kupchan, Charles A., Lin, Cristina and Nowak, Bartlomiej E. (2014) *Liberal Order in a Post-Western World*. Washington, DC: Transatlantic Academy.

Förster, Annette (2012) *Decent Peace, Stability and Justice: John Rawls's International Theory Applied*. PhD Dissertation: London School of Economics and Political Science.

Forsythe, David P. (1978) *Humanitarian Politics: The International Committee of the Red Cross*. Baltimore, MD: Johns Hopkins University Press.

Franck, Thomas (1992) 'The emerging right to democratic governance', *The American Journal of International Law*, 86 (1): 46–91.

Franck, Thomas (2000) *One Market Under God: Extreme Capitalism, Market Populism and the End of Economic Democracy*. New York: Doubleday.

Freeman, Samuel (2007) *Rawls*. London: Routledge.

Freedman, Lawrence (1993) *The Gulf Conflict, 1990–1991: Diplomacy and War in the New World Order*. London: Faber and Faber.

Freedman, Lawrence and Karsh, Ephraim (2000) 'Victims and victors: reflections on the Kosovo War', *Review of International Studies*, 26 (3): 335–58.

Friedman, Milton (1966 [1953]) 'The methodology of positive economics', in Milton Friedman, *Essays in Positive Economics*. Chicago, IL: University of Chicago Press.

Frost, Mervyn (1986) *Towards a Normative Theory of International Relations*. Cambridge: Cambridge University Press.

Frost, Mervyn (1996) *Ethics in International Relations: A Constitutive Theory*. Cambridge: Cambridge University Press.

Frost, Mervyn (2009) *Global Ethics: Anarchy, Freedom and International Relations*. London: Routledge.

Fukuyama, Francis (1989) The end of history, *The National Interest*, (Summer).

Fukuyama, Francis (2012) *The End of History and the Last Man*. Re-issue edition. London: Penguin (1st edition, 1992).

Gat, Azar (2007) 'The return of authoritarian great powers', *Foreign Affairs*, 86 (4).

Gat, Azar, Deudney, Daniel, Ikenberry, G. John, Inglehart, Ronald and Welzel, Christian (2009) 'Which way is history marching – debating the authoritarian revival', *Foreign Affairs*, 88.

Gentry, Caron E. and Eckert, Amy (eds) (2014) *The Future of Just War: New Critical Essays*. Athens, GA: University of Georgia Press.

George, Jim (1995) 'Realist "ethics", international relations, and post-modernism: Thinking beyond the egoism-anarchy thematic', *Millennium: Journal of International Studies*, 24 (2): 195–223.

Georgia Journal of International and Comparative Law (2005) Symposium on the Limits of International Law, 34 [v].

Geras, Norman (1995) *Solidarity in the Conversation of Humankind: The Ungroundable Liberalism of Richard Rorty*. London: Verso.

Geras, Norman (1999) *The Contract of Mutual Indifference* London: Verso.

Geras, Norman (2009) Brian Berry 1936–2009. *Normblog*, (http://normblog.typepad.com/normblog/2009/03/brian-barry-19362009.html)

Geuss, Raymond (2008) *Philosophy and Real Politics*. Princeton, NJ: Princeton University Press.

Ginbar, Yuval (2008) *Why Not Torture Terrorists?: Moral, Practical, and Legal Aspects of the 'Ticking Bomb' Justification for Torture*. Oxford: Oxford University Press.

Glennon, Michael J. (2010) *The Fog of Law: Pragmatism, Security, and International Law*. Washington, DC: Woodrow Wilson Center Press.

Glenny, Misha (1996) *The Fall of Yugoslavia: The Third Balkan War*. 3rd edition. London: Penguin.

Goldsmith, Jack L. and Posner, Eric A. (2005) *The Limits of International Law*. Oxford: Oxford University Press.

Gong, Gerritt W. (1984) *The Standard of 'Civilization' in International Society*. Oxford: Clarendon Press.

Goodin, Robert E. (1985) 'Nuclear disarmament as a moral certainty', *Ethics*, 95 (3): 641–58.

Goodin, Robert E. (1995) *Utilitarianism as a Public Philosophy*. Cambridge: Cambridge University Press.

Gourevitch, Philip (1999) *We Wish to Inform You That Tomorrow We Will be Killed With Our Families: Stories from Rwanda*. New York: Picador.

Gow, James (1997) *Triumph of the Lack of Will: International Diplomacy and the Yugoslav War*. London: Hurst.

Greenberg, Karen (2006) *The Torture Debate in America*. Cambridge; New York: Cambridge University Press.

Greenberg, Karen (2009) *The Least Worse Place: Guantanamo's First 100 Days*. Oxford: Oxford University Press.

Greenberg, Karen and Dratel, Joshua (eds) (2005) *The Torture Papers: The Road to Abu Ghraib*. New York: Cambridge University Press.

Greenwald, Glen (2014) *No Place to Hide: Edward Snowden, the NSA and the Surveillance State*. London: Penguin.

Gregory, Daniel (2011) 'From a view to kill: Drones and late modern war', *Theory, Culture & Society*, 28 (7–8): 188–215.

Gross, Michael L. (2009) *Moral Dilemmas of Modern War: Torture, Assassination, and Blackmail in an Age of Asymmetric Conflict*. Cambridge: Cambridge University Press.

Gross, Michael L. (2013) 'Just War and guerrilla war', in Anthony Lang, Cian O'Driscoll and John Williams (eds), *Just War*. Washington, DC: Georgetown University Press.

Guilhot, Nicholas (2011) *The Invention of International Relations Theory: Realism, the Rockefeller Foundation, and the 1954 Conference on Theory*. New York: Columbia University Press.

Haacke, Jürgen (2009) 'Myanmar, the Responsibility to Protect, and the need for practical assistance', *Global Responsibility to Protect*, 1 (2): 156–84.

Haas, Michael (2013) *International Human Rights: A Comprehensive Introduction*. 2nd edition. London: Routledge.

Habermas, Jürgen (1990) *Moral Consciousness and Communicative Action*. Cambridge, MA: MIT Press.

Hanson, Victor Davis (1990) *The Western Way of War*. Oxford: Oxford University Press.

Harding, Luke (2014) *The Snowden Files*. London: Faber/Guardian.

Hehir Aidan (2012) *The Responsibility to Protect: Rhetoric, Reality and the Future of Humanitarian Intervention*. Basingstoke: Palgrave Macmillan.

Hehir, Aidan (2013) 'The permanence of inconsistency: Libya, the Security Council, and the Responsibility to Protect', *International Security*, 38 (1): 137–59.

Hehir, Aidan and Murray, Robert (2013) *Libya, the Responsibility to Protect and the Future of Humanitarian Intervention*. London: Palgrave Macmillan.

Held, David (1987) *Models of Democracy*. Cambridge: Polity Press.

Held, David (2004) *Global Covenant: The Social Democratic Alternative to the Washington Consensus*. Oxford: Polity.

Herz, John (1959) *International Politics in the Atomic Age*. New York: Columbia University Press.

Hitchens, Christopher (2003) *A Long Short War: The Postponed Liberation of Iraq*. New York: A Plume Book.

Hobbes, Thomas (1651/1994) *Leviathan: With Selected Variants from the Latin Edition of 1668*. Indianapolis, IN: Hackett Publishing Company.

Hobson, John (2012) *The Eurocentric Conception of World Politics*. Cambridge: Cambridge University Press.

Hochschild, Adam (1999) *King Leopold's Ghost: A Story of Greed, Terror, and Heroism in Colonial Africa*. Boston, MA: Houghton Mifflin.

Hochschild, Adam (2005) *Bury the Chains: The British Struggle to Abolish Slavery*. Basingstoke: Macmillan.

Holbrooke, Richard C. (1999) *To End a War*. New York: Modern Library.

Holmes, George (1992) *The Oxford History of Medieval Europe*. Oxford: Oxford University Press.

Holzgrefe, J.L. and Keohane, Robert O. (eds) (2003) *Humanitarian Intervention: Ethical, Legal, and Political Dilemmas*. Cambridge: Cambridge University Press.

Hopgood, Stephen (2008) 'Saying no to Wal-Mart. Money and morality in professional humanitarianism', in Michael Barnett and Thomas Weiss (eds), *Humanitarianism in Question*. Ithaca, NY: Cornell University Press.

Hopgood, Stephen (2013) *The Endtimes of Human Rights*. Ithaca, NY: Cornell University Press.

Hume, David (1985) *Essays: Moral, Political & Literary*. Indianapolis, IN: Liberty Classics.

Hurrell, Andrew (2007) *On Global Order: Power, Values, and the Constitution of International Society*. Oxford: Oxford University Press.

Hutchings, Kimberly (1999) *International Political Theory: Rethinking Ethics in a Global Era*. London: Sage.

Hutchings, Kimberly (2000) 'Towards a feminist international ethics', *Review of International Studies*, 26 (5): 111–30.

Hutchings, Kimberly (2005) '"Speaking and hearing": Habermasian discourse ethics, feminism and IR', *Review of International Studies*, 31 (1): 155–65.

Hutchings, Kimberly (2008) *Time and World Politics: Thinking The Present*. Manchester: Manchester University Press.

Hutchings, Kimberly (2010) *Global Ethics – An Introduction*. Cambridge: Polity Press.

Hutchings, Kimberly (2011) 'What is orientation in thinking?: On the question of time and timeliness in cosmopolitical thought', *Constellations*, 18 (2): 190–204.

Ignatieff, Michael (2003) *Empire Lite: Nation Building in Bosnia, Kosovo, Afghanistan*. London: Vintage.

Ignatieff, Michael (2004) *The Lesser Evil: Political Ethics in an Age of Terror*. Princeton, NJ: Princeton University Press.

Ikenberry, G. John (2011a) 'The future of the liberal world order: Internationalism after America', *Foreign Affairs*, 90: 56.

Ikenberry, G. John (2011b) *Liberal Leviathan: The Origins, Crisis, and Transformation of the American World Order*. Princeton, NJ: Princeton University Press.

International Commission on Intervention and State Sovereignty (2001) *Responsibility to Protect*. Ottawa: International Development Research Centre (http://responsibilitytoprotect.org/ICISS%20Report.pdf).

International Affairs (2009) Special Issue: The War Over Kosovo: Ten Years On, 85(3).

Ivison, Duncan (2008) *Rights*. Durham: Acumen Publishing.

Jackson, Robert H. (1990) *Quasi-states: Sovereignty, International Relations, and the Third World*. Cambridge: Cambridge University Press.

Jackson, Robert H. (2003) *The Global Covenant: Human Conduct in a World of States*. Oxford: Oxford University Press.

Jackson, Robert H. (2007) *Sovereignty: The Evolution of an Idea*. Cambridge: Polity Press.

Jagger, Alison (ed.) (2010) *Thomas Pogge and His Critics*. Cambridge: Polity Press.

James, Alan (1993) 'System or society?', *Review of International Studies*, 19 (3): 269–88.

Johnson, James Turner (1985) *Just War Tradition and the Restraint of War*. Princeton, NJ: Princeton University Press.

Johnson, James Turner (1986) *Can Modern War be Just?* New Haven, CT: Yale University Press.

Johnson, James Turner (2001) *Morality & Contemporary Warfare*. New Haven, CT: Yale University Press.

Johnson, James Turner (2005) *The War to Oust Saddam Hussein: Just War and the New Face of Conflict*. Lanham, MD: Rowman & Littlefield.

Johnson, James Turner (2011) *Ethics and the Use of Force*. Farnham: Ashgate.

Jones, Peter (1994) *Rights*. London: Macmillan.

Jones, Roy E. (1981) 'The English School of international relations: a case for closure', *Review of International Studies*, 7 (01): 1–13.

Journal of International Criminal Justice (2005) Special Issue on Rwanda, 3 (4).

Journal of Intervention and Statebuilding, (2010) Special Issue: Critical Perspectives on R2P, 4 (1).

Kagan, Robert (2004) *Paradise and Power: America and Europe in the New World Order*. New edition. London: Atlantic Books.

Kagan, Robert (2012) *The World America Made*. New York: Vintage.

Kaldor, Mary (1999) *New and Old Wars: Organized Violence in a Global Era*. Cambridge: Polity Press.

Kalmo, Hent and Skinner, Quentin (eds) (2011) *Sovereignty in Fragments*. Cambridge: Cambridge University Press.

Kant, Immanuel (1983) *Perpetual Peace and other Essays*. Trans. Ted Humphrey. Indianapolis, IN: Hackett Publishing Co.

Kaufmann, Chaim D. and Pape, Robert A. (1999) 'Explaining costly international moral action: Britain's sixty-year campaign against the Atlantic slave trade', *International Organization*, 53 (4): 631–68.

Keene, Edward (2002) *Beyond the Anarchical Society: Grotius, Colonialism and Order in World Politics*. Cambridge: Cambridge University Press.

Keene, Edward (2005) *International Political Thought: A Historical Introduction*. Cambridge: Polity Press.

Kelly, Paul (ed.) (1998) *Impartiality, Neutrality and Justice: Re-reading Brian Barry's Justice as Impartiality*. Edinburgh: Edinburgh University Press.

Kennedy, Paul (1989) *The Rise and Fall of Great Powers*. London: Fontana Press.

Kersten, Mark (forthcoming) *Justice in Conflict: The Effects of the International Criminal Court's Investigations and Indictments on Peace and Justice Processes in northern Uganda and Libya*. PhD Dissertation: London School of Economics and Political Science.

Klabbers, Jan (2013) *International Law*. Cambridge: Cambridge University Press.

Klein, Naomi (2001) *No Logo: No Space, No Choice, No Jobs*. London: Flamingo.

Koenig-Archibugi, Mathias (2011) 'Is global democracy possible?', *European Journal of International Relations*, 17 (3): 519–42.

Koskenniemi, Martti (1990) 'The politics of international law', *European Journal of International Law*, 1 (1).

Koskenniemi, Martti (2002) *The Gentle Civilizer of Nations: The Rise and Fall of International Law, 1870–1960*. Cambridge: Cambridge University Press.

Koskenniemi, Martti (2011) *The Politics of International Law*. Oxford: Hart.

Krasner, Stephen D. (1999) *Sovereignty: Organized Hypocrisy*. Princeton, NJ: Princeton University Press.

Kratochwil, Friedrich (1989) *Rules, Norms and Decisions*. Cambridge: Cambridge University Press.

Kratochwil, Friedrich (1995) 'Sovereignty as dominium: Is there a right of humanitarian intervention?', in Gene M. Lyons and Michael Mastanduno (eds), *Beyond Westphalia? State, Sovereignty and International Intervention*. Baltimore, MD: Johns Hopkins University Press.

Kratochwil, Friedrich (2014) *The Status of Law in World Society*. Cambridge: Cambridge University Press.

Kroslak, Daniela (2007) *The Role of France in the Rwandan Genocide*. London: Hurst.

Kupchan, Charles (2012) *No One's World: The West, the Rising Rest and the Coming Global Turn*. New York: Oxford University Press.

Kuperman, Alan J. (2000a) 'Rwanda in retrospect', *Foreign Affairs*, 79 (1): 94–118.

Kuperman, Alan (2000b) 'Kuperman Replies', *Foreign Affairs* 79 (3)

Kuperman, Alan J. (2013) 'A model humanitarian intervention? Reassessing NATO's Libya Campaign', *International Security*, 38 (1): 105–36.

Kymlicka, Will (1995) *The Rights of Minority Cultures*. Oxford: Oxford University Press.

Landes, David S. (1998) *Wealth And Poverty Of Nations*. New edition. London: Abacus.

Lang, Anthony F. (2003) *Just Intervention*. Washington, DC: Georgetown University Press.

Lang, Anthony F. and Beattie, Amanda (2009) *War, Torture and Terrorism: Rethinking the Rules of International Security*. London: Routledge.

Lang, Anthony F., O'Driscoll, Cian and Williams, John (eds) (2013) *Just War: Authority, Tradition, and Practice: Authority, Tradition, and Practice*. Washington, DC: Georgetown University Press.

Laughland, John (2008) *A History of Political Trials: From Charles I to Saddam Hussain*. Oxford: Peter Lang.

Leigh, David and Harding, Luke (2010) *Wikileaks: Inside Julian Assange's War on Secrecy*. London: Guardian Books.

Lemkin, Raphael (1946) 'Genocide', *The American Scholar*, 15 (2): 227–30.

Lemkin, Raphael (1947) 'Genocide as a crime under International Law', *The American Journal of International Law*, 41 (1): 145–51.

Levy, Jack S. (2010) *Causes of War*. Malden, MA: Wiley-Blackwell.

Levinson, Sanford (2004) *Torture: A Collection*. Oxford: Oxford University Press.

Lewis, Ioan and Mayall, James (1996) 'Somalia', in James Mayall (ed.), *The New Interventionism, 1991–1994: United Nations Experience in Cambodia, Former Yugoslavia and Somalia*. Cambridge: Cambridge University Press.

Linklater, Andrew and Suganami, Hidemi (2007) *The English School of International Relations: A Contemporary Reassessment*. Cambridge: Cambridge University Press.

Linklater, Andrew (2011) *The Problem of Harm in World Politics*. Cambridge: Cambridge University Press.

Little, Richard (2000) 'The English School's contribution to the study of international relations', *European Journal of International Relations*, 6 (3): 395–422.

Little, Richard (2003) 'The English School vs. American Realism: A meeting of minds or divided by a common language?', *Review of International Studies*, 29 (3): 443–60.

Long, David and Wilson, Peter (eds) (1995) *Thinkers of the Twenty Years' Crisis: Inter-war Idealism Reassessed*. Oxford: Oxford University Press.

Lucas, Edward (2013) *The Snowden Operation*. Amazon: Kindle Single.

Lynch, Joseph (1992) *The Medieval Church: A Brief History*. London: Routledge.

Lyons, Gene M. and Mastanduno, Michael (1995) *Beyond Westphalia? State Sovereignty and International Intervention*. Baltimore, MD: Johns Hopkins University Press.

Lyons, Gene M. and Mayall, James (2003) *International Human Rights in the 21st Century: Protecting the Rights of Groups*. Lanham, MD: Rowman & Littlefield Publishers.

MacKinnon, Catherine A. (1989) *Towards a Feminist Theory of The State*. Cambridge, MA: Harvard University Press.

MacKinnon, Catherine A. (1993) *Only Words*. Cambridge, MA: Harvard University Press.

MacKinnon, Catherine A (2006) *Are Women Human? And Other International Dialogues*. Cambridge, MA: Belknap Press of Harvard University Press.

Makinda, Samuel M. (1993) *Seeking Peace from Chaos: Humanitarian Intervention in Somalia*. Boulder, CO: Lynne Rienner.

Malcolm, Noel (1994) *Bosnia: A Short History*. London: Macmillan.

Malcolm, Noel (2002) *Kosovo: A Short History*. London: Pan.

Mamdani, M. (2010) 'Responsibility to protect or right to punish?' *Journal of Intervention and Statebuilding*, 4 (1): 53–67.

Mandle, Jon and Reidy, David A. (2013) *A Companion to Rawls*. Oxford: Wiley Blackwell.

Mann, Michael (2005) *The Dark Side of Democracy: Explaining Ethnic Cleansing*. New York: Cambridge University Press.

Mansell, Wade (2004) 'Goodbye to all that? The rule of law, international law, the United States, and the use of force', *Journal of Law and Society*, 31 (4): 433–56.

Maogoto, Jackson N. (2004) *War Crimes and Realpolitik: International Justice from World War I to the 21st Century*. Boulder, CO: Lynne Rienner Publishers.

Martin, Rex and Reidy, David (2006) *Rawls's Law of Peoples: A Realistic Utopia*. Oxford: Wiley Blackwell.

Mattox, John Mark (2006) *St. Augustine and the Theory of Just War*. London: Bloomsbury Publishing.

Mayall, James (1990) *Nationalism and International Society*. Cambridge: Cambridge University Press.

Mayall, James (ed.) (1996) *The New Interventionism, 1991–1994: United Nations Experience in Cambodia, Former Yugoslavia, and Somalia*. Cambridge: Cambridge University Press.

McCormack, Tara (2010) 'The Responsibility to Protect and the end of the Western century', *Journal of Intervention and Statebuilding*, 4 (1): 69–82.

McGoldrick, Dominic, Rowe, Peter and Donnelly, Eric (2004) *The Permanent International Criminal Court: Legal and Policy Issues*. Oxford: Hart Publishing.

McKrisken, Trevor (2013) 'Obama's Drone War', *Survival* (55) 2: 97–122.

McMahan, Jeff (2008) 'The morality of war and the law of war', in David Rodin and Henry Shue (eds), *Just and Unjust Warriors: The Moral and Legal Status of Soldiers*. Oxford: Oxford University Press.

McMahan, Jeff (2009) *Killing in War*. Oxford: Oxford University Press.

McMahan, Jeff (2011) 'Duty, obedience, desert, and proportionality in war: A response', *Ethics*, 122 (1): 135–67.

Megret, Frederic (2001) 'Epilogue to an endless debate: The ICC's third party jurisdiction and the looming revolution of international law', *European Journal of International Law*, 12 (2): 247–68.

Megret, Frederic (2002) 'The politics of international criminal justice', *European Journal of International Law*, 13 (5): 1261–84.

Megret, Frederic (2005) 'In defense of hybridity: Towards a representational theory of international criminal justice', *Cornell International Law Journal*, 38: 725.

Meierhenrich, Jens (2014) *Genocide: A Reader*. New York: Oxford University Press.

Melvern, Linda (2000) *A People Betrayed: The Role of the West in Rwanda's Genocide*. London: Zed Books.

Melvern, Linda (2006) *Conspiracy to Murder: The Rwandan Genocide*. London: Verso.

Miller, David (1995) *On Nationality*. Oxford: Oxford University Press.

Miller, David (2005) 'Against global egalitarianism', *The Journal of Ethics*, 9 (1–2): 55–79.

Miller, David and Walzer, Michael (eds) (1995) *Pluralism, Justice and Equality*. Oxford: Oxford University Press.

Moghalu, Kingsley Chiedu (2006) *Global Justice: The Politics of War Crimes Trials*. Westport, CT: Praeger Security International.

Moore, Jonathan (1998) *Hard Choices: Moral Dilemmas in Humanitarian Intervention*. Lanham, MD: Rowman & Littlefield.

Morgenthau, Hans J. (1947) *Scientific Man vs. Power Politics*. London: Latimer House Ltd.

Morgenthau, Hans J. (1970) *Truth and Power: Essays of a Decade, 1960–70*. London: Pall Mall.

Moyn, Samuel (2010) *The Last Utopia: Human Rights in History*. Cambridge, MA: Harvard University Press.

Moyo, Dambisa (2010) *Dead Aid: Why Aid Is Not Working and How There Is a Better Way for Africa*. London: Penguin.

Mueller, John E. (2004) *The Remnants of War*. Ithaca, NY: Cornell University Press.

Nabulsi, Karma (2006) 'Conceptions of justice in war: from Grotius to modern times', in Richard Sorabji and David Rodin (eds), *The Ethics of War – Shared Problems in Different Traditions*. Farnham: Ashgate.

Nagel, Thomas (2005) 'The problem of global justice', *Philosophy & Public Affairs*, 33 (2): 113–47.

Nardin, Terry (1983) *Law, Morality, and the Relations of States*. Princeton, NJ: Princeton University Press.

Nardin, Terry (2005) 'Humanitarian imperialism', *Ethics & International Affairs*, 19 (2): 21–6.

Nardin, Terry (2008) 'International ethics', in Christian Reus-Smit and Duncan Snidal (eds) *The Oxford Handbook of International Relations*. Oxford: Oxford University Press.

Nardin, Terry and Mapel, David R. (eds) (1992) *Traditions of International Ethics*. Cambridge: Cambridge University Press.

Nardin, Terry and Williams, Michael S. (eds) (2006) *Humanitarian Intervention NOMOS XLVII*. New York: New York University Press.

Navari, Cornelia (ed.) (2009) *Theorising International Society: English School Methods*. London: Palgrave.

Navari, Cornelia (ed.) (2013) *Ethical Reasoning in International Affairs*. London: Palgrave.

Newman, Michael (2009) *Humanitarian Intervention: Confronting the Contradictions*. London: Hurst.

Norman, Richard, (1995) *Ethics, Killing and War*. Cambridge: Cambridge University Press.

Norton, Anne (2001) 'Review essay on Euben, Okin, and Nussbaum', *Political Theory*, 29 (5): 736–49.

Nussbaum, Martha (2000) *Women and Human Development: The Capabilities Approach*. Cambridge: Cambridge University Press.

Nussbaum, Martha (2001) *The Fragility of Goodness: Luck and Ethics in Greek Tragedy and Philosophy*. New edition. Cambridge: Cambridge University Press (1st edition, 1986).

Nussbaum, Martha (2011) *Creating Capabilities: The Human Development Approach*. Cambridge, MA: Harvard University Press.

Nussbaum, Martha and Glover, Stephen (eds) (1995) *Women, Culture, and Development: A Study of Human Capabilities*. Oxford: Oxford University Press.

Nussbaum, Martha and Sen, Amartya (eds) (1993) *The Quality of Life*. Oxford: Oxford University Press.

O'Brien, Conor Cruise (2011) *To Katanga and Back: A UN Case History*. London: Faber and Faber.

O'Connell, M.E. (2010) 'Responsibility to peace: A critique of R2P', *Journal of Intervention and Statebuilding*, 4 (1): 39–52.

O'Donovan, Oliver (1996) *The Desire of the Nations: An Outline for Political Theology*. Cambridge: Cambridge University Press.

O'Donovan, Oliver (2003) *The Just War Revisited*. Cambridge: Cambridge University Press.

O'Driscoll, Cian (2008) 'James Turner Johnson's Just War idea: Commanding the headwaters of tradition', *Journal of International Political Theory*, 4 (2): 189–211.

O'Neill, Onora (1986) *Faces of Hunger: An Essay on Poverty, Justice and Development*. London: Allen & Unwin.

O'Neill, Onora (1991) 'Transnational Justice', in David Held (ed.), *Political Theory Today*, Cambridge: Polity Press.

Oakeshott, Michael (1975) *On Human Conduct*. Oxford: Clarendon Press.

Odysseos, Louiza, and Petito, Fabio (2007) *The International Political Thought of Carl Schmitt: Terror, Liberal War and the Crisis of Global Order*. London: Routledge.

Ofek, Hillel (2010) 'The tortured logic of Obama's drone war', *The New Atlantis*, (27): 35–44.

Okin, Susan Moller (ed.) (1999) *Is Multiculturalism Bad for Women?* Princeton, NJ: Princeton University Press.

Orend, Brian (2006) *The Morality of War*. Plymouth: Broadview Press.

Orford, Anne (2011) *International Authority and the Responsibility to Protect*. Cambridge: Cambridge University Press.

Osiander, Andreas (1994) *The States System of Europe, 1640–1990*. Oxford: Oxford University Press.

Osiander, Andreas (2001) 'Sovereignty, International Relations, and the Westphalian myth', *International Organization*, 55 (2): 251–87.

Pannikar, K.M. (1961) *Asia and Western Dominance: A Survey of the Vasco Da Gama Epoch of Asian History 1498–1945*. London: George Allen & Unwin.

Patman, Robert G. (ed.) (2000) *Universal Human Rights?* Basingstoke: Macmillan.

Pattison, James (2010) *Humanitarian Intervention and the Responsibility to Protect: Who Should Intervene?* Oxford: Oxford University Press.

Peters, Jan and Wolper, Andrea (1995) *Women's Rights, Human Rights: International Feminist Perspectives*. London: Routledge.

Peterson, Scott (2000) *Me Against My Brother: At War in Somalia, Sudan and Rwanda: A Journalist Reports from the Battlefields of Africa*. London: Routledge.

Peterson, V. Spike (1990) 'Whose rights? A critique of the 'givens' in human rights discourse', *Alternatives: Global, Local, Political*, 15 (3): 303–44.

Phillips, Anne (2001) 'Feminism and liberalism revisited: Has Martha Nussbaum got it right?' *Constellations*, 8 (2): 249–66.

Philpott, Dan (2001) *Revolutions in Sovereignty: How Ideas Shaped Modern International Relations*. Princeton, NJ: Princeton University Press.

Pilger, John (2003) *The New Rulers of the World*. London: Verso.

Pinker, Steven (2012) *The Better Angels of Our Nature: A History of Violence and Humanity*. London: Penguin.

Pogge, Thomas (1989) *Realizing Rawls*. Ithaca, NY: Cornell University Press.

Pogge, Thomas (1992) 'Cosmopolitanism and sovereignty', *Ethics*, 103 (1): 48–75.

Pogge, Thomas (1994) 'Cosmopolitanism and sovereignty', in Chris Brown (ed.), *Political Restructuring in Europe*. London: Routledge.

Pogge, Thomas (1999) 'Human flourishing and universal justice', *Social Philosophy and Policy*, 16 (1): 333–61.

Pogge, Thomas (2005) 'Real world justice', *The Journal of Ethics*, 9 (1–2): 29–53.

Pogge, Thomas (ed.) (2007) *Freedom from Poverty as a Human Right: Who Owes What to the Very Poor?* Oxford: Oxford University Press.

Pogge, Thomas (2008) *World Poverty and Human Rights: Cosmopolitan Responsibilities and Reforms*. 2nd edition. Cambridge: Polity Press.

Pogge, Thomas and Horton, Keith (eds) (2007) *Global Ethics: Seminal Essays*. St. Paul, MN: Paragon House.

Pogge, Thomas and Moellendorf, Darrel (eds) (2008) *Global Justice: Seminal Essays*. St. Paul, MN: Paragon House.

Political Studies (1996) A Symposium: Brian Barry's Justice as Impartiality, 44(2).

Pollis, Adamantia and Schwab, Peter (1979) *Human Rights: Cultural and Ideological Perspectives*. New York: Praeger.

Porter, Bernard (2007) *Critics of Empire: British Radicals and the Imperial Challenge*. London: I.B.Tauris.

Posner, Eric A. (2009) *The Perils of Global Legalism*. Chicago: University of Chicago Press.

Power, Samantha (2002) *'A Problem from Hell': America and the Age of Genocide*. New York: Basic Books.

Prunier, Gérard (1995/revised 1998) *The Rwanda Crisis, 1959–94: History of a Genocide*. London: Hurst.

Prunier, Gérard (2005) *Darfur: The Ambiguous Genocide*. London: C Hurst & Co.

Prunier, Gérard (2011) *Africa's World War: Congo, the Rwanda Genocide and the Making of a Continental Catastrophe*. New York: Oxford University Press.

Rabkin, Jeremy (2005) 'Global criminal justice: An idea whose time Has passed', *Cornell International Law Journal*, 38, 753.

Ralph, Jason (2004) 'The ICC and the "uneasy revolution" in international society', *International Journal of Human Rights*, 8 (2): 235–47.

Ramsbotham, Oliver and Woodhouse, Tom (1996) *Humanitarian Intervention in Contemporary Conflict: A Reconceptualization*. Cambridge: Polity Press.

Ramsey, Paul (1961) *War and the Christian Conscience: How Shall Modern War be Conducted Justly?* Durham, NC: Duke University Press.

Rawls, John (1970) *A Theory of Justice*. Cambridge, MA: Harvard University Press.

Rawls, John (1993) *Political Liberalism*. New York: Columbia University Press.

Rawls, John (1994) 'The Law of Peoples', in Stephen Shute and S.I. Hurley, *On Human Rights: The Oxford Amnesty Lectures, 1993*. New York: Basic Books.

Rawls, John (1999) *The Law of Peoples and the Idea of Public Reason Revisited*. Cambridge, MA: Harvard University Press.

Rengger, N.J. (2005) 'Reading Charles Beitz: twenty-five years of *Political Theory and International Relations*', *Review of International Studies*, 31 (2): 361–9.

Rengger, N.J. (2013) *Just War and International Order: The Uncivil Condition in World Politics*. Cambridge: Cambridge University Press.

Renteln, Alison D. (1990) *International Human Rights: Universalism vs. Relativism*. Newbury Park, CA: Sage.

Reus-Smit, Christian (2003) 'Politics and international legal obligation', *European Journal of International Relations*, 9 (4): 591–625.

Reus-Smit, Christian (2004) *The Politics of International Law*. Cambridge: Cambridge University Press.

Review of International Studies, (2005) Special Section on 25 Years of Charles Beitz *Political Theory and International Relations*, 31 (02).

Rieff, David (2002) *A Bed for the Night*. New York: Vintage.

Rieff, David (2006) *At the Point of a Gun: Democratic Dreams and Armed Intervention*. New York: Simon & Schuster.

Risse, Mathias (2005a) 'Do we owe the global poor assistance or rectification?', *Ethics & International Affairs*, 19 (1): 9–18.

Risse, Mathias (2005b) 'How does the global order harm the poor?', *Philosophy & Public Affairs*, 33 (4): 349–76.

Risse, Mathias (2012) *On Global Justice*. Princeton, NJ: Princeton University Press.

Roberts, Adam (1993) 'Humanitarian war: Military intervention and human rights', *International Affairs*, 69 (3): 429–49.

Roberts, Adam and Guelff, Richard (eds) (2000) *Documents on the Laws of War*. 3rd edition (with revisions and additions). Oxford: Oxford University Press.

Robertson, Geoffrey (2012) *Crimes Against Humanity: The Struggle for Global Justice*. London: Penguin.

Rodin, David (2011) 'Justifying harm', *Ethics*, 122 (1): 74–110.

Rodin, David and Shue, Henry (eds) (2008) *Just and Unjust Warriors: The Moral and Legal Status of Soldiers*. Oxford: Oxford University Press.

Rorty, Richard (1989) *Contingency, Irony and Solidarity*. Cambridge: Cambridge University Press.

Rorty, Richard (1990) 'Postmodernist bourgeois liberalism', in Richard Rorty, *Objectivity, Relativism and Truth*. Cambridge: Cambridge University Press.

Rorty, Richard (1994) 'Human rights, rationality and sentimentality', in Stephen Shute and S.L. Hurley (eds), *On Human Rights: The Oxford Amnesty Lectures 1994*. New York: Basic Books.

Rorty, Richard (1996) 'Who are we? Moral universalism and economic triage', in Thomas Pogge and Keith Norton (eds), *Global Ethics: Seminal Essays*. St. Paul, MN: Paragon House.

Rorty, Richard (1998) 'Human rights, rationality, and sentimentality', in Richard Rorty, *Truth and Progress*. Cambridge: Cambridge University Press.

Rorty, Richard (1999) *Philosophy and Social Hope*. London: Penguin.

Rorty, Richard (2007) *Philosophy as Cultural Politics*. Cambridge: Cambridge University Press.

Rose, Michael (1999) *Fighting for Peace: Lessons from Bosnia*. London: Warner.

Rudolph, Christopher (2001) 'Constructing an atrocities regime: The politics of war crimes tribunals', *International Organization*, 55 (3): 655–91.

Sachs, Jeffrey (2005) *The End of Poverty: How We Can Make it Happen in Our Lifetime*. London: Penguin.

Sahnoun, Mohamed (1994) *Somalia: The Missed Opportunities*. Washington, DC: United States Institute of Peace.

Salomon, Margaret E. (2007) *Global Responsibility for Human Rights: World Poverty and the Development of International Law*. Oxford: Oxford University Press.

Sands, Philippe (2006) *Lawless World: Making and Breaking Global Rules*. London: Penguin.

Scanlon, Thomas M. (2000) *What We Owe to Each Other*. Cambridge, MA: Belknap Press.

Schabas, William (2000) *Genocide in International Law: The Crime of Crimes*. New York: Cambridge University Press.

Schabas, William (2007) *An Introduction to the International Criminal Court*. 3rd edition. Cambridge: Cambridge University Press.

Scheuerman, William E. (2011) *The Realist Case for Global Reform*. Cambridge: Polity Press.

Schmitt, Carl (2003) *The Nomos of the Earth in the International Law of the Jus Publicum Europaeum*. New York: Telos Press.

Scott, Len (2011) 'Intelligence and the Risk of Nuclear War: Able Archer-83 Revisited', *Intelligence and National Security*, 26 (1): 759–77.

Sen, Amartya (1990) 'More than 100 million women are missing', *The New York Review of Books*, (www.nybooks.com/articles/archives/1990/dec/20/more-than-100-million-women-are-missing/).

Sen, Amartya (2005) 'Human rights and capabilities', *Journal of Human Development*, 6 (2): 151–66.

Sen, Amartya (2006a) *Identity and Violence: The Illusion of Destiny*. New York: W. W. Norton & Co.

Sen, Amartya (2006b) *The Argumentative Indian: Writings on Indian History, Culture and Identity*. London: Penguin.

Sen, Amartya (2009) *The Idea of Justice*. London: Allen Lane.

Serrano, Monica (2010) 'Implementing the Responsibility to Protect: The power of R2P talk', *Global Responsibility to Protect*, 2 (1): 167–77.

Shapcott, Richard (2010) *International Ethics: A Critical Introduction*. Cambridge: Polity Press.

Shapiro, Ian and Brilmayer, Lea (eds) (1998) *Global Justice*. New York: New York University Press.

Shapiro, Ian and Kymlicka, Will (eds) (1997) *Ethnicity and Group Rights*. New York: New York University Press.

Shaw, Martin (2007) *What is Genocide?* Cambridge: Polity Press.

Shklar, Judith N. (1996) 'The liberalism of fear', in Judith N. Schklar, *Political Liberalism: Variations on a Theme*. Albany, NY: State University of New York Press.

Shklar, Judith N. and Yack, Bernard (eds) (1996) *Liberalism Without Illusions: Essays on Liberal Theory and the Political Vision of Judith N. Shklar*. Chicago, IL: University of Chicago Press.

Shue, Henry (1980) *Basic rights: Subsistence, Affluence, and U.S. Foreign Policy*. Princeton, NJ: Princeton University Press.

Shute, Stephen and Hurley, S.L. (1994) *On Human Rights: Amnesty Lectures 1993*. New York: Basic Books.

Simms, Brendan (2001) *Unfinest Hour: Britain and the Destruction of Bosnia*. London: Allen Lane.

Simms, Brendan (2013) *Europe: The Struggle for Supremacy, 1453 to the Present: A History of the Continent Since 1500*. London: Allen Lane.

Simms, Brendan and Trim, David (eds) (2011) *Humanitarian Intervention: A History*. Cambridge: Cambridge University Press.

Simpson, Gerry (2004) *Great Powers and Outlaw States: Unequal Sovereigns in the International Legal Order*. Cambridge: Cambridge University Press.

Simpson, Gerry (2007) *Law, War and Crime: War Crimes Trials and the Reinvention of International Law*. Cambridge: Polity Press.

Singer, Peter (1972) 'Famine, affluence and morality', *Philosophy & Public Affairs*, 1 (3): 229–43.

Singer, Peter (2010) *The Life You Can Save: How to Play Your Part in Ending World Poverty*. London: Picador.

Singer, Peter (2011) *The Expanding Circle: Ethics, Evolution, and Moral Progress.* Princeton, NJ: Princeton University Press.

Slaughter, Anne-Marie (2004) *A New World Order.* Princeton, NJ: Princeton University Press.

Smith, Karen E. and Light, Margot (eds) (2001) *Ethics and Foreign Policy.* Cambridge: Cambridge University Press.

Smith, Michael J. (1998) 'Humanitarian intervention: An overview of the ethical issues', *Ethics & International Affairs*, 12 (1): 63–79.

Smith, Thomas W. (2002) 'Moral hazard and humanitarian law: The International Criminal Court and the limits of legalism', *International Politics*, 39 (2): 175–92.

Snyder, Jack and Vinjamuri, Leslie (2004) 'Trials and errors: Principle and pragmatism in strategies of international justice', *International Security*, 28 (3): 5–44.

Social Theory and Practice (2008) Special Issue on 'Ideal Theory, Non Ideal Circumstance', 34 (3).

Sorabji, Richard and Rodin, David (eds) (2006) *The Ethics of War – Shared Problems in Different Traditions.* Burlington: Ashgate.

Springborg, Patricia (ed.) (2007) *The Cambridge Companion to Hobbes's Leviathan.* Cambridge: Cambridge University Press.

Stahn, Carsten, Easterday, Jennifer and Iverson, Jen (eds) (2014) *Jus Post Bellum: Mapping the Normative Foundations.* Oxford: Oxford University Press.

Steans, Jill (2007) 'Debating women's human rights as a universal feminist project: defending women's human rights as a political tool', *Review of International Studies*, 33 (1): 11–27.

Steans, Jill (2013) *Gender and International Relations.* Cambridge: Polity.

Sterne, Laurence (2008) *A Sentimental Journey and Other Writings.* Parnell, T. and Jack, I. (eds). Oxford: Oxford University Press.

Stiglitz, Joseph E. (2004) *Globalization and Its Discontents.* New York: W.W. Norton & Company.

Stiglitz, Joseph E. (2007) *Making Globalization Work: The Next Steps to Global Justice.* London: Penguin.

Strawser, Bradley Jay (ed.) (2013) *Killing By Remote Control: The Ethics of an Unmanned Military.* New York: Oxford University Press.

Sutch, Peter (2000) 'Human rights as settled norms: Mervyn Frost and the limits of Hegelian human rights theory', *Review of International Studies*, 26 (2): 215–31.

Tamir, Yael (1993) *Liberal Nationalism.* Princeton, NJ: Princeton University Press.

Tan, Kok-Cho (2000) *Toleration, Diversity, and Global Justice.* University Park, PA: Penn State University Press.

Tan, Kok-Cho (2012) *Justice, Institutions, and Luck: The Site, Ground, and Scope of Equality.* Oxford: Oxford University Press.

Tang, James Tuck-Hong (ed.) (1994) *Human Rights and International Relations in the Asia-Pacific Region.* London: Pinter.

Taylor, A.J.P. (1971) *The Struggle for Mastery in Europe.* New edition. Oxford: Oxford University Press.

Taylor, Charles, Appiah, Kwame Anthony, Habermas, Jürgen, Rockefeller, Stephen C. , Gutman, Amy, Walzer, Michael and Wolf, Susan (1994) *Multiculturalism: Examining the Politics of Recognition.* Princeton, NJ: Princeton University Press.

Teitel, Ruti (2005) 'The law and politics of contemporary transitional justice', *Cornell International Law Journal*, 38: 837.

Tesón, Fernando R. (2005a) 'Ending tyranny in Iraq', *Ethics & International Affairs*, 19 (2): 1–20.

Tesón, Fernando R. (2005b) *Humanitarian Intervention: An Inquiry Into Law and Morality.* 3rd edition. Ardsley: Transnational Publishers.

Tesón, Fernando R. (2005c) 'Of tyrants and empires', *Ethics & International Affairs*, 19 (2): 27–30.

Thakur, Ramesh C. (2006) *The United Nations, Peace and Security: From Collective Security to the Responsibility to Protect.* Cambridge: Cambridge University Press.

Thucydides (2009) *The Peloponnesian War.* Translated Martin Hammond. Oxford: Oxford University Press.

Todorov, Tzvetan (1984) *The Conquest of America: The Question of the Other.* New York: Harper & Row.

Toulmin, Stephen (1992) *Cosmopolis: The Hidden Agenda of Modernity.* Chicago, IL: University of Chicago Press.

Tuck, Richard (2000) *The Rights of War and Peace.* Oxford: Oxford University Press.

Tuck, Richard (2002) *Hobbes: A Very Short Introduction.* Oxford: Oxford University Press.

Tully, James (1995) *Strange Multiplicities: Constitutionalism in an Age of Diversity*. Cambridge: Cambridge University Press.
United Nations (1945) Charter of the United Nations. www.un.org/en/documents/charter/
United Nations (1948) The Universal Declaration of Human Rights. www.un.org/en/documents/udhr/
UNESCO (1949) *Human Rights: Comments and Interpretations: A Symposium*. Maritain, J. (ed.). New York: Allan Wingate.
Uvin, Peter (2001) 'Reading the Rwandan genocide', *International Studies Review*, 3 (3): 75–99.
Vincent, Andrew (2010) *The Politics of Human Rights*. Oxford: Oxford University Press.
Vincent, R.J. (1986) *Human Rights and International Relations*. Cambridge: Cambridge University Press.
Waddell, Nicholas and Clark, Phil (2008) *Courting Conflict? Justice, Peace and the ICC in Africa*. London: Royal African Society.
Wallis, Andrew (2006) *Silent Accomplice: The Untold Story of France's Role in the Rwandan Genocide*. London: I.B. Tauris.
Walt, Stephen (2013) 'Snowden deserves an immediate presidential pardon', *Financial Times*, 9 July.
Waltz, Kenneth N. (1979) *Theory of International Politics*. Boston, MA: McGraw-Hill.
Walzer, Michael (1965) *The Revolution of the Saints*. Cambridge, MA: Harvard University Press.
Walzer, Michael (1970) *Obligations: Essays on Disobedience, War, and Citizenship*. Cambridge, MA: Harvard University Press.
Walzer, Michael (1973) 'Political action: The problem of dirty hands', *Philosophy & Public Affairs*, 2 (2): 160–80.
Walzer, Michael (1983) *Spheres of Justice: A Defense of Pluralism and Equality*. New York: Basic Books.
Walzer, Michael (1993) *Interpretation and Social Criticism Interpretation and Social Criticism*. Cambridge, MA: Harvard University Press.
Walzer, Michael (1994) *Thick and Thin: Moral Argument at Home and Abroad*. Notre Dame, IN: University of Notre Dame Press.
Walzer, Michael (1995) 'The politics of rescue', *Social Research*, 62 (1): 53–66.
Walzer, Michael (2005) *Arguing About War*. New Haven, CT: Yale University Press.
Walzer, Michael (2006) *Just and Unjust Wars: A Moral Argument with Historical Illustrations*. 4th edition. New York: Basic Books (1st edition, 1976).
Walzer, Michael (2007) *Thinking Politically: Essays in Political Theory*. New Haven, CT: Yale University Press.
Watson, Adam (1992) *The Evolution of International Society: A Comparative Historical Analysis*. London: Routledge.
Weber, Max (1949) *On the Methodology of the Social Sciences*. New York: Free Press.
Weiss, Thomas G. (1999) 'Principles, politics, and humanitarian action', *Ethics & International Affairs*, 13 (1): 1–22.
Weiss, Thomas G. (2007) 'Halting genocide: Rhetoric versus reality', *Genocide Studies and Prevention*, 2 (1): 7–30.
Weiss, Thomas G. (2011) 'RtoP alive and well after Libya', *Ethics & International Affairs*, 25 (3): 287–92.
Weiss, Thomas G. (2012) *Humanitarian Intervention: Ideas in Action*. 2nd edition. Cambridge: Polity Press.
Weller, Marc (1999) 'The Rambouillet Conference on Kosovo', *International Affairs*, 75 (2): 211–51.
Weller, Marc (2002) 'Undoing the global constitution: UN Security Council action on the International Criminal Court', *International Affairs*, 78 (4): 693–712.
Weller, Marc (2008) 'Kosovo's final status', *International Affairs*, 84 (6): 1223–43.
Weller, Marc (2009) *Contested Statehood: Kosovo's Struggle for Independence*. Oxford: Oxford University Press.
Welsh, Jennifer (2002) 'From right to responsibility: Humanitarian intervention and international society', *Global Governance*, 8, 503.
Welsh, Jennifer (2007) 'The Responsibility to Protect: Securing the individual in international society', *Security and Human Rights*, 363–83.

Welsh, Jennifer (2010a) 'Implementing the "Responsibility to Protect": Where expectations meet reality', *Ethics & International Affairs*, 24 (4): 415–30.

Welsh, Jennifer (2010b) 'Turning words into deeds? The implementation of the "Responsibility to Protect"', *Global Responsibility to Protect*, 2 (1): 149–54.

Welsh, Jennifer (2011) 'Civilian protection in Libya: Putting coercion and controversy back into RtoP', *Ethics & International Affairs*, 25 (3): 255–62.

Wenar, Leif (2008) 'Property rights and the resource curse', *Philosophy & Public Affairs*, 36 (1): 2–32.

Wenar, Leif (2013) 'Fighting the resource curse', *Global Policy*, 4 (3): 298–304.

Wendt, Alexander (2003) 'Why a world state is inevitable', *European Journal of International Relations*, 9 (4): 491–542.

Wenman, Mark (2013) *Agonistic Democracy: Constituent Power in the Era of Globalisation.* Cambridge: Cambridge University Press.

Wheeler, Nicholas J. (1992) 'Pluralist or solidarist conceptions of international society: Bull and Vincent on humanitarian intervention', *Millennium: Journal of International Studies*, 21 (3): 463–87.

Wheeler, Nicholas J. (2000) *Saving Strangers: Humanitarian Intervention in International Society.* Oxford: Oxford University Press.

Wheeler, Nicholas J. and Dunne, Tim (1996) 'Hedley Bull's pluralism of the intellect and solidarism of the will', *International Affairs*, 72 (1): 91–107.

Whetham, David (2009) *Just Wars and Moral Victories.* Leiden: Brill.

Wight, Martin (1960) 'Why is there no International Theory?', *International Relations*, 2 (1): 35–48.

Williams, Bernard (2005) *In the Beginning was the Deed: Realism and Moralism in Political Argument.* Princeton, NJ: Princeton University Press.

Williams, Bernard (2006) *Ethics and the Limits of Philosophy.* London: Routledge.

Williams, Howard, Wright, Morehead and Evans, Tony (eds) (1993) *A Reader in International Relations and Political Theory.* Buckingham: Open University Press.

Williams, Michael C. (1999) 'Perceptions of the war in Bosnia', *International Affairs*, 75 (2): 377–81.

Williamson, Roger (ed.) (1998) *Some Corner of a Foreign Field: Intervention and World Order.* Basingstoke: Macmillan.

Wilson, Peter (2009) 'The English School's approach to International Law', in Cornelia Navari (ed.), *Theorising International Society.* London: Palgrave.

Woolsey, R. James (ed.) (2003) *The National Interest on International Law and Order.* New Brunswick, NJ: Transaction Publishers.

Yan, Xuetong (2011) *Ancient Chinese Thought, Modern Chinese Power.* Princeton, NJ: Princeton University Press.

Young, Shaun P. (2004) *Political Liberalism: Variations on a Theme.* Albany, NY: State University of New York Press.

Zhang, Yongjin and Buzan, Barry (2012) 'The Tributary System as International Society in Theory and Practice', *Chinese Journal of International Politics*, 5 (1): 3–36.

INDEX

Main entries in **bold**

Printed in Great Britain
by Amazon